To Don & Keith —
God Bless you!

[signature]
Rom 12:1-2

Praise for *Your Reasonable Service*

"The subject of spiritual gifts should awaken the tenderest mercies of a living, serving church. Instead, the frequent misinterpretation of the subject causes incredible strife. Every Christian ought to read *Your Reasonable Service: Understanding Your Motivation for Ministry* by Dr. Thomas Rush, pastor and scholar, for that reason. Rush has understood the whole subject of spiritual gifts and given it a turn that will bless every church. I am thankful for this remarkable assessment."
—**Paige Patterson, President**
Southwestern Baptist Theological Seminary
Fort Worth, Texas

"It is a wonderful and encouraging reality that God through the Holy Spirit has already gifted every Christian to do whatever it is God has called us to do. Every Christian has been blessed with one or more gifts of the Spirit. Discovering your spiritual gift is an exciting adventure, and Dr. Tom Rush is just the one to lead you on that adventure. You will find this book, based in the study of God's Word, to be an enlightening and helpful manual on the spiritual gifts. It would be an excellent resource for personal and group study."
—**J. Robert White, Executive Director**
Georgia Baptist Mission Board

"*Your Reasonable Service: Understanding Your Motivation for Ministry* is an incredible and useful resource for any Christian serious about serving others for Jesus' sake. The motivational gifts found in Romans 12 are those God has built into us and made part of us, to be used for the benefit of others and for His glory. They are called "motivational" because they are the motivating force for our lives; gifts that even shape our personalities and give us greater effectiveness for evangelism. They define how the Holy Spirit works in and through the believer to meet needs within the body of Christ. Tom Rush uniquely explains the spiritual gifts the way God intended them to operate. Page after page, you will be both blessed and encouraged in your service for the Lord as you read this book."
—**Johnny Hunt, Pastor**
First Baptist Church
Woodstock, Georgia

"The church today is urgently in need of biblical wisdom regarding spiritual gifts. Tom Rush, a faithful pastor and careful teacher of the Bible answers that need in *Your Reasonable Service: Understanding Your Motivation for Ministry.* This book will help every Christian to understand the spiritual gifts and to be a

more faithful disciple and church member. I am thankful for Tom Rush and for the wisdom in this book."
—R. Albert Mohler, Jr., President
The Southern Baptist Theological Seminary
Louisville, Kentucky

"With precision befitting his background as a military officer, love revealing a pastor's heart, and skill honed by years as a faithful expositor, Tom Rush has presented the church with a valuable resource. *Your Reasonable Service: Understanding Your Motivation for Ministry*, unwraps the Spirit's gifts and puts their meaning in reach of every recipient. A church in which each member is serving according to his or her giftedness - this book makes that vision both explainable and attainable. It will bless you and your church to read it."
—Dan Spencer, Pastor
First Baptist Church
Sevierville, Tennessee

"Because the doctrine of the Holy Spirit is so abused, particularly in regards to the gifts of the Spirit, few people dare to write on the subject. That is tragic, because the church is to fulfill its mission on earth as people utilize their spiritual gifts in harmony with God's divine plan. Tom Rush has tackled this difficult subject and given a clear and certain sound about the gifts of the Spirit. The chapters on *The Proper Foundation for Discovering Your Spiritual Gifts and Basic Truths about Spiritual Gifts* are a must for every serious believer. I commend Dr. Rush for the extensive thought and labor necessary to produce this excellent volume; and I heartily recommend it to those who desire to grow in the grace and knowledge of our dear Savior."
—Gerald Harris, Editor
The Christian Index
Duluth, Georgia

"Tom Rush has written more than a blueprint for discovering your own spiritual gifts. Your Reasonable Service is a key to living the Christian life in general. Spiritual maturity is not just for the "super spiritual." All believers are supposed to be growing in Christ-likeness toward spiritual maturity. How? By following the clear direction of Scripture and applying it to the situations and circumstances of life. This work guides the reader along the correct path toward the level of maturity God desires us to achieve.

One can understand spiritual gifts and still battle dissatisfaction during challenging periods of life. However, as this book offers, the believer can continue to grow and mature in Christ, no matter the circumstances.

Gifts are significant in the life of the church. It will be increasingly critical in the years to come that we faithfully commit ourselves to discover and use our giftedness to further the Kingdom. As the author explains, the benefits of identifying and understanding your spiritual gifts are many:

It will build up the fellowship,
cause members of the body to respect the function of others,
help you accept responsibility in line with what God has gifted you to do,
help you seek to develop the gifts of others,
gives praise to God for the manifestation of the gifts,
will cause all things done in the church to be judged on the basis of whether
they bring praise to God and edification to the body,
and, will cause a desire for balance in the manifestation of the gifts.

I highly recommend *Your Reasonable Service: Understanding Your Motivation for Ministry.* It will teach, challenge, inspire, refresh and refocus every reader to allow their own spiritual gifts to impact this generation and beyond."
—**Joel H. Horne**
121 Mentoring Partners
Vision Caster
Clovis, New Mexico

YOUR REASONABLE SERVICE

Understanding Your Motivation for Ministry

THOMAS E. RUSH

WESTBOW
P R E S S®
A DIVISION OF THOMAS NELSON
& ZONDERVAN

WestBow Press books may be ordered through booksellers or by contacting:

WestBow Press
A Division of Thomas Nelson & Zondervan
1663 Liberty Drive
Bloomington, IN 47403
www.westbowpress.com
1 (866) 928-1240

ISBN: 978-1-5127-8242-4 (sc)
ISBN: 978-1-5127-8243-1 (hc)
ISBN: 978-1-5127-8241-7 (e)

Library of Congress Control Number: 2017905288

Print information available on the last page.

WestBow Press rev. date: 4/26/2017

Word Definitions were taken from the following resources:

Word definitions marked (BAGD) are taken from the Arndt, W., F. W. Gingrich, F. W. Danker, and W. Bauer. *A Greek-English Lexicon of the New Testament and Other Early Christian Literature*. Chicago: University of Chicago Press, 1979.

Word definitions marked (DBL) are taken from the Swanson, J. *A Dictionary of Biblical Languages with Semantic Domains: Greek (New Testament)*. Oak Harbor: Logos Research Systems Inc., 1997. Electronic edition.

Word definitions marked (ESL) are taken from the Strong, J. *Enhanced Strong's Lexicon*. Bellingham, WA: Logos Bible Software, 2001.

Word definitions marked (GEL) are taken from the Liddell, H., ed. *A Lexicon: Abridged from Liddell and Scott's Greek-English Lexicon*. Oak Harbor, WA: Logos Research Systems Inc., 1996.

Word definitions marked (JHT) are taken from the Thayer, Joseph Henry. *A Greek-English Lexicon of the New Testament*. Grand Rapids: Baker Book House, 1977.

Word definitions marked (SCDBW) are taken from the Strong, J. *A Concise Dictionary of the Words in the Greek Testament and the Hebrew Bible*. Bellingham, WA: Logos Bible Software, 2009.

Word definitions marked (TDNT) are taken from the Kittel, G., G. W. Bromiley, and G. Friedrich, eds. *Theological Dictionary of the New Testament*. Grand Rapids, MI: Eerdmans, 1964. Electronic edition.

Word definitions marked (TDNTA) are taken from the Kittel, G., G. W. Bromiley, and G. Friedrich, eds. *Theological Dictionary of the New Testament, Abridged in One Volume*. Grand Rapids, MI: W. B. Eerdmans, 1985.

Word definitions marked (VINE) are taken from the Vine, W. E. *An Expository Dictionary of New Testament Words.* Old Tappan, NJ: Fleming H. Revell Co., 1940.

Word definitions marked (WSGNT) are taken from the Wuest, K. S. *Wuest's Word Studies from the Greek New Testament: For the English Reader.* Grand Rapids: Eerdmans, 1997.

In Memory Of My
Mentor and Dear Friend,
Dr. Sam Cathey,
Whose Godly Influence On My Life, My Family, and My Ministry
Will Be Forever Cherished

August 30, 1934-March 8, 2016
Precious in the sight of the Lord is the death of His saints.
—Psalm 116:15

Acknowledgements

I am deeply grateful for the support of my wife, Victoria. We have been married over thirty-nine years, and she has supported my ministry every step of the way. She has provided wise counsel as we have discussed the subject of the gifts over the years. She has used her gift of exhortation to be an encouragement to me, to our family, and to the churches we have been privileged to serve. She has been a particular encouragement to me in the writing of this book!

The study of the spiritual gifts has been an eventful journey, which got off to a solid start in the early days of my ministry. After seminary, I had the privilege of going to pastor a church in South Georgia. While there, in the gracious providence of God, I came under the preaching of Dr. Sam Cathey, "Papa Sam." He became both a mentor and a friend to me. His teaching and preaching on the subject of spiritual gifts revolutionized my conceptual understanding of the subject. I knew there was a systematic and practical way to approach the teaching, discovery, and use of the gifts, but I had not grasped it well until I heard Dr. Cathey teach on the subject.

Any similarity to what you may have heard him teach about the spiritual gifts, which is found in this book, is intentional! Thank you, Dr. Cathey, for your faithfulness to the true gospel of Jesus Christ and for your friendship to me and my family, you are a blessing beyond words. (At the time of the initial writing of the acknowledgments, Dr. Cathey—at the end of a lengthy illness—went on to be with the Lord, on March 8, 2016. This book is dedicated to his memory.)

I am also indebted to the work of Bill Gothard on spiritual gifts. I first heard of the gifts in the early seventies at a Basic Youth Conflicts seminar. While I do not agree with all of Mr. Gothard's conclusions, particularly when it comes to Old Testament applications, his work on spiritual gifts was well thought-out and has been helpful, particularly in the chapters dealing with the specific characteristics and potential misuses of the seven motivational gifts.

One of the great joys of my life is to have a son in the ministry. Nathan, who serves as a pastor in Kansas, is a competent theologian and an excellent wordsmith. His assistance with both the content and style of the book has been priceless. Thank you, Nathan, for your faithfulness to the Lord and your assistance with this work. You are a great blessing to my life.

I am grateful to my dear friends Ken and Beth Williams, whose contribution to this work is known to the Lord and much appreciated by this pastor.

I am very grateful to WestBow Press for their assistance in getting this work completed.

Above all, my thanks and praise are offered to the Lord Jesus Christ, who saved me and gifted me for ministry in these days. It is a joy and privilege to have been called into the gospel ministry, and I am humbled by the call and opportunity to serve the Lord. I trust this work will be a blessing to all who read it.

Contents

Foreword

I felt very humbled and honored when Dr. Rush asked me to write the foreword for his marvelous work. After reading it, I felt so unworthy because it made my work on this subject seem so shallow. I heartily commend this work to both pastors and laymen alike. The principles elucidated in this work regarding Holy Spirit motivation for ministry could bring both revitalization and renewal to any church, and perhaps even revival!

I stumbled onto the Scriptural emphasis on spiritual gifts when I was in my early twenties and did, what I thought, was a thorough examining of what the Bible says about the subject. It shook me when I saw that every believer has at least one gift that motivates them to a particular pursuit of lifestyle and ministry. With that conclusion, I sought to list and define each of the gifts. I quickly found that there were seven strong gifts that I called controlling gifts, and the rest were manifestations of them.

After seeing my own gift, I soon was able to define gifts in others. These seven motivational gifts, from Romans 12, and all their companions, are still at work today in the church. They serve to shape the function of every believer in the life and ministry of the local church.

Most of the difficulties and divisions in today's church are created because of the ignorance of the people regarding their gifts. I contend that no one is "at home" in their ministry participation until this truth is revealed, embraced, and used!

Over the course of my pastoral ministry, I found that my church members were misplaced until they found their gift, lined their ministry up with it, and helped others do the same! Of course, the main reason there is "trouble in Zion" is that many are not even saved!

Dr. Rush is more than a competent scholar, and you can trust his research and presentation. Find your gift, scripturally, and go for God. *Your Reasonable Service* will be a precious help to that end.

—Dr. Sam Cathey
Oklahoma City, Oklahoma
September 2015

Introduction

The very mention of spiritual gifts can cause some Christians to run and hide. Many of God's people are confused about the gifts, either assuming that somehow they may have been left out, or perhaps they simply have never been taught how to discover their gift. Some think that when spiritual gifts are discussed, they refer only to what are sometimes called the *sign* gifts, such as tongues and healing. Since they do not understand such gifts, or perhaps have a fear of them, they avoid the topic. Others, because they do not think they have a gift or believe they are not worthy of one, also avoid the topic.

To others, it is more than confusion. It is a controversy. They have heard pastors tell them that in order to demonstrate that they are saved, or that they have the Holy Spirit indwelling them, they must evidence it by speaking in tongues or some other mystical manifestation of the power of the Spirit. On the other hand, they have heard pastors tell them that such manifestations are either fake or demonic. They have been told such gifts have ceased and are no longer a part of the spiritual-gifts inventory.

The controversy rages in some churches. The phenomenon of "charismatic"[1] practices have crossed denominational lines for many years. Practice of the sign or revelatory gifts common in Pentecostal churches came over into fundamental and evangelical churches with varied acceptance and success. Many are the evangelical churches

---

[1] There is a proper and biblical use of the term charismatic, but in this work, I shall use the term as it is understood in the modern church to refer to the "charismatic movement" with its overemphasis on miracles, unknown tongues, and prosperity.

that have split over the issue. But the controversy has taken its toll in more ways than just splitting churches and causing disagreements between pastors. Because of the controversial nature of the spiritual gifts, many pastors, churches, and individual believers have chosen just to ignore the subject.

Sometimes it seems that the work of the Holy Spirit has been left to the Charismatic Movement; and the rest of the church has, in a sense, allowed them to steal much truth from the church while they progressed onward in their errors. Baptists became scared of raising a hand in worship or expressing their emotion in any way whatsoever for fear of being thought too "charismatic."

Thankfully, there has been a renewed interest in the gifts over the last few decades. More believers are interested; more churches are providing teaching and tools for their members to discover their gifts. This renewed emphasis on the gifts should be welcomed and will be of great help to the church, provided it maintains a biblical balance.

One major area of confusion in the study of the spiritual gifts is that vast difference you find in various authors about how many gifts the Bible makes available. Some say seven, some eighteen, and some thirty or more! We will address this concern and try to bring some biblical balance to the question.

Another issue that clouds and confuses the understanding of the spiritual gifts even further is the modern tendency to combine the study of the spiritual gifts with studies of human personality traits. These approaches often speak of the need for "self-discovery" and lead one down a long path of researching their personality, human abilities, life experiences, and even one's "passions" (meaning, what one is passionate about in life). The popularity of such systems is immense, and they are used in many churches. I am not questioning the sincerity of those who have built these systems. I believe that many of them have a strong desire to see believers discover their gifts and use such gifts in faithful service to the Lord through the church. What I question is the biblical foundation of such methods.

The purpose of this book is to bring clarification to the issue of spiritual gifts. It will be my purpose to answer a number of important questions about the subject. At the foundation of these questions will be an honest attempt to discover what the Bible says about the gifts. How many spiritual gifts are there? How do I discover my gift? Can I have more than one gift? Should I have all the gifts? Can I have all the gifts (as is taught by many in the charismatic movement)? How can I most effectively use my gifts? Do my personality traits or natural human abilities have any bearing on my giftedness? What is the purpose of spiritual gifts—in other words, why were they given? How can I know how other Christians are gifted, and what does that mean for me? What impact does a proper biblical understanding of the gifts have on the local church? What significance do the gifts have in my family?

If the purpose is to bring clarification, the goal is to provide a tool that pastors, churches, and laypersons can use to determine God's design for their service to the Lord. The church of today is weak and inept, often overrun by an enemy of ignorance and indifference, especially when it comes to the work of the Holy Spirit. I will readily admit that this book in no way purports to be a definitive work on ministry of the Holy Spirit (other and more capable men than me have provided numerous such works[2]). But one area of the Spirit's work that surely needs emphasis in the church today is the work that God desires to do through His church by the exercise of the spiritual gifts given to each and every saint.

The bottom-line objective is to help each believer, each church member, discover their Holy Spirit-given motivation for ministry. As we will discover, that motivation *is* your spiritual gift. God the Holy Spirit gifted you to motivate you toward a ministry that He would bless. It is His desire to use you in the service of your Savior, to advance the cause of the kingdom, and to be a blessing to your fellow believers. The truth is, we have all been called into ministry. The work of the ministry is not solely the work of the pastor or the paid church staff (Eph. 4:11-16).

---

[2] Works on the Holy Spirit that might be useful to the serious Bible student include *The Baptism and Fullness: The Work of the Holy Spirit* by John R. W. Stott, *The Silent Shepherd* by John MacArthur, and *Holy Spirit Power* by Charles H. Spurgeon.

A great motto for a church would be, "Every member a minister." Of course, for that to happen, the pastor and membership would need to get serious about understanding and discovering the spiritual gifts of each member. I believe that any Bible-believing church would find the results of such an effort to be a tremendous blessing. For most churches, the time comes around every year when the nominating committee, deacons, or elders begin the labor of filling all the positions of service needed in the church.

In theory, if all the members knew and practiced their spiritual gifts, there would be no need for a nominating committee! People would be much more satisfied and fulfilled in their work in the church! There would likely be a waiting list to serve. Rather than begging someone to teach a Sunday school class, for example, a person would come to the pastor and say, "I have the gift of teaching, and I'd like to teach a class." He would then respond, "We'll put you on a waiting list!" Or he might make them an assistant teacher or have them start a new class. There is no question that the church would be blessed and more effective in ministry if all the members were serving just as God had gifted them.

"Your reasonable service" (cf. Rom. 12:1-2) is to present your body as "a living sacrifice...to God." God saved you in order to use you in His service! In Romans 12, Paul shows us clearly how we can be the living sacrifices He desires through discovering and using the motivational spiritual gifts we have been given by the Holy Spirit. That will be the aim of this book, to help pastors and church members discover their gifts for the glory of the Lord, the furtherance of His kingdom, and the good of the church.

> "Now we must all ask ourselves, do we truly encourage the Holy Spirit to work in our churches today? Are we truly teaching that each born-again Christian is gifted for service by the Holy Spirit to bless their local church and to be an effective member of that church for local testimonial effect for the Gospel and to spread the Gospel, both here and abroad?"
> —Dr. James I. Stewart, Immanuel Bible College

Part I

Concepts
Understanding the Basics
of Spiritual Gifts

1

God's Purpose and Plan for the Spiritual Gifts

How confusion and controversy over the gifts hold back the church from the ministry God has called it to accomplish

*Now concerning spiritual gifts, brethren, I
do not want you to be ignorant.*
—1 Corinthians 12:1

*But the manifestation of the Spirit is given
to each one for the profit of all.*
—1 Corinthians 12:7

As mentioned in the introduction, there is an unfortunate amount of confusion and even controversy over the nature and use of spiritual gifts in the church. The result—at least to some degree—is that the church has ignored, downplayed, or overlooked the important purpose of the spiritual gifts. This has held the church back in its effectiveness in ministry.

Paul's letters to the church at Corinth indicate that he had some serious concerns about that church. In his first letter to them, he was answering questions they had sent to him about various issues and problems within the fellowship. While the church had numerous problems, we discover that they were not lacking in spiritual gifts.

> I thank my God always concerning you for the grace of God which was given to you by Christ Jesus, that you were enriched in everything by Him in all utterance and all knowledge, even as the testimony of Christ was confirmed in you, *so that you come short in no gift*, eagerly waiting for the revelation of our Lord Jesus Christ, who will also confirm you to the end, that you may be blameless in the day of our Lord Jesus Christ. God is faithful, by whom you were called into the fellowship of His Son, Jesus Christ our Lord. (1 Cor. 1:4-9, *emphasis mine*)

While they were not lacking in any spiritual gift, their questions revealed that they were confused about them (1 Cor. 12-14). Apparently, they were "ignorant" about the nature and operation of the gifts (1 Cor. 12:1). The word used is ἀγνοέω (*agnoeō*), which literally means "not to know." Paul uses the word again in First Corinthians 14:38, where it has the meaning of "not paying attention." Peter uses the word to speak of false teachers who do not "understand" what they are talking about (2 Pet. 2:12). To Paul, such a condition in a local church was clearly unacceptable. We should know the gifts, their purpose, and how they operate. In other words, we should know God's plan for the implementation of a spiritual-gifts ministry in the local church. Under the inspiration of the Holy Spirit, this is Paul's aim in First Corinthians 12-14: to clarify the purpose of the gifts. He will show how they are organized and what the result of their proper understanding and use will be to the church.

God's Purpose for Spiritual Gifts

God's purpose for the spiritual gifts is stated best in First Corinthians 12:7: "But the manifestation of the Spirit is given to each one for the profit of all." The gifts were given to be a benefit and blessing to the fellowship of the church. They were designed to allow you to serve others for Jesus's sake (2 Cor. 4:5). This is the bottom line of the Christian faith. We are called by God to minister to one another. Surely we would be better off in the church if each member understood the work and ministry of the Holy Spirit and how He has gifted us to minister to one another.

In addition to the passage in the Corinthian correspondence, Paul deals with spiritual gifts in Romans 12. We will demonstrate in part II of this book, where we will look at the characteristics of the primary motivational gifts, that the Romans passage is foundational to our understanding of the gifts. In this passage, Paul makes several things clear, not the least of which is the fact that the gifts were given for the purpose of ministry to others. He says, "So we being many, are one body in Christ, and individually members of one another." The context of the passage makes it clear that the focus is God's call to the church to be about the business of encouraging and supporting one another.

What is critical in all of this is to realize that the gifts are not given for the purpose of feeling better about yourself or having the Holy Spirit minister to you in some way. This is often said of those who engage in the so-called gift of unknown tongues.[1] As a justification for practicing this gift, the user calls it a "personal, private prayer language," and its use is purported to bring the user closer to God. But the spiritual gifts were not meant to be a blessing to the believer; they were meant to make the believer a blessing to others! This should not be taken to mean that there is no benefit to the believer in the exercise of the spiritual gifts; in fact, the benefits and blessings are many.

As Christians, we should know that we are always blessed through our obedience to the Lord. When we truly "present our bodies as a living sacrifice" through our service to others, we sense both a personal satisfaction and humble gratefulness that one unworthy could be used by the Lord to bless another. There is a rejoicing that comes on the heels of doing what God has called us to do. Hence, the

---

[1] Please see chapter 15 for a complete treatment of this issue in the life of the modern church.

primary motivation for spiritual gifts has to do with being a benefit and blessing to others.

Much of the dissatisfaction, unhappiness, defeat, and even depression in the church today comes from the frustration over not knowing the what, how, and why of God's will for service. Many church members deeply desire to serve the Lord and want to do so with effectiveness and Holy Spirit power. But their area of service is likely to be that which they have had their arm twisted to do. Under pressure from the nominating committee, the pastor, or a staff member, they have reluctantly agreed to serve because there was a need. This is not all bad. Sometimes we do need to pitch in and serve where the needs are greatest. But to serve where we are gifted and motivated by the Holy Spirit is the only way to serve with lasting results and spiritual satisfaction.

We will have more to say about discovering your gift, but it stands to reason that if the Holy Spirit is the One who has gifted you, His design would be both that which brings glory to God and be a source of gratification and not frustration.

Some years ago, a couple came into my office. They had been working in the student ministry primarily in a teaching role. The wife was clearly frustrated. I am referring to a committed and faithful family who were consistent in attendance and service. I asked her what her spiritual gift was, and she was not sure. After discussing the gifts and giving her a survey to complete, we determined her gift was administration, with a secondary giftedness in the area of exhortation. At the time, I needed someone to coordinate and administer our prayer ministry. She took the job, and the Spirit immediately began to work in and through her. Her frustration was gone, and she continued to work in the student ministry, encouraging and praying for the students and assisting our student pastor in any way she could.

Blessed is the congregation who has been taught the spiritual gifts and then encouraged to find a ministry that fits their individual giftedness. This church will be more faithful, more effective, and have a greater impact for the kingdom. This church will be filled with members who get along with one another because they understand that God has gifted each one differently but that all the gifts are needed and important. There is less chance of one-upmanship, selfish motives, and personal ambitions getting in the way of ministry.

When Paul was addressing the church at Philippi, he warned about the danger of selfishness. While he was not speaking directly to spiritual gifts, it is easy to see that he was getting at the idea. He says, "Do nothing from selfish ambition or conceit, but in humility count others more significant than yourselves. Let each of you look not only to his own interests, but also to the interests of others" (Phil. 2:3-4, ESV).

How better to "count others more significant than yourselves" than to serve faithfully and efficiently in our Holy Spirit motivated spiritual gifts? That is the whole point of God's purpose and plan in the gifts. The first two verses of Philippians 2 read like an instruction manual on preparedness for learning and using your Spirit motivation to serve:

> Therefore if there is any consolation in Christ, if any comfort of love, if any fellowship of the Spirit, if any affection and mercy, fulfill my joy by being like-minded, having the same love, being of one accord, of one mind.

Dr. Johnny Hunt says in his series on the motivational gifts that they are for the purpose of serving others:

> We employ them to benefit one another. These are the gifts God has built into us, made part of us, to be used for the benefit of others and for His glory. They are called motivational because they are the motivating force for our lives. They are the gifts that shape our personalities. Since God has created us with a free will, we can choose to *use* our gifts appropriately, or we can choose to *neglect* them, or even *abuse* them. We must learn what they are and how they function.

Dr. Hunt makes a very good point here. It is the Holy Spirit who shapes your personality through the motivational gift that He has given you. And, may I add, not the other way around! Far too many spiritual-gift inventories, tests, and systems have a greater emphasis on trying to help you determine your personality traits than to discover and develop your gift. Your personality isn't the primary issue. We will deal with this more at length in Part II when we get into the specifics of discovering and developing your gift, but the reality is that you must be genuinely saved to have a spiritual gift. When you are saved, the Holy Spirit indwells your life (Rom. 8:6-11).

At the very moment you were saved, the Holy Spirit took over your personality! In a very real sense, He has become your personality. You have become a servant of the Most High God! Sometimes we have some difficulty overcoming the old personal habits and mentalities we had before we were saved. The flesh is still at work in us. In fact, that was one of the very issues Paul was dealing with in the case of the Corinthians (1 Cor. 12:1-3). But at the moment you were saved, not only did the Holy Spirit indwell your life but He gave you at least one motivational spiritual gift from the list in Romans 12:6-8.

It is very possible that the Holy Spirit considered your personality and gifted you in accordance with your natural human tendencies. But it is also very likely that He completely ignored your personality, your past, your natural abilities, and gifted you for the purpose and plan He already laid out for you in eternity past. I know this is the case in my own life. If you had known me as a boy, you would never have picked me out to be a preacher, much less to have the gift of prophecy. My personality as a child just wouldn't naturally fit that. But when God saved me, He gifted me. As I grew up, and particularly as I grew in my faith, my personality began to change. The more submissive I was to the leadership of the Holy Spirit in my life, the more I noticed that I was changing from the inside out!

As we study the gifts together in this context, there will be no emphasis on personality traits, natural abilities, life experiences, or psychological testing. All these things could have an impact on your service for the Lord, but at the same time, all of them should be subject to the Word of God and the leading of the Holy Spirit. We are going to approach the task from the standpoint that if you are saved, you have at least one motivational spiritual gift from the list in Romans 12 (prophecy, service, teaching, exhortation, giving, leading, or mercy). The design of this book is to help you discover, develop, and utilize your gift for the glory of God and the good of your local church.

God's Plan for Spiritual Gifts

If we are to understand and properly utilize our spiritual gifts, it is imperative that we know what the Word of God teaches in regard to the nature and function of the gifts. There are several important passages in the New Testament that contain instruction on spiritual gifts. The mention of the gifts is somewhat limited in volume as New Testament subjects go, but it is not lacking in scope. The four primary passages are Romans 12, First Corinthians 12-14, Ephesians 4:7-16, and First Peter 4:10-12. A firm grasp of these passages will go a long way in clearing away much of the confusion that exists on the subject today.

There are two primary Greek words used in the New Testament that relate to the discussion of spiritual gifts. Those words are χάρισμα (*charisma*) and πνευματικός (*pneumatikos*). They are not interchangeable or direct synonyms, but both are used to refer to the spiritual gifts.

The word χάρισμα (*charisma*) is found sixteen times in Paul's letters and once in Peter (1 Pet. 4:10). It is connected to χαρις (*charis*), which is translated as "grace." The word is hard to find in Greek prior to the Pauline letters, but it is not supposed that Paul coined the term. It essentially means "something grace has bestowed."[2] It is defined as "a gift (freely and graciously given), a favor bestowed" (BAGD) and as "a gracious gift" (DBL).

This is where the term *grace-gift* originates. The spiritual gifts then should be seen as "grace-gifts" given to us from God for the purpose of carrying out His will. God never commands us to do that which He has not empowered us to do. Paul's use of the term applies to

---

[2] For a more detailed explanation of the words, see D. A. Carson's Showing the Spirit (Grand Rapids: Baker Books, 1987), 19-24.

several things that we sometimes do not think of in terms of spiritual gifts, including salvation. This should give us some important insight on the nature of spiritual gifts.

The first and most significant spiritual gift is the very gift of salvation itself. "For the wages of sin is death, but the *gift* [*charisma*] of God is eternal life in Christ Jesus our Lord" (Romans 6:23, emphasis mine). Paul contrasts the death sentence received through our connection to Adam with the life-giving grace that came through Christ:

> But the *free gift* [*charisma*] is not like the offense. For if by the one man's offense many died, much more the grace [*charis*] of God and the gift [*dorea*] by the grace [*charis*] of the one Man, Jesus Christ, abounded to many. And the gift [*dorema*] is not like that which came through the one who sinned. For the judgment which came from one offense resulted in condemnation, but the *free gift* [*charisma*] which came from many offenses resulted in justification." (Rom. 5:15-16, *emphasis mine*)

The primary word in Greek for a gift that is given to someone is δωρεά (*dorea*) or δώρημα (*dorema*). These words come from the word δίδωμι (*didomi*), which means "to give"; "a prolonged form of a primary verb...to give; to give something to someone, of one's own accord to give one something; to bestow a gift" (ESL). We notice that in the passage above, Paul uses these words with *charisma* in describing what God has done in the redemptive act of Christ in saving us from sin, death, and hell. In a sense, both the sentence of death received from being a descendant of Adam and the grace of God in salvation are gifts. But one, thankfully, is very much unlike the other in that it is a gift of grace! "For by grace [*charis*] you have been saved through faith, and that not of yourselves; it is the gift [*doron*] of God, not of works, lest anyone should boast" (Eph. 2:8-9).

The significance of this is great in relation to spiritual gifts. *The gifts are for the saved only!* There is no sense in talking about how one is gifted if you have not received the most important and original *gift* of salvation.[3] In fact, this was the very intent of Paul's letter to the Romans. He was desirous of going to Rome and speaking to the church in person. His letter is an attempt to accomplish that which he would love to do in person. He says, "For I long to see you, that I may impart to you some spiritual [*pneumatikon*] gift [*charisma*], so that you may be established" (1:11).

The book of Romans has as its primary and first subject a discussion of salvation, what it means, and how it is accomplished (chs. 1-11). Paul then moves to the issue of sanctification beginning in chapter 12, how to live once you are saved! And we should note that the very first thing in how to live as a saved person (at least from Paul's approach in Romans) is to understand and utilize your spiritual gift. We'll have more to say about this in part II, but for now, let's settle on the fact that salvation means being indwelt by the Holy Spirit, and the evidence of such indwelling will be noticeable in every believer through the believer's walk in the Spirit and exercise of the spiritual gifts given to him.

Later in Romans, Paul uses this word again in reference to the election of Israel. It is not my purpose here to discuss the doctrine of election but to note what this verse teaches about the gifts of God. "For the gifts [*chaismata*] and the calling of God are irrevocable" (11:29). I understand that there is a particular application of this statement to Israel and God's sovereign design for their eventual salvation. But it is interesting to me that Paul mentions here both the gifts and calling of God. To me, the connection is significant. Those whom God calls (saves) are the very same ones He gifts to serve Him.

Baptists are fond of the saying, "Once saved, always saved." While concurring most wholeheartedly with the statement, I believe it to be the result of a doctrine, not the doctrine itself. The doctrine is more properly stated, "The perseverance of the saints" (Matt. 10:22, 24:13; 1 Cor. 3:14; 2 Tim. 2:12; James 5:11). The better way to use the phrase might be to say, "Once saved, always *serving*." Surely the true evidence

---

[3] For a discussion on what it means to be truly saved, please refer to chapter 14.

of salvation is the faithful service of a child of God in the work of the kingdom of our Lord and Savior.

Paul also uses the word *charisma* to refer the prayers offered by "many" (presumably the Corinthian believers) as a "gift" granted to himself and Timothy (2 Cor. 1:11). I would take this to mean that he had been the recipient of the manifold grace of God through the Corinthians coming to understand and utilize their spiritual gifts more effectively on the basis of his instruction in the first letter. Their gifts had been used through the prayer ministry of the church, and God had been pleased to deliver them from death. Paul was certain that the protection would be extended in that he was trusting God for future deliverance. The Corinthians could share in this victory because they had prayed for it (cf. context of 2 Cor. 1:8-11).

The rest of the uses of this word in the New Testament refer directly to spiritual gifts. In the Pastoral Epistles, Paul uses the word twice to refer to the gift that had been given to Timothy (1 Tim. 4:14, 2 Tim. 1:6). The gift given to him was either recognition of his motivational spiritual gift (which was very likely service and/or teaching) or the gift of his call to the ministry (as pastor of the church at Ephesus, cf. Eph. 4:11). The word is then used in relation to the motivational gifts in Romans 12:6-8 and in the First Corinthians 12-14 passage where the primary subject is the spiritual gifts. Peter uses the word also to refer directly to spiritual gifts in First Peter 4:10-11.

The word is used in one other instance by Paul, and it provides an important point for us to understand in the overall scope of spiritual gifts. One of the confusing issues related to the gifts is the insistence by many (particularly of the charismatic persuasion) that a true Christian should possess all the spiritual gifts. However, in First Corinthians 7:7, Paul says (emphasis mine), "For I wish that all men were even as I myself. But each one has his own *gift* [*charismata*] from God, one in this manner and another in that." In the context, the *this* and *that* refer to marriage and celibacy. It seems rather obvious to me that you cannot have both of those at the same time!

Some years ago, I was in a discussion about the gifts with a gentlemen of the charismatic persuasion. He was one of those of the opinion that one should have, or at least aspire to have, all the gifts. He was certain, upon questioning, that he did indeed possess and use all the spiritual gifts. I noticed that he was wearing a wedding band on his left ring finger. So assuming he was married, I asked, "So you have a celibate marriage?" He was confused by the question, and I explained the First Corinthians 7 passage to him and told him that the only way you can have all the gifts is to be both married and celibate at the same time. By definition of the terms, that is impossible. I'm not sure I convinced him, but I did make a point that he could not refute.

The point of this for our consideration at this conjuncture is that God gifts each of us differently. We don't have all the gifts. We are motivated by the Spirit in a particular direction, and the goal is to discover how God has gifted us so that we might serve Him "acceptably with reverence and godly fear" (Heb. 12:28).

The second word we need to consider is πνευματικός (*pneumatikos*). Paul uses this word to refer to several concepts. In his discussion with the church at Corinth on spiritual gifts (ch. 12), he opens the chapter with the phrase, "Now concerning spiritual *gifts...*" The word *gifts* will be found in italics in most translations because it does not actually appear in the Greek text. It literally says, "but concerning spirituals." The word is simply *pneumatikon*, but it is clear in the passage that Paul is introducing the topic of gifts since that is the subject considered over the next three chapters.

The word means either a spiritual one or a spiritual thing. "In the great majority of cases it refers to the divine πνεῦμα [*pneuma*, or Spirit]...caused by or filled with the (divine) Spirit, pertaining or corresponding to the (divine) Spirit" (BAGD). As Carson points out, the word is used by Paul in the masculine to refer to "spiritual people" (cf. 2:15, 3:1, 14:37) or in the neuter to refer to "spiritual things" (such as gifts, cf. 9:11, 12:1, 14:1, 15:46).[4] How it is to be taken in chapter 12 verse 1 is based on the context, and the universal opinion is that, in this case, he is clearly referring to spiritual gifts. But let it suffice

---

[4] D. A. Carson, *Showing the Spirit* (Grand Rapids: Baker Books, 1987), 22.

to say that spiritual people are the ones who have an interest in spiritual things. Paul left no doubt about that earlier in the letter (cf. 1 Cor. 2-3).

The problem at Corinth wasn't the lack of gifts having been distributed to God's people. The problem was a lack of spiritual maturity. That is true in your church and mine! We are not held back from serving the Lord because we have an inadequately gifted congregation. We are held back because we have not demonstrated the spiritual maturity necessary to grow in our faith, discern and develop our gifts, and then to use them in and through the various offices and ministries of the church.

Notice what Paul told them in chapter 2 verse 2: "Now we have received, not the spirit of the world, but the Spirit who is from God, that we might know the things that have been freely given to us by God." Here, he must have in mind the spiritual gifts, perhaps along with the knowledge of the gospel—"Jesus Christ and Him crucified." Paul had been telling them about the need for the wisdom of God, which had been revealed to them through the Spirit. The Holy Spirit, who has indwelt and gifted us, is our teacher of spiritual things (John 14:15-17, 26; 16:13-15). This is where our emphasis must fall.

Paul goes on, "These things we also speak, not in words which man's wisdom teaches but which the Holy Spirit teaches, comparing spiritual things with spiritual. But the natural man does not receive the things of the Spirit of God, for they are foolishness to him; nor can he know them, because they are spiritually discerned. But he who is spiritual judges all things, yet he himself is *rightly* judged by no one. For 'who has known the mind of the Lord that he may instruct Him?' But we have the mind of Christ. And I, brethren, could not speak to you as to spiritual people but as to carnal, as to babes in Christ." (1 Corinthians 2:13-3:1).

It was one thing for the "natural man" not to get it but quite another for the true believers in the church. But if we do not mature in our faith and grow in our walk in the Spirit, we will fail to be all that we could be for the sake of the kingdom. You have likely heard of the pastor who called in one of his deacons and said, "I believe

I have discovered the two biggest problems in our church, and I believe they are ignorance and indifference. What do you think?" The deacon thought for a moment and replied, "I don't know, and I don't care!" While this is sadly true in many churches, and with some in all churches, there are many who deeply care and who want to know how to make their church more effective in its fulfillment of the Great Commission and Great Commandment.

The relation of the two words we have studied brings us to this conclusion. Since both can refer to the spiritual gifts, we have then a foundational truth that whatever is thought of as "spiritual" is nothing less than a gracious gift from the Almighty. The Corinthians seemed to be self-focused. The danger in the church today is that in the quest for "spirituality," however it might be expressed, we miss the source and power behind the true expression of spiritual gifts, which is the grace of God. We are saved and sanctified by the grace of God, and we serve in and through the grace of God (Eph. 2:8-10). Let us then grow to spiritual maturity, not being ignorant of the spiritual gifts but giving ourselves to the discovery and development of the gifts for the glory of God and the good of the church.

2

The Biblical System of Spiritual Gifts

Motivation for a ministry that manifests the power of God

For I say, through the grace given to me, to everyone who is among you, not to think of himself more highly than he ought to think, but to think soberly, as God has dealt to each one a measure of faith. For as we have many members in one body, but all the members do not have the same function, so we, being many, are one body in Christ, and individually members of one another. Having then gifts differing according to the grace that is given to us, let us use them: if prophecy, let us prophesy in proportion to our faith; or ministry, let us use it in our ministering; he who teaches, in teaching; he who exhorts, in exhortation; he who gives, with liberality; he who leads, with diligence; he who shows mercy, with cheerfulness.
—Romans 12:3-8

There are diversities of gifts, but the same Spirit. There are differences of ministries, but the same Lord. And there are diversities of activities, but it is the same God who works all in all. But the manifestation of the Spirit is given to each one for the profit of all.
—1 Corinthians 12:4-7

Any work on spiritual gifts will have a listing of the gifts taken from several places in scripture. The gifts are listed, categorized, packaged, and explained in multiple ways, depending on the take of the author or ministry providing the resource. Sometimes gifts from different places in the Bible that appear similar are lumped together, sometimes not. If this were not confusing enough in and of itself, there are those that add "gifts" to the list that are not in scripture. Usually, these are more along the lines of natural abilities such as "music" or "visitation." We should not categorize anything as a spiritual gift without specific scriptural warrant.

It is my belief that the apostle Paul was very orderly in his presentation of that which he received under the inspiration of the Holy Spirit. That being the case, a careful study of First Corinthians 12:4-7 will reveal a very distinct three-part breakdown of the design, organization, and effect of spiritual gifts, concluding with the overall purpose. What Paul reveals in this passage is that your motivational gift (from the list of seven in Romans 12) establishes your ministry. As you use your *motivational* gift through a *ministry* of the local church, the Holy Spirit then *manifests* His gifts to other believers (cf. "Spiritual Gifts Organizational Chart" on p. 47).

The Motivational Gifts

In First Corinthians 12:4, we read, "There are diversities of gifts [*charismaton*, the same term Paul uses in Romans 12:6], but the same Spirit." This is a reference to what I call the *motivational gifts*, which are listed in Romans 12. They are "gifts differing according to the grace of God." These gifts form the primary key to understanding how the Holy Spirit works in our lives and in the local church. These are the gifts that should receive the emphasis of our study. Indeed, if the emphasis were placed here, there would be much less abuse and division over the more popular gifts such as tongues and miracles. This failure has caused many Christians, churches, and even entire denominations to miss completely the true meaning of tongues and miracles.

Part of the goal in this study is to lay a foundation for a deeper understanding of the work of the Holy Spirit. The Spirit has three primary tasks in regard to believers: 1) to glorify God by lifting up and honoring Jesus (John 15:26, 1 John 5:6); 2) to teach believers, equipping them for the service of Almighty God (via the motivating gifts; John 14:26); and 3) to comfort or encourage us (John 14:15-18; cf. 2 Cor. 1:3-7). Interestingly, our motivational gifts allow the Spirit of God to work through us to accomplish the above works in others! The Holy Spirit is equipping us to establish a ministry that actually meets the needs of other believers.

The seven gifts listed in Romans 12:6-8 are the *major motivational gifts*. Those gifts are elucidated in the seven verses that follow the list of the gifts (Rom. 12:9-15). I want to emphasize again that the study of spiritual gifts is *not* a study in personality types or temperaments. When you are saved by the grace of God, the Holy Spirit takes up residence in your life, and He takes control of your personality! He motivates and empowers you to serve God. As our motivational gifts are exercised, normally through a ministry gift, the Holy Spirit manifests a work (or gift) in another person. We will do a thorough breakdown of the motivational gifts in part II.

The Ministry Gifts

The next area of focus is the *ministry gifts*, which Paul explains in verse 5 of First Corinthians 12: "There are differences of ministries [*diakanion*], but the same Lord." The ministries available through the local church are numerous. I believe it was Paul's intention to name those ministries in First Corinthians 12:27-31 and Ephesians 4:11-13.

> Now you are the body of Christ, and members individually. And God has appointed these in the church: first apostles, second prophets, third teachers, after that miracles, then gifts of healings, helps, administrations, varieties of tongues. Are all apostles? Are all prophets? Are all teachers? Are all workers of miracles? Do all have gifts of healings? Do all speak with tongues? Do all interpret?

> But earnestly desire the best gifts. And yet I show you a more excellent way. (1 Cor. 12:27-31)

This list in Ephesians 4 is very similar:

> And He Himself gave some to be apostles, some prophets, some evangelists, and some pastors and teachers, for the equipping of the saints for the work of ministry, for the edifying of the body of Christ, till we all come to the unity of the faith and of the knowledge of the Son of God, to a perfect man, to the measure of the stature of the fullness of Christ. (Eph. 4:11-13)

We should note very clearly that no believer has all the gifts. Paul's questions are rhetorical, and each implies an obvious no answer. The reason is simple. He is here referring to the ministries established in a local church. It takes many people to accomplish all that God wants done through the local assembly of believers. So in the church, "God has appointed" these various or different ministries. This is a very key point—the ministries mentioned have clear and distinct *differences*. The word is used in verse 4 to indicate the "diversities" of the motivational gifts and in verse 6 to indicate the "diversities" of the results or "activities" of the Spirit. The word is διαίρεσις (*diairesis*) and is used only in these three verses in the New Testament. Its meaning is "division, distribution...distinction, difference; in particular, a distinction arising from a different distribution to different persons" (ESL). The most natural translation might be "distributions."

Of this word in the context, Vincent says, "It may also be rendered distributions. There is no objection to combining both meanings, a distribution of gifts implying a diversity. Ver. 11, however, seems to favor distributions."[1] Verse 11 summarizes in this way (emphasis mine): "But one and the same Spirit works all these things, *distributing* to each one individually as He wills." So whether we are talking about the gift the Holy Spirit gives you as your motivation, the ministry He

---

[1] M. R. Vincent, *Word Studies in the New Testament* (New York: Charles Scribner's Sons, 1887).

places you in to exercise that gift, or the activity that He produces in another through the gift given, they are all done individually and as He directs.

Since we know from this passage that there are different ministries that the Holy Spirit will establish, we can be certain that, at some point, He would reveal some structure for understanding them. As we see from the two passages above (1 Cor. 12:27-31 and Eph. 4:11-13), the various ministries are clearly conveyed as distinct. They could properly be called gifts, but they are not gifts to the believer; rather, they are gifts to the church. It seems obvious that these types of ministries should be established in each local church.

Apostles and Prophets

We should note that the official offices of apostle and prophet as were known in biblical days are gone. There are several reasons for this. Apostolic authority was used to establish the church and verify the writing of the New Testament. Once those tasks were completed, there was no longer a need for the office.[2] While there remains a gift of prophecy there is no need for the office of Prophet. The Prophet heard directly from God and was the one through whom God communicated His Word (2 Pet. 1:19-21; 2 Tim. 3:16; John 6:63; 2 Sam. 23:2). He was a "forth"-teller because he spoke forth the Word of God. Sometimes his "forth"-telling was also foretelling. As God gave the Word to His prophets, that Word sometimes spoke to future events. So in reality, only God was foretelling.

The prophetic predictions for the future closed with the New Testament. All that will happen from now to the end of time has

---

[2] The office of apostle had several requirements according to Dr. Robert L. Thomas. He says, "What might be called 'natural prerequisites' for holding this office included personal contact with the Lord Jesus while He was on earth, followed by the experience of seeing Him alive after His resurrection (Acts 1:22-23; 1 Cor. 9:1-2). In addition, it was required that an apostle have a direct appointment from the Lord Jesus to this office (Luke 6:13; Rom. 1:1)." -Robert L. Thomas, *Understanding Spiritual Gifts* (Grand Rapids: Kregel Publications, 1978), 58-59.

already been predicted from a biblical point of view. There are no more new revelations to be given. In fact, the Bible closes with an admonition that one should not add to nor take away from scripture (Rev. 22:18-19; cf. Deut. 4:2, Prov. 30:6).

That being said, the concept of an apostolic and prophetic type of ministry still exists. An apostle was, in the simplest terms, one sent on behalf of another with a message. We in the church have our marching orders from the Lord, the Great Commission (Matt. 28:16-20, Acts 1:8). We are to take the message of the gospel to the nations. Therefore, one of the ministries of a church should be missions, or the sending of missionaries. This corresponds to the original idea of an apostle in the New Testament.[3]

Evangelist

Another office was that of evangelist, mentioned in the Ephesians 4 passage. There is certainly no reason to think this office would have been eliminated. But there is some confusion related to this gift. We are speaking here of ministry gifts. The evangelist is a gift to the church. This is a man called of God to be a revivalist, a preacher of the gospel, whose main focus is the presentation of the gospel so that souls might be brought to saving faith. Either as a member of a church or in an itinerant ministry, this man is effective in teaching, modeling, and organizing evangelistic efforts in the local church. He might be called a Great Commission specialist. From a Great Commission

---

[3] It is very important to note that the offices of apostle and of prophet are no longer in place. In the previous footnote, we clarified why this is true, and that explains why no one could be considered an apostle today. There is, however, a movement within the modern church known as the New Apostolic Reformation. It has gone under different names in the past, such as the Latter Rain. Leaders of this unbiblical movement claim that offices of apostle and prophet have been restored and that the miraculous things the original apostles did are occurring again today. This movement is led by false teachers connected to the Word of Faith and prosperity gospel movements and should be rejected by all Bible-believing Christians. An excellent source of information on this movement is available at Brannon Howse's ministry website: www.worldviewweekend.com.

perspective, sometimes the evangelist is one who teaches the church all that God has commanded (Matt. 28:19-20).

Confusion sometimes arises because there are some who think this establishes or refers to a "gift of evangelism." There is no gift of evangelism because evangelism is a command to every believer (Acts 1:8). We will deal with this issue at length in chapter 13.

Teachers

In the Corinthians passage, the term is simply *teachers*; but in Ephesians, it is *pastor-teachers*. I don't think the distinction is significant, but one thing is clear: proper biblical instruction was very important to Paul (1 Cor. 14:19). Truth properly communicated to the church is the foundation of correct Christian conduct. One of the grave errors of the modern church has been the elevation of experience over scripture as the standard for faith and practice. The early apostles, along with Paul, understood that this was a dangerous approach. That is why we find these men consistently teaching the Word.

In its infancy, the church's leadership quickly discovered that the administrative and pastoral demands on the time of the church's pastors and elders were something that would take away from their primary task. The *twelve* (the first apostles) realized that they needed to secure help in dealing with everyday matters of ministry in order not to be distracted from the main thing God had called them to do. They said to the disciples,

> It is not desirable that we should leave the word of God and serve tables. Therefore, brethren, seek out from among you seven men of good reputation, full of the Holy Spirit and wisdom, whom we may appoint over this business; but we will give ourselves continually to prayer and to the ministry of the word. (Acts 6:2-4)

Most believe that the men selected in this process were the first deacons. If they were not the first deacons, they were certainly the forerunners of that office. But the point here pertains to the importance that was placed on teaching, on communicating the truth of God's Word. As you read through the book of Acts, you find that this was the primary task and emphasis of the apostles (Acts 11:1, 20-21; 13:5, 15, 42, 49; 14:3, 7, 15, 21; 16:10; 17:11, 18; 18:11; 19:9-10; 20:17-32). Paul also made this clear in the pastoral epistles, emphasizing the need for sound doctrine in the churches (1 Tim. 1:3, 10; 4:6, 13-16; 6:3; 2 Tim. 2:2, 15, 25; 3:16-17; 4:1-5; Titus 1:9; 2:1, 12).

Pastoral ministries such as hospital visitation, funeral ministry, weddings, nursing-home and homebound ministry, counseling, church administration, staff oversight, and facility maintenance and upkeep all have their proper place. But blessed of God is the church that realizes that the pastor's most significant and important task is to preach and teach the Word of God. And if they realize this, then they will make certain the pastor isn't overburdened with things that distract him from the ministry of the Word and prayer.

So in the church, you have the office of pastor-teacher. This is the senior pastor, the one with the primary teaching responsibility of the church's pulpit. The one thing every pastor-search team should be concerned about is whether or not a potential candidate for the office of pastor has a thorough knowledge of Bible doctrine and that he can communicate it effectively. The church also has a Bible-teaching ministry that can be staffed by lay teachers or other staff pastors. The office of teacher is a gift to the church. And those who teach in the Sunday school, small group ministry, or discipleship-training ministry of the church should have a speaking gift (prophecy, teaching, or exhortation), and they should be sound in their doctrine.

Miracles

The word in Greek is δύναμις (*dunamis*) and is the word from which we get our English word *dynamite*. If you were to approach the gifts from the perspective of the charismatic movement, you would be told that this has to do with the working of miraculous events outside the natural realm—in other words, the demonstration of supernatural power. Since the next gift mentioned is "gifts of healings," you would think this then referred to supernatural events other than those of physical healing. But I believe we need to approach this from an entirely different standpoint.

It is true that in the New Testament, the ministry of the original apostles was accompanied with signs and wonders to verify the truth of the message they were preaching. Once that was established and the New Testament was written, the requirement of such signs and wonders was rendered unnecessary. Many believe in what is sometimes referred to as *cessation*. In other words, at a distinct point in time, certain of these gifts ceased to operate. I would not argue with the logic of that position. However, I assert that God is still a miracle-working God and that the gift still applies to the church, but in a way much different from how it would be perceived in the charismatic movement.

Consider this—the greatest miracle of all is the salvation of a soul. What could be a greater miracle then that which was dead coming alive (cf. Eph. 2:1-10)? Consider also that much of the greatness of the ministry that took place in the days of the early church was a direct result of prayer. The very coming of the Holy Spirit at Pentecost directly followed the church's prayers. The Bible says they "continued with one accord in prayer and supplication…and they prayed…they were all with one accord in prayer" (Acts 1:14-2:1). Then in Acts 10, we read of Cornelius being saved in response to prayer. Peter was set free from prison as the church was praying for him (Acts 12). Paul and Barnabas were sent on the first missionary journey after the church had prayed and fasted.

Further, let's consider what the Bible says. "Then He [Jesus] spoke a parable to them, that men always ought to pray and not lose heart" (Luke 18:1). Jeremiah reveals to us this promise, "And you will seek Me and find Me, when you search for Me with all your heart" (Jer. 29:13). If this is true, then the key to a mighty outpouring of power in the church is directly related to its prayer ministry. Anyone who has studied the Great Awakenings and revival through the history of the church knows that prayer was the vital element.

Prayer is a relationship with God.[4] When we learn to pray in an effective and biblical way, we are brought into the presence of God. I am not speaking of some mystical thing where you see visions and hear voices. I am talking about going to God with clean hands and a pure heart, confessing and repenting of your sin, praising and adoring Him, and taking your requests to Him with thanksgiving (Ps. 139:23-24, Phil. 4:6). The health of any church and the impact of its ministry will be greatly energized if the prayer meeting of the church becomes the main focus. Through this ministry, the church is enabled, emboldened, and energized to see the power of God manifested in the lives of those it is attempting to reach. In other words, souls will be saved, and the saved will be sanctified! In most churches, that should be considered nothing less than miraculous.

Gifts of Healings

This is another area that creates not only confusion but controversy when spiritual gifts are discussed. Some believe this is a person who has the ability to physically heal others through some special giftedness from God. There is no lack of televangelists claiming such power. Others say this is one of those gifts used to authenticate the gospel message in the apostolic age and that it has ceased. You can see where the controversy starts.

The best solution is to begin with a study of the words used in the text. The phrase is ετα χαρίσματα ἰαμάτων (*eta charismata*

---

[4] The importance of a prayer ministry in the church cannot be overstated. But the truth is, effective prayer ministries in a church come from effective prayer lives that have developed in the membership. I highly recommend the work of Dr. Gregory Frizzell as an aid to any church seeking to improve both the corporate and personal prayer life of the church. Consider the following: *Returning to Holiness* (Bethany Press, 2000) and *How to Develop a Powerful Prayer Life* (Bethany Press, 1999). These and other resources can be obtained from http://frizzellministries.org.

iamaton). We clearly see the word *gift*, which we have previously defined and shown its connection to grace. This is the grace-gift or ministry of healing (from *iama*) that Liddel says is "a means of healing, remedy, medicine" (GEL). Some of the lexicons define the word as the "power to heal" but don't specify whether that is through medicine or miracle. One of the definitions given is "cure" (SCDBW). That would seem to indicate a medicinal approach.

What seems very clear is that God is still in the business of healing physical diseases. Often He does so in answer to prayer, and that is why this ministry gift follows "miracles" (a prayer ministry) in the list. An effective prayer ministry, while it should not be focused on physical needs alone, will have a positive impact on the healing of the sick. We are instructed in scripture to pray for one another.

> Is anyone among you suffering? Let him pray. Is anyone cheerful? Let him sing psalms. Is anyone among you sick? Let him call for the elders of the church, and let them pray over him, anointing him with oil in the name of the Lord. And the prayer of faith will save the sick, and the Lord will raise him up. And if he has committed sins, he will be forgiven. Confess your trespasses to one another, and pray for one another, that you may be healed. The effective, fervent prayer of a righteous man avails much. (James 5:13-16)

While we believe in the power of God to heal, we do not believe in faith healers. But this gift is not referring to someone who has some sort of New Testament-like apostolic power to heal. We are talking about the church in prayer seeking the will of the Heavenly Father on behalf of others. Sometimes God is pleased to answer those prayers with healing; other times He answers and does not heal. But if we look carefully at the text from James, we discover that it is *not* primarily a plea for physical healing.

James admonishes the believers he is addressing to "confess your trespasses one to another and pray for one another." Why would it be necessary to "confess" sins to be "healed?" Is all sickness a result of sin? It certainly is not. James is referring to "fervent prayer," which avails absolutely in spiritual areas only. It should be obvious that James's primary consideration here has little, if anything, to do with physical illnesses.

Many of us would say, "But I don't want anyone to know about my sin." Exactly, and the devil and his demons would agree. The less confession of sin in the fellowship of the church, the less power the church has. Sin is most dangerous to a segregated believer. Satan has always operated on the principle of divide and conquer. Honesty and integrity are great helps to our spiritual progress. That's why we need the fellowship of the church. But this is not a suggestion that every single sin needs to be publicly confessed, nor that the details need to be shared. However, some will not even go to the altar in church to do business with God for fear that someone else will think they must be guilty. We are guilty! We have sinned and transgressed God's commands.

Again in this passage, the word *healed* is the word *iaomai,* "to heal, cure; or restore." The usual word for healing of physical illness is *therapeuo. Iama,* the root, as we have said, primarily signifies spiritual restoration or forgiveness of sin. It is used in Hebrews 12:12-13 and again in First Peter 2:24—where, in both instances, it clearly refers to spiritual healing. Jesus also used it in this context: "For the hearts of this people have grown dull. Their ears are hard of hearing, And their eyes they have closed, Lest they should see with *their* eyes and hear with *their* ears, Lest they should understand with *their* hearts and turn, So that I should *heal* them" (Matt. 13:15; emphasis mine).

Dr. W. A. Criswell told of the final year of Dr. George Truett's life, his predecessor at First Baptist Dallas. Apparently, Dr. Truett suffered terribly during that last year. But through it all, Dr. Criswell noted that his friend maintained a great faith in God and believed until the end in the tremendous goodness of God. He repeated what he oft preached, "Not my will, but thine be done." It was in that yielded state of submission that Dr. Truett died. Criswell says,

That is what it is to be a Christian. Anyone can sing songs and be happy when all is well. But what happens when the dark day comes, when the valley stretches endlessly ahead, when illness racks, and the bed is itself an affliction? That is when we glorify God, singing songs in the night, trusting in the goodness of the Lord. We take it to God in prayer, and ask the pastor and people who believe in the Lord to pray. We use every means God has given us—the doctor, the pharmacist, the hospital—then having prayed, having done all that we know how to do, yielded, submissive, we leave the final verdict in God's hands. If it is God's will that we live, may we praise the Lord in the gift of days. If it is God's will that our lives be closed like a book and the last chapter be written, then may we have the faith to believe that God will heal us over there. This is what it is to be a Christian.[5]

Let's go back to our main text in the Corinthians passage. The word *healings* is plural and so would indicate that we are dealing with ministry to many different spiritual, social, and physical needs. That there are sick and hurting people who could benefit from medical, social, and counseling assistance from the church is obvious. Churches where they can should establish clinics to minister to these needy persons in their church and community. This could include dental and health care, as well as crisis pregnancy centers, alcohol and drug rehabilitation centers, and shelters for the homeless.

Obviously, many churches are too small to operate effective ministries of this type on their own. That is where a church should consider partnering with other like-minded churches, denominational ministries, or parachurch groups that have established such ministries. This will give members of the church additional opportunities to find places to exercise their motivational gifts.

---

[5] W. A. Criswell, *Expository Sermons on the Epistle of James* (Grand Rapids: Zondervan, 1975), 115.

Helps

In reality, the miracles, gifts of healings, and helps-type ministries should build one upon another and often go hand in hand. Some believe that this gift and the gift of service from Romans 12:7 are the same. The gift of service is a motivational gift whereas this refers to the ministry areas in a church that are designed to meet the needs of others and where the gift of service might readily be demonstrated.

The word itself is rich with meaning. It comes from a root word meaning "to grasp" or "lay hold of." The word is ἀντίλημψις (*antilēmpsis*), "to "help" in the general sense (i.e., not of miracles but of loving action [cf. Acts 6:1ff]) (TDNTA). John MacArthur gives an excellent definition: "to take the burden off someone else and place it on oneself."[6] He goes on to point out that this area of ministry is vitally important in supporting those who minister in other areas and with different gifts. Paul used the term when speaking to the elders from Ephesus when he met with them in Miletus (emphasis mine): "I have shown you in every way, by laboring like this, that you must *support* the weak. And remember the words of the Lord Jesus, that He said, 'It is more blessed to give than to receive'" (Acts 20:35).

For practical purposes, we are talking about everything from a clothing closet and food pantry to rescue missions and orphanages. There are no specific helping areas of ministries that are required for any church, and this is for good reason. Every church's ministry field is different. But it is reasonable to believe that the Lord wants each church to determine what needs exist within the membership and in the surrounding community. It might also be in the scope of this area of ministry to consider what kind of helping ministries might be established on the mission field.

It is wise for churches not to waste resources and gifts on ministries that would duplicate what other churches or ministries are already doing. In one case, it seemed reasonable to close down the

---

[6] John MacArthur, *The MacArthur New Testament Commentary: 1 Corinthians* (Chicago: Moody Press, 1984), 324.

clothing-closet ministry of the church I was serving as pastor at the time. The building that housed the ministry was on the verge of being condemned, and the decision had been made to take the building down rather than try to renovate it. The old building was taking up space needed for parking. Just down the road from our church was a very effective city rescue mission that had a thrift-shop ministry. They were better equipped to handle the distribution of the clothes to the needy than we were.

Some of the people working in our clothing closet were upset that they were losing their place of service. But I involved them in the transfer of the clothes, hangers, racks, and other miscellaneous equipment that had been gathered over a number of years to the rescue mission. The mission was thrilled to receive the items. As it turned out, they needed help to work in their thrift shop, and our church members were able to take their gifts and serve there.

This is one of the keys to effectively establishing a spiritual gifts ministry in your church. First you must teach and train the congregation in the motivational gifts. Then you find ministries within the church or community where they can put their gifts to use in the Lord's work.

Administrations

The previous three ministry areas require a great deal of administration. They need direction, accountability, and excellence. But there are many other areas in a church that need the oversight of good and godly people. Administrative ministries can include a number of things, from support staff to ministry teams or committees, depending on how a church is organized. There are many who complain that they don't like "organized" religion. Well, I for one don't like "unorganized" religion! One cannot read the Bible, and in particular the New Testament, and not see that God has laid out a very specific organization for the church to follow. It is not rigid by any means, but it does have some very specific areas that are clearly set out as important.

Let's consider the organization of the church. It is a local body of regenerated, baptized believers. The term for church is *ekklesia*, or "the called out." It originally meant "an assembly of people who were called together to consider matters of public interest." In the New Testament, the word was used to describe the church, which was a visible body of people gathered for a specific purpose. The word is never used in the New Testament to refer to a national or international body, group, or organization. My friend Dr. Jimmy Millikin says,

> The New Testament knows nothing of a nebulous, indefinable, invisible, scattered church. It only knows a church which has regular meetings (1 Cor. 5:4; 11:19, 33-34; 16:2; 14:19; Heb. 10:25); prescribed officers (1 Tim. 3:1-13, Eph. 4:8-11); observes tangible ordinances (1 Cor. 11:23-34); and disciplines its members (1 Cor. 5:4, Matt. 18:15-17).[7]

Sometimes we get labeled as only being concerned about buildings, budgets, and baptisms. It is true that Baptists and other evangelicals are number crunchers at times. But I would contend that as long as we understand what the numbers represent (souls and opportunity for service), we are only enhancing our ministry effectiveness if we do it with excellence. No doubt there are many things more important than buildings and budgets, but very few churches could operate in an efficient manner without them. God has gifted—motivated, if you will—some of our members with the gifts of leading, serving, and giving to meet these administrative needs in the church. Many pastors and elders, whose primary gifts are speaking gifts, will have a secondary gift in leading. In fact, the pastors of a church are charged with the responsibility for the oversight and management of the church (1 Pet. 5:1-5, Acts 20:17-32).

The word is κυβέρνησις (*kubernesis*) and comes from the root verb that means "to steer" and, thus, "to rule." The noun form is *helmsman*

---

[7] Jimmy Millikin, *Christian Doctrine for Everyman* (Southaven, MS: The King's Press, 1976), 85.

(used in Acts 27:11). It means literally "steering" and figuratively "government" and "divine direction" (TDNTA). Another definition given is "guidance, administration, analogous to the piloting of a ship" (DBL). The church is like the great ship Zion, and it needs to be guided safely to its desired haven.

I have some experience driving ships, and that helps me understand what Paul was getting at with this word choice. Many years ago, I was standing watch as officer of the deck on a US Navy-guided missile cruiser. We were pulling into a port along the east coast of Africa, a place that no US Navy ship had been in many years. The harbor was small, and there was only one pier where we could safely dock. It would be a tight fit, and getting in and out would be difficult. Due to engineering problems with our steam plant, we only had one screw (propeller) operational. Maneuvering 8,500 tons is much easier when both screws can be used against each other to turn the ship. A local pilot was taken aboard, and tugs were standing by.

In looking over the port through my binoculars, I noticed that an old wreck was docked at our pier! I knew there was no way we would be able to dock at that pier, and that was where the pilot was taking us. I took the *con* (control of the helm and lee helm) back from the pilot, to the surprise of the captain, and ordered our one operating engine room to "all back full." I pointed out the problem in the harbor to the captain. One thing a Navy captain and his subordinate officers do not want to do is run a Navy ship aground!

One thing a pastor never wants to do is run one of God's churches aground. The pastor and the people of each church should understand the motivational gifts, know who is properly gifted, and find a way to get those people into the positions of leadership and administration of the church's ministries. Piloting or navigating a seagoing vessel requires knowledge of the forces of the sea, skill in plotting and maintaining a course, and serious study of the navigational charts. It is also critical to know the rules of the road and then to keep a steady and consistent watch.

It's a big ocean, but all the ships use the same routes! It is no less important for the leadership of a church to know where they are going and what God has called the church to do. You can't just get out on the sea and double your speed. You must know your course (where you are headed) and then be ever vigilant for the dangers that will come (1 Pet. 5:8-10). The various ministries of the church might be likened to a formation of ships. All have somewhat different responsibilities, but all are headed in the same direction with the same goals and objectives. We all should be pursuing excellence in the prosecution of the Great Commission and Great Commandment.

Varieties of Tongues

Tongues and their interpretation go together as we know from the fact that in Paul's list of rhetorical questions, he includes interpreting (1 Cor. 12:30). When we come to discuss this gift, we are mindful of the controversy that surrounds it. My contention is that this is primarily referring to language missions. There are many who believe that the gift of tongues ceased at the close of the apostolic age. Once the New Testament was written and the church was well established, the need for tongues no longer existed. The argument for cessation is strong. Properly understood, and regardless of what one believes about whether tongues have ceased, the biblical gift had to do with speaking (and hearing) known languages.

There is nothing in the New Testament to commend the use of unknown tongues or babble as is practiced in many charismatic style churches today.[8] One of the reasons the gift of tongues is no longer necessary is the fact that learning a foreign language is something almost anyone is capable of doing. But I believe the key here is to understand that the "varieties of tongues" actually sets up a ministry in the local church. It is a necessary and critical ministry due to the fact that we have been commanded to take the gospel to the nations, to the very end of the earth (Matt. 28:16-20). The phrase is γένη

---

[8] Chapter 15 deals extensively with this issue.

γλωσσων (*gene glosson*) and literally means the "languages of the nations." I believe this ministry is critical to any church. There should be support for missions across the globe.

As a Southern Baptist, I am grateful to be able to partner with thousands of other churches to send missionaries through our International Mission Board. Our church prays for many of our missionaries and gives financially to support them on the field. But in addition to that, I think it is important for a church to plan and carry out short-term mission trips to foreign countries.

I have been taking mission trips to Brazil for several years. While my Portuguese is not very good, I have been able to work with some terrific translators and have seen God work through those mission efforts to extend the reach of the gospel. On my first trip to Brazil, my host pastor's English was not very good (it has since improved significantly). We were having a discussion about the very subject of spiritual gifts, and there was a growing interest in tongues coming from the influence of an associate pastor in his church. We laid our Bibles side by side, English and Portuguese, and by the grace of God, were able to communicate with each other.

I would like to say of a church's involvement in supporting missions through praying, giving, and going: it's not something you have to do; it's something you get to do! There is no greater joy than partnering with fellow church members and often other churches and going out to share the gospel message with the lost. This, after all, is the one of the primary reasons the church exists.

Once you discover your motivational gift (which will be our topic in part II) and recognize its characteristics, you can then move into a ministry established in your church by the Holy Spirit. It is important to note that a church does not necessarily need to establish a ministry in each one of these areas. Just as the motivational gifts that are distributed to individual believers are different (Rom. 12:4-5), so there are "differences of ministries" (1 Cor. 12:5) that churches are called to function in. Each church must determine how the Holy Spirit is leading it to operate in its sphere of influence.

The Manifestation Gifts

Through the exercise of your motivational gift in a ministry of the local church, the Holy Spirit will work in the life of others. This is what I call a *manifestation gift*. It is an operation, activity, or working out in the lives of those to whom you have the opportunity to minister. "There are diversities of activities, but it is the same God who works all in all. But the manifestation of the Spirit is given to each one for the profit of all" (1 Cor. 12:6-7). In other words, the result of the Spirit motivating you to ministry is that others might receive one of the manifestations listed:

> For to one is given the word of wisdom through the Spirit, to another the word of knowledge through the same Spirit, to another faith by the same Spirit, to another gifts of healings by the same Spirit, to another the working of miracles, to another prophecy, to another discerning of spirits, to another different kinds of tongues, to another the interpretation of tongues. But one and the same Spirit works all these things, distributing to each one individually as He wills. (1 Cor. 12:8-11)

This passage reveals the work of the Holy Spirit through your ministry. The word *activities* is ἐνέργημα (*energēma*), which is where we get the English word *energy*. It is translated "operations" in the KJV, the NASB uses the word *effects*, and the NIV says *workings*. It is the "thing wrought...[the] effect [of the] operation" (ESL). Therefore, it is "an effect—[an] operation, [a] working" (SCDBW). The word is repeated at the end of the verse when it plainly says, "The same God who works [*energeo*] all in all." The point is clear: when we exercise our spiritual gifts, we are living the Christian life exactly as God intended, for this is indeed Christ living His life through you (Gal. 2:20).

In verse 7, the effect is said to be a "manifestation of the Spirit," which is given for the purpose of benefitting others. The word *manifestation* is φανέρωσις (*phanerosis*), which is best translated "manifestation" or "appearance." It carries the idea of making something known, clear, or evident. The work of the Holy Spirit is made known to others through the outworking of your spiritual gift. Of course, it's not really you, it's Him! What a blessed privilege this is to be indwelt by the Holy Spirit and then to be used by Him in ministry to others.

Paul then gives us a list of those things we can imagine and expect the Holy Spirit to do as a result of the ministry that we accomplish using our gifts. For example, my motivational gift is prophecy. I primarily exercise that gift as I serve as a pastor-teacher and preach the Word to my congregation. As I preach, a number of things happen. I pray before each service, welcoming the presence of the Holy Spirit in our time of corporate worship. You don't have to "invite" Him if you are worshiping in the name of the One Living and True God, Jesus Christ, because He has already promised that He will be there (Matt. 18:20).

I ask the Holy Spirit to do His work of the conviction of sin, righteousness, and judgment (John 16:8-11). I ask for a hedge of protection over the congregation, that our minds will be open to hear from God through His Word. I am not surprised then when a member of the congregation says something like this after the service: "Pastor, I understand that passage now" or "Now I have the wisdom to put that principle into practice" or "My faith was encouraged by the message."

It is not a surprise to see people at the altar at the close of the service doing business with God because they have come under conviction. They have recognized (discerned) something that God wants them to do or stop doing. This is how the Spirit works. So these gifts are not gifts that individuals have and use but rather gifts that the Holy Spirit activates or operates in their life as a result of His work through a fellow believer who was exercising their motivational gift!

We should note that through the entire process, the work is all of God. In fact, we have a very clear presentation of the Trinity in First Corinthians 12:4-6. "The same Spirit" in verse 4 is the one who gives us our motivational gift. "The same Lord" in verse 5 is the Lord Jesus who directs the different ministries of the local church. In fact, it should always be Jesus who directs us to set up any ministry we undertake in the church. "It is the same God who works, all in all" in verse 6. The Father is active in producing results in our lives as the gifts operate in His church.

Let's consider the activity of the Holy Spirit as we minister through spiritual gifts.

The Word of Wisdom

The term σοφία (*sophia*) is a general term for "wisdom" and "is used most often to refer to the ability to understand God's will and apply it obediently (see, e.g., Matt. 11:19, 13:54; Mark 6:2; Luke 7:35; Acts 6:10; James 1:5; 3:13, 17; 2 Pet. 3:15."[9] The point of the spiritual gifts would be to lead people to know and apply the truth to their everyday lives. Proverbs says that wisdom is very important: "Wisdom is the principal thing; therefore get wisdom. And in all your getting, get understanding" (Prov. 4:7). The spiritual gifts are designed so that others "profit" by learning how to apply the truths of God's Word to their situations and circumstances.

The Word of Knowledge

Like the "word of wisdom," the "word of knowledge" is not some mystical thing where wisdom and words fall from the sky into your brain. When you hear someone preaching or teaching and they look up and claim that God has just spoken to them, you can rest assured that what they are about to say has no substance or truth to it. I don't want to say that God cannot, or will not, impress a thought or direction on the mind of the preacher while he is in the act of preaching. But God never says anything that contradicts His Word. The best way to preach is to study the Word and get a word from the Word before you approach the pulpit!

Paige Patterson says of these, "Both…must be understood to involve special spiritual enlightenment. This is not the mere exercise

---

[9] MacArthur, *The MacArthur New Testament Commentary*, 298.

of human abilities." I certainly agree. Patterson goes on to give a word of caution: "This 'word of knowledge' and 'word of wisdom' will never, under any circumstance, be in violation of or contradiction with the revealed truth of God as recorded in Scripture."[10]

So what then is the "word of knowledge"? This is simply gaining, or being given, knowledge about the truths of God. Wisdom is knowing how to apply the truth; knowledge is knowing the truth. It is grasping the meaning of the Word. It is knowing the doctrine (1 Tim. 4:16).

Perhaps the best passage to gain an understanding of what the Spirit does in manifesting these two "words" in the lives of believers is found in one of Paul's prayers:

> For this reason we also, since the day we heard it, do not cease to pray for you, and to ask that you *may be filled with the knowledge of His will in all wisdom and spiritual understanding*; that you may walk worthy of the Lord, fully pleasing Him, being fruitful in every good work and increasing in the knowledge of God; strengthened with all might, according to His glorious power, for all patience and longsuffering with joy; giving thanks to the Father who has qualified us to be partakers of the inheritance of the saints in the light. He has delivered us from the power of darkness and conveyed us into the kingdom of the Son of His love, in whom we have redemption through His blood, the forgiveness of sins." (Col. 1:9-14, emphasis mine)

Paul prayed that the believers in Colosse would know God's will, have the wisdom to carry out it out, and that they would be blessed with spiritual understanding about His will. The intended result was that they would walk worthy, please God, and be fruitful in good works (cf. 1 Thess. 4:1-8). But we also note an additional result that Paul desired: that they would increase in the "knowledge of God." There is an important distinction here. Knowing His will is different from knowing Him! The point is that if we are filled,

---

[10] Paige Patterson, *The Troubled, Triumphant Church* (Nashville: Thomas Nelson, 1983), 211-212.

controlled, by the knowledge of His will, our conduct and service will be right and honoring to Him; and in the process, we will get to know Him. We will grow in our walk and fellowship with the Lord. We will then be strengthened by God for all that He has called us to do.

Faith

Some think there is a new category of gifts starting with this and the following ones because of the fact that Paul uses a different word for *another* here. The word ἄλλος (*allos*) means "another of the same kind." That word is used before each of the gifts in this list except "faith." Here, he says "to another" (ἕτερος [*heteros*]), which means "another of a different kind" or "to a different one." I think the distinction, if any, is minimal. It might be said that every believer desperately needs both words of knowledge and wisdom. One cannot effectively live the Christian life without knowing the will of God and how to apply it to their life. So the rest of these manifestations of the Spirit may not be as essential, but they are certainly things we should hope the Holy Spirit would grant to us.

Faith is the word πίστις (*pistis*). It is "faithfulness, reliability... trust, confidence, faith in the active sense" (BAGD). It is obvious that we have something more here than saving faith. Every Christian must believe and place their faith in Christ for salvation. But this is the kind of faith that the disciples wanted: "And the apostles said to the Lord, 'Increase our faith'" (Luke 17:5). It is what the father of the demon-possessed boy was asking for when he cried out to Jesus to heal his son: "Jesus said to him, 'If you can believe, all things are possible to him who believes.' Immediately the father of the child cried out and said with tears, 'Lord, I believe; help my unbelief!'" (Mark 9:23-24).

To grow in faith is a worthy goal for every believer. As we exercise our gifts, the Holy Spirit works in the lives of others to build their faith. For one thing, they can see the evidence of the Holy Spirit in our lives as we are serving Him, and this encourages them to serve the Lord more faithfully.

Healing

Here we find the same word that we looked at under the ministry gifts, and there we discovered that it is not the usual Greek word for physical healing. This refers to the work of healing that the Spirit does in the life of another person as the gifts are exercised. In this case, the word is in the singular whereas in the ministry gifts list, it is plural. This refers to a healing of the spirit and soul as much, if not more so, than of the physical body. As the Word is taught or preached, as one with the gift of exhortation is counseling or encouraging, as one with gift of mercy is extending comfort, the Holy Spirit does a work of healing.

This work by the Spirit may come on the heels of repentance, brokenness, or someone grasping the power of forgiveness. Broken hearts are mended, families are restored, friends are reconciled, and sins are forsaken. When the Spirit of God is alive and active in the life of a church that is pressing forward in its understanding of the spiritual gifts, amazing things can happen. In fact, this creates an environment in the church where church discipline will be accepted, exercised, and effective.

I have always said that church discipline never works when you don't do it! But when the Spirit of God is working and people are yielding to the Spirit's control, impressive things can and do happen. I recall a situation where one of our men got in trouble with the law. I sadly read of his failure in the local newspaper. When I confronted him, he confessed. But not only did he confess, he repented. He asked if he could share with the congregation. With a broken heart, he asked the church to forgive him. I am happy to report that they did! He went to prison for his crime. During the short time he was incarcerated, he led several other inmates to Christ. His actions had cost him his job, and his finances were wiped out. But the church that forgave him prayed for him. Soon he was married, employed, and serving the Lord faithfully.

I believe this was a result of the Holy Spirit creating an atmosphere of love and mutual trust in our church, where the heart-healing activity of the Spirit could flourish. It was a God thing, no doubt. But I am convinced that the congregation had set the tone, the atmosphere, for such things to happen. It was a year in which over one hundred people were saved and baptized in the church. I don't think such things in the church happen by accident.

Miracles

We are looking at the same word we had under the ministry gifts, which we learned actually refers to the prayer ministry of the church. Here, the reference is to the results that come in response to the prayers of God's people. These are the answers to prayer, the natural or supernatural events caused by God with precise timing to bring glory to Himself.

Most of what happens in the church today can be explained by the programs and efforts of the people in the church. What we need are those things that we simply have to look at and say, "I have no idea how that happened. It must have been God's doing." Prayer is the key behind this, not just the corporate prayer times of the church but the growth in prayer of the congregation in their daily lives. The church has long emphasized praying for the sick. I sometimes to refer to the prayers of the church as *organ* prayers. It seems we are only praying for all the sick "organs" of the elderly folk.

Don't get me wrong. Praying for the sick and asking for healing for those who are in need is perfectly acceptable. But if that is all we are focused on, then we have completely missed what Jesus really meant when He said, "That men always ought to pray and not lose heart" (Luke 18:1). We need to learn to confess and repent; to worship and adore the Lord our God; to cry out for holiness, sanctification, and revival; to seek the face of the Lord for the lost.

What we have here is proof positive that God still answers prayer!

God still saves souls! God still changes lives! God still restores that which was lost! God is still in the miracle business!

Prophecy

We will learn more about prophecy as we study the motivational gift of prophecy in chapter 4. There, it is a speaking gift, and the word is the same here as in Romans 12:6. I believe that here we have the result, or the work that Holy Spirit does as a manifestation in the life of a believer. That work is the conviction of sin leading to repentance. The word is προφητεία (*propheteia*). In both passages, it is a noun in the singular feminine. The only difference in syntax is that here it is nominative while in Romans it is accusative. The nominative means it is the subject of a verb or noun, and in this case, it is the subject of the Spirit who gives or activates it.

Consequently, we are talking about a result, an activity or operation that works in someone's life. Here, the meaning is that a profound prophetic work has occurred. The word preached has taken root and brought about the desired result. Conviction of things done or left undone has made a mark. The accusative case in Romans means that the word is the direct object—in other words, it is one of the "gifts...that is given" to a member of the body of Christ; and thus, there it is a motivational speaking gift.

Discerning of Spirits

When the gifts are properly exercised, one of the activities of the Holy Spirit is to assist us in clearly recognizing right from wrong, differentiating the godly from the ungodly, knowing the difference in truth and error. *Discerning* is διάκρισις (*diakrisis*), which can mean "to distinguish." It is defined as "distinguishing, differentiation of good and evil" (BAGD).

This is not always popular in church, but one of the things that should be happening is that people should be learning the difference in right and wrong. What is right is not up for a vote. It is not a matter of, "Here is what God says. Now do whatever you want." When the gifts are being properly exercised, the Holy Spirit teaches us that God's standards are not only correct but the best choice for our lives. His Word is not up for discussion.

Oftentimes the question is asked, "What does this verse or passage mean to you?" It is totally irrelevant what it means to you or any other person. What matters is "what saith the Lord!" And, of course, what He means by what He has said. This is the focus of preaching and teaching the Word: to say what God said and what He actually meant by what He said. The proper question to ask is, "What would God have me do about this instruction in His Word?"

Since the phrase includes specifically *discerning of spirits*, there is likely a recognition of the need for spiritual warfare. The Holy Spirit wants us to know the difference in His work and that of our enemy. It would do us well to remember that we have an enemy of our soul. John admonishes us to be able to "test the spirits" (1 John 4:1-6; cf. 1 Pet. 5:8-11, 2 Cor. 10:3-6). In order to test the spirits, we need the Holy Spirit's assistance in discernment. Victory over the enemy will come as we surrender to the lordship of Christ in every area of our lives. Here, we have the promise that the Holy Spirit will be there to provide the conviction and guidance we need.

Different Kinds of Tongues—The Interpretation of Tongues

I believe the simplest way to put this in terms of an activity or result of the work of the Holy Spirit is that it is the praise and worship of God through language and music. We communicate through words. Semantics is important. The definition of words is important. When we are communicating with someone from another area of the country, and especially with someone who speaks another language, we have to be careful with our words. We want to make sure that the precious message of the gospel is communicated correctly. We will look more closely at the gift of tongues in chapter 15.

A final word about the manifestation gifts comes from Paul's summary of those gifts in verse 11: "But one and the same Spirit works all these things, distributing to each one individually as He wills." There is no question that this verse shows that these gifts are "operations" of the Holy Spirit in the lives of individual believers. They are things that only the Holy Spirit could produce, so attempts to work them up in the flesh will not produce lasting results. To appropriate this list as an additional permanent list of gifts for believers to use is to miss the point of the passage entirely.

There is good news for all who desire to be used by God to minister to others. If you will both submit to the lordship of Christ and then discern, learn, and use the spiritual gifts the indwelling Holy Spirit has given you, He will work through you to manifest His glory in the lives of others. I cannot imagine anything that would please God more or create more good in the life of the church!

The Miscellaneous Gifts

A fourth category of gifts is that which I call *miscellaneous*. They are those given the same terminology in the scripture as the areas we have discussed but are not found in those lists. There are at least three that deserve our serious consideration in a work on spiritual gifts.

Salvation

No one could argue about the fact that salvation is a gift of God's grace (Eph. 2:8-9). It is perhaps the foremost and most significant of the spiritual gifts, for without it, we would not have a motivational gift with which to serve the Lord. We will bring attention to the importance of this when we look at the proper foundation for the discovery of the gifts in chapter 3. But let's note how the terminology is used by Paul.

> But *the free gift* [*charisma*] is not like the offense. For if by the one man's offense many died, much more *the grace* [*charis*] of God and *the gift by the grace* [*dorea en charis*] of the one Man, Jesus Christ, abounded to many. And *the gift* [*dorema*] is not like that which came

through the one who sinned. For the judgment which came from one offense resulted in condemnation, but *the free gift* [*charisma*] which came from many offenses resulted in justification." (Rom. 5:15-16) For the wages of sin is death, but *the gift* [*charisma*] of God is eternal life in Christ Jesus our Lord." (Rom. 6:23)

No question about it, the greatest gift of all is the gracious gift of salvation provided to the believer through the person and work of our Lord Jesus Christ. Paul notes that the gift of salvation is very much unlike the result ("the gift," if you will) of the "offense." The gift you got from the offense of sin was death, separation from God forever, judgment, and condemnation. But the gift of God's grace resulted in your justification before God. "Thanks be to God for His indescribable gift!" (2 Cor. 9:15).

The Election of Israel

The election of Israel[11] is defined as a spiritual gift given from God. Paul explains,

> And so all Israel will be saved; just as it is written, *"The Deliverer will come from Zion, He will remove ungodliness from Jacob." "This is My covenant with them, When I take away their sins."* From the standpoint of the gospel they are enemies for your sake, but from the standpoint of God's choice they are beloved for the sake of the fathers; for the *gifts* [*charismata*] and the calling of God are irrevocable." (Rom. 11:26-29, NASB).

John MacArthur explains this in his commentary:

> When the Lord elected (by divine *choice*) the nation of Israel to be His own people, He bound Himself by His own promises to bring the Jews to salvation and to be forever His *beloved* and holy people. During this present age, Israel might be called the

---

[11] See chapter 1, God's Plan for Spiritual Gifts, pages 7-10 for additional comments on this point.

"beloved" enemies of God. Because of unbelief, they are, like all the unsaved, at enmity with God (Rom. 5:10; 8:7). But God's eternal election guarantees that their enmity is not permanent, *for the gifts and calling of God are irrevocable. Gifts* translates *charismata,* which carries the fuller connotation of grace gifts, gifts flowing from the pure and wholly unmerited favor of God.[12]

One day, all Israel will come to the knowledge of salvation because this is a spiritual gift that God Himself has promised to them.

Marriage or Celibacy

We covered this in chapter 1 when dealing with the definition of the word *charismata.* In First Corinthians 7:7, Paul says, "For I wish that all men were even as I myself. But each one has his own *gift* [*charismata*] from God, one in this manner and another in that." In the context, the *this* and *that* refers to marriage and celibacy, each being a spiritual gift granted by God (cf. ch. 1, pages 10-11).

The Mistaken Gifts

There are several other scriptural areas where there are those who find texts that command or admonish action on the part of the believer; and such is considered, or taken to be, a spiritual gift incorrectly. The most common of these is the so-called gift of evangelism.[13] *Evangelism is a command, not a gift!* There is the gift of an evangelist, a God-called preacher whose ministry is to reach the lost and who is himself a gift to the church to assist it in fulfilling the Great Commission. Other commands sometimes confused with a gift are hospitality (1 Pet. 4:9) and benevolence (1 Cor. 13:2-3). Some have even taken First Corinthians 13:3 to mean that martyrdom is

---

[12] John MacArthur, *The MacArthur New Testament Commentary: Romans 9-16* (Chicago: Moody Press, 1994), 131-132.

[13] A complete discussion of evangelism and its relationship to the spiritual gifts is covered in chapter 13.

a gift. It is not a gift but rather an event that does sometimes befall God's precious saints.

Why would someone call a command a gift? If we can say that a command is a gift, we have a ready excuse not to follow the command by saying, "Hey, that's not my gift!" If I do not want to be hospitable, then I just say that I don't have the gift. Then I don't have to feel guilty for not providing hospitality where it is needed and where I am perfectly capable of meeting the need.

At the end of this chapter, there is an organizational chart that lists all the spiritual gifts in their appropriate categories. The process is clear and direct. You discover the motivational gift that the Holy Spirit has given you. You find a ministry in your church that fits into one or more of the categories of ministry gifts. As you exercise your motivational gift, the Holy Spirit operates in the lives of others to manifest (literally to energize) a work in their life from the list of manifestation gifts.

The privilege to serve God is a great one. Discovering and developing your spiritual gift is one of the most important things you can do in your Christian life. This is the way the Holy Spirit has designed the church to operate. It is His organization, and He knows best! Your satisfaction in ministry will increase exponentially when you learn and use your motivational gift for His glory and the good of your church.

Spiritual Gifts Organizational Chart

Motivational Gifts
Romans 12:6-8

- Prophecy*
- *Service***
- Teaching*
- Exhortation*
- *Giving***
- *Administration*
  *(Or Leading)***
- *Mercy***

First Peter 4:10-11 refers to *speaking and ***serving* gifts, easily seen in their division in the list of motivational gifts

Ministry Gifts
1 Corinthians 12:27-31,
Ephesians 4:11-13

- Apostles
  (Missions ministries
  and missionaries)
- Prophets (preachers)
- Evangelists
- Teachers (pastor-
  teachers and other
  teachers in the church)
- Miracles (prayer)
- Healing (medical
  missions)
- Helps (service or social
  ministry)
- Governments
  (administrative
  ministries)
- Tongues (language
  missions)

Manifestation of Gifts
1 Corinthians 12:8-11

- Word of wisdom
- Word of knowledge
- Faith
- Gifts of healings
  (Of the spirit and soul,
  and sometimes the
  body)
- Working of miracles
  (Answers to prayer)
- Prophecy
  (Conviction of sin
  leading to repentance)
- Discerning of spirits
  (Recognizing right
  from wrong)
- Different kinds of
  tongues and the
  interpretation of
  tongues (praise and
  worship of God through
  language and music)

Miscellaneous Gifts
Salvation (Rom. 5:15-16, 6:23)
The election of Israel (Rom. 11:29)
Marriage or celibacy (1
Cor. 7:7)

Part II

Characteristics
Learning to Use the
Spiritual Gifts

3

The Proper Foundation for Discovering Your Spiritual Gifts

Understanding your place in the body of Christ

As each one has received a gift, minister it to one another, as good stewards of the manifold grace of God. If anyone speaks, let him speak as the oracles of God. If anyone ministers, let him do it as with the ability which God supplies, that in all things God may be glorified through Jesus Christ, to whom belong the glory and the dominion forever and ever. Amen.
—1 Peter 4:10-11

For as the body is one and has many members, but all the members of that one body, being many, are one body, so also is Christ.
—1 Corinthians 12:12

But now God has set the members, each one of them, in the body just as He pleased.
—1 Corinthians 12:18

Now you are the body of Christ, and members individually.
—1 Corinthians 12:27

*For as we have many members in one body, but all the members
do not have the same function, so we, being many, are one
body in Christ, and individually embers of one another.*
—Romans 12:4-5

The Bible is clear that when we are saved, we are placed, or baptized, into the body of Christ (1 Cor. 12:13). In other words, when God saves us, He makes us part of something bigger than ourselves. His purpose in doing this is to get us in on what He is doing. He knows that we do not have the capability in and of ourselves to serve Him as we should. This is the reason that Jesus had to leave the earth and send the Holy Spirit to be our guide and teacher. The method God has chosen to put us into the service of the kingdom is that of spiritual gifts. Peter says plainly that each of us has received a gift, and we are commanded to use it to minister to one another (1 Pet. 4:10-11).

In both Romans and First Corinthians, Paul makes it plain and unambiguous that we have been made part of the family of God. We have been made an individual member of a body, God has placed us where we are, and determined our sphere of service through the gifts He gave us, just as it pleased Him (1 Cor. 12:18).

That being the case, it is essential that we discover our spiritual gifts and begin to use them to serve Christ and His church. The most important biblical data on spiritual gifts is found in Romans 12:1-15. It is imperative that every Christian study these verses and seek to discover their spiritual gift. A most significant fact is that every Christian has at least one spiritual gift. No believer in the Lord Jesus Christ is left out. Furthermore, the gift each one has is designed for the purpose of edifying the body of Christ. The gift is not for yourself but for the good of others and the glory of God (1 Cor. 12:7).

As we grow in our understanding of spiritual gifts, we will discover that the key to understanding others is found in recognizing the correct operation of the spiritual gifts in their lives. Every area of our lives ought to be approached through the operation of our spiritual gift.

A Proper Foundation for Spiritual Gifts

We need to obtain a proper foundation for a complete understanding of spiritual gifts. The apostle Paul provides this for us in the context of Romans 12:1-5. One of the great weaknesses in the area of spiritual-gifts studies and ministries is that of taking verses out of their intended context. This, is a problem in any area of scripture study. Perhaps the key to grasping the spiritual gifts is to base our understanding of them on all that has preceded this chapter in Romans. Note that he begins by saying "therefore." This forces us to recall what the book of Romans teaches as a necessary background. That which is written about the spiritual gifts hinges on what Paul has already said.

Romans is a book on *redemption*. Paul deals with *sin* and *salvation*. He begins with man's complete ruin (Rom. 1-3) and God's perfect remedy in Christ (Rom. 3-5). He emphasizes the need to overcome sin and to learn to walk in the Spirit (Rom. 6-8). Then he deals with Israel's unbelief and the nation's rejection of the offer of redemption (Rom. 9-11). As he often does in his letters, Paul shifts his emphasis from doctrine to duty; in this case, from sin and salvation to *sanctification*, in chapters 12-16. Our sanctification is the process of our being set apart unto God. It is living a holy life, which is the proper behavior for a child of God. Right living can never occur without right belief. Our behavior is based on our belief. Correct doctrine is essential for proper application of biblical truth in our lives.

It is not our purpose to deal with *soteriology* (the doctrine of salvation), but what we need to clarify is this: a person must be genuinely saved to have and understand the operation of the spiritual gifts. The Holy Spirit is the one who gives each spiritual gift, and He controls its operation within us. Every believer receives the Holy Spirit at the moment of salvation (Rom. 8:9-11). Therefore, every believer receives his or her spiritual gift(s) at the moment of salvation.

God's truth on spiritual gifts is not hidden. It is revealed in scripture, and your personal study and prayerful approach to this topic will be a great benefit to you in discovering your spiritual giftedness. It is true that your pastor and other Christian leaders may be able to help you determine your gift, but you must be aware that it is your responsibility to discover your gift and to use it in the service of God.

Believers are commanded in scripture to live out the concepts of each of the seven gifts. Yet it is very clear from Romans 12 that God has specifically gifted us in at least one area. That is where we need to maximize our service for the Lord. You may or may not have every single characteristic of the gift, but you will notice a tendency toward one gift or another.

Your gift is your major motivation for ministry. Perhaps you have been a Christian for some time but have never really found or been active in a place of service or ministry in the local church. The reason could well be that you have never discovered your spiritual gift. This book has been written with the prayer that the reader will discern what gift(s) the Holy Spirit has bestowed upon them and then enter into the greatest days ever of service to our glorious King and Master, the Lord Jesus Christ.

We will consider Romans 12:1-5 in this chapter to prepare our hearts and minds for understanding the gifts.

> I beseech you therefore, brethren, by the mercies of God, that you present your bodies a living sacrifice, holy, acceptable to God, which is your reasonable service. And do not be conformed to this world, but be transformed by the renewing of your mind, that you may prove what is that good and acceptable and perfect will of God. For I say, through the grace given to me, to everyone who is among you, not to think of himself more highly than he ought to think, but to think soberly, as God has dealt to each one a measure of faith. For as we have many members in one body, but all the members do not have the same function, so we, being many, are one body in Christ, and individually members of one another.

There are four issues we find that are necessary prerequisites to discerning our gifts:

1. Presenting our bodies to God (v. 1)
2. Proving His will (v. 2)
3. Properly appraising ourselves (v. 3)
4. Taking our proper place in the body (vv. 4-5)

When Paul says, "I beseech you therefore, brethren, by the mercies of God," he is pleading with them to realize that what they are is based solely on the mercy of God. "Therefore" refers back to the whole concept of salvation that he has most effectively shared in the previous chapters.

Each person reading this book must realize who they are — you are either lost and in need of salvation, or you have been saved and lifted out of the sea of sin. If you are not saved, I urge you to consider the importance of surrendering your all to Christ before it is eternally too late. (For help on knowing how to be saved, please refer to chapter 14.)

I trust that you are saved, that you have yielded your life to Christ. If you are saved, then salvation is no longer a possibility but a fact! Now, think about the greatness of this mercy of God of which you have become a recipient. Think of who you were before and what you are now in Christ (2 Cor. 5:17, Col. 1:28). We live on the ground of these "mercies"; therefore, we ought to sense the greatness of our debt to God and the level of gratitude we should have for what He has done for us.

That is why I cannot understand a professing believer who has no bona fide interest in the things of God. They seem content with a casual Christianity, utilizing the faith for their own benefit but with little or no motivation to serve the Lord with fervor and zeal. It seems sometimes that false religions and cults are more zealous for a lie than are God's people for the truth!

Presenting Our Bodies to God (Rom. 12:1)

Man is made up of three parts: body, soul, and spirit. The Bible says, "Now may the God of peace Himself sanctify you completely; and may your whole *spirit, soul,* and *body* be preserved blameless at the coming of our Lord Jesus Christ" (1 Thess. 5:23; cf. Matt. 10:28). Our physical body is the earthly tent God has given us in which we live and move (Acts 17:28). The soul, housed in the body, is the seat of our emotions, our mind, intellect, and will. It is the part of us that actually makes us who we are, the inner man. It is the seat of our decision-making. The soul is sometimes referred to as the heart in scripture.

The spirit of man is yet a third part of our makeup. The spirit is the center of our being, and a lost man's spirit is controlled by the devil. But when we are saved, the Bible teaches us that our spirit is sealed unto the day of redemption.

> In Him you also trusted, after you heard the word of truth, the gospel of your salvation; in whom also, having believed, you were sealed with the Holy Spirit of promise. (Eph. 1:13-14; cf. 4:30).

At the very moment of salvation, the Holy Spirit comes to indwell our life, His Spirit taking up residence in our spirit and sealing us, which guarantees us that we are God's purchased possession, that we are forever His.

God is Trinitarian in essence with three natures: Father, Son, and Spirit (1 John 5:6-8). In like manner, man is trichotomous — body, soul, and spirit — as we were made in God's image (Gen. 1:26). In our text, Paul says that we are to present our bodies to Him. Presenting our bodies represents all that we are, including soul and spirit. The Christian faith is a heart relationship, yet we live in a physical world that requires our bodies being brought into subjection and being yielded to the lordship of Christ.

The Christian life is a war, and that war must be waged in our bodies (Eph. 6:10-18; 2 Cor. 10:3-6; 1 Pet. 5:8-10). It would help us to understand the basics of spiritual warfare; otherwise, we will be rendered useless in the area of service through our spiritual gifts. The Bible teaches us that there is a battle going on for control of our soul. The center of our being is our soul. Your body, which houses the soul and spirit, becomes subject to temptation of the world and the devil.

Decisions are made in the soul, the seat of our mind, will, and emotions. We can obey the Spirit. a godly influence, or we can obey the flesh, the world, or the devil through our senses (the body). Sin attacks on every level! Sin is *supernatural*, from the devil or his demons. It is *social*, from the world. And it is *selfish*, or personal, from the flesh (1 John 2:15-16, 4:1; James 4:1-10; Eph. 6:12; 1 Pet. 5:8). Don't spend forty years in the wilderness defeated by the enemy and missing God's best for your life.

Of course, the cause of our problem is sin! We are attacked and often fall into the "trap of temptation." This creates a downward path that can lead to our destruction. At the very least, it defeats us in our attempts to serve God through the spiritual gifts.

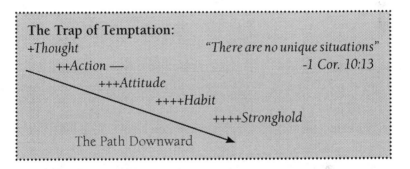

The Trap of Temptation:
+Thought   *"There are no unique situations"*
    ++Action —   *-1 Cor. 10:13*
        +++Attitude
            ++++Habit
                ++++Stronghold
    The Path Downward ➤

The chart above represents what I call *the path downward*. It all begins with unconfessed sin. We start with a thought that gives way to an act of sin. We develop an attitude about our sin that includes our justifying the acts of sin on one basis or another. This is our human reasoning working with influence from the enemy. Sadly, we fall into habits that we find very hard to break. Normally, by the time a sin has become a habit, we recognize it as sin and try through willpower and other means to rid ourselves of it. This usually proves futile.

Once the habit develops into a stronghold (2 Cor. 10:3-6), the enemy often has us hooked. At this point, one may hate the sin but will feel powerless to overcome it. Willpower and self-help programs are ineffective in overcoming the enemy. But there is good news. "He who is in you is greater than he who is in the world" (1 John 4:4). If you are saved, you have been indwelt by the Holy Spirit, and He can lead you to overcome the enemy. But if we are to get the victory over sin, we must win the battle for the soul, and the process is that we must *renew our minds!* Since sin starts with a thought, we must go to the root of the problem.

The only way to behave in a godly manner is to think in a godly way. We must control what we allow into our minds, and we must think like God thinks; which means saturating our minds with God's Word. That is what Paul is getting at in Romans 12:2 when he commands, "And do not be conformed to this world, but be transformed by *the renewing of your mind*, that you may prove what is that good and acceptable and perfect will of God" (Rom. 12:2).[1]

Let us note that Paul says, "That you present your bodies a living sacrifice...which is your reasonable service." Your body represents everything that you are and have. Why is it that God expects nothing more and nothing less than all we are, all that we have, and all that we ever hope to be? We have no more to give than all, and how could we ever think of offering less? God is never pleased with the leftovers of our time, talent, and treasure. The true Christian life is being sold out to the Lord, yielding everything to Him. As Isaac Watts so beautifully said, "Love so amazing, so divine, demands my soul, my life, my all" ("When I Survey the Wondrous Cross").

Paul reminds the Corinthians of their need to yield their bodies to the Lord. "Now the body is not for sexual immorality but for the Lord, and the Lord for the body. And God both raised up the Lord and will also raise us up by His power" (1 Cor. 6:14). In Ephesians 3:16, Paul says "that He [Jesus] would grant you, according to the riches of His glory, to be strengthened with might through His Spirit in the inner man." Through our inner man, our soul, in response to the prompting of our spirit, which is indwelt by the Holy Spirit, comes before God and presents the body as a living sacrifice to God, giving

---

[1] For a complete study of the issues of spiritual warfare, I highly recommend Dr. Sam Cathey's sermon series on the subject, *Our Spiritual Warfare*, available for MP3 download at: https://app.box.com/s/sm7o04brf4b51xwqpw3el5zoec3e3pd8.

all to Him. One of my favorite old hymns was 350 in the *1956 Baptist Hymnal*, "Is Your All on the Altar of Sacrifice Laid?"

> Is your all on the altar of sacrifice laid?
> Your heart does the Spirit control?
> You can only be blessed,
> And have peace and sweet rest,
> As you yield Him your body and soul.[2]

If we are going to be prepared to use our gifts, we must first present our bodies to Him, representing all that we are. Now we note that Paul says we are to be a "living sacrifice." What Paul is getting at is complete surrender—literally giving all to the Lord. This is the Christ-life. Christianity is *not* what *you* do for God; it is what *God* does in and through your life. So Paul is advocating our giving of ourselves over to the Lord so that He may use us and do with us as He desires.

A "living sacrifice" is a contrast to a dead-animal sacrifice. It is the praise offering of ourselves to God. It is essentially summed up in the word *obedience*. Sacrifice is not giving up what is near and dear to us. It is offering ourselves as a living sacrifice of praise to God, offered up by the operation of the Holy Spirit within.

The Old Testament prophets understood this concept. The people of Israel thought their religion would satisfy God. But Christianity is not a religion - it is a relationship! Amos reminds the Israelites,

> Seek good and not evil, That you may live; So the Lord God of hosts will be with you, As you have spoken. Hate evil, love good; Establish justice in the gate. It may be that the Lord God of hosts Will be gracious to the remnant of Joseph…Woe to you who desire the day of the Lord! For what good is the day of the Lord to you? It will be darkness, and not light. It will be as though a man fled from a lion, And a bear met him! Or as though he went into the house, Leaned his hand on the wall, And a serpent bit him! Is not the day of the Lord darkness, and not light? Is it not very dark, with no brightness in it? "I hate, I despise your feast days, And I

---

[2] Public Domain, *Baptist Hymnal* (Nashville: Convention Press, 1956), 350.

do not savor your sacred assemblies. Though you offer Me burnt offerings and your grain offerings, I will not accept them, Nor will I regard your fattened peace offerings. Take away from Me the noise of your songs, For I will not hear the melody of your stringed instruments. But let justice run down like water, And righteousness like a mighty stream." (Amos 5:14-15, 18-24).

God is not primarily interested in our religious activity. He is interested in us. He wants our full and complete devotion. This is clearly what Paul is advocating. Isaiah also understood this. He said,

> Hear the word of the Lord, You rulers of Sodom; Give earto the law of our God, You people of Gomorrah: "To what purpose is the multitude of your sacrifices to Me?" Says the Lord. "I have had enough of burnt offerings of rams And the fat of fed cattle. I do not delight in the blood of bulls, Or of lambs or goats. When you come to appear before Me, Who has required this from your hand, To trample My courts? Bring no more futile sacrifices; Incense is an abomination to Me. The New Moons, the Sabbaths, and the calling of assemblies—I cannot endure iniquity and the sacred meeting. Your New Moons and your appointed feasts My soul hates; They are a trouble to Me, I am weary of bearing them. When you spread out your hands, I will hide My eyes from you; Even though you make many prayers, I will not hear. Your hands are full of blood. Wash yourselves, make yourselves clean; Put away the evil of your doings from before My eyes. Cease to do evil, Learn to do good; Seek justice, Rebuke the oppressor; Defend the fatherless, Plead for the widow. Come now, and let us reason together," Says the Lord, "Though your sins are like scarlet, They shall be as white as snow; Though they are red like crimson, They shall be as wool. If you are willing and obedient, You shall eat the good of the land; But if you refuse and rebel, You shall be devoured by the sword;" For the mouth of the Lord has spoken. (Isa. 1:10-20)

It is important for us to understand what a true sacrifice would look like. The truth is that we can have no personal sacrifice that would be acceptable to the Lord. If we had something worthy to sacrifice to Him, that would render the Lord's sacrificial death on Calvary unnecessary. We are told, "There no longer remains a sacrifice for sins" (Heb. 10:26). While there is much in the Old Testament about the saints of God making sacrifices to the Lord *for sin*, there is no such thing in the New Testament. There we find references to the Old Testament's sacrificial system, which was a type and forerunner of the final once-for-all sacrifice of the God-man, Jesus Christ. His sacrifice is set forth as once for all and complete (cf. Heb. 9-10).

So if we are talking about the believers' sacrifice in the New Testament, we are limited to a few verses, the primary of which is the one we are now considering (Rom. 12:1-2). That sacrifice is the giving of our entire being to Him for Him to do as He pleases with us! The imagery of the New Testament in relation to the believer is one of slavery (cf. Rom. 6). So how do you become a "living sacrifice"?

We are not talking about making a sacrifice but rather *being* a sacrifice. Some think that if they do not sin, they have made a sacrifice. It is very important that we understand this truth : *it is not a sacrifice not to sin!* For example, if someone says to me on Sunday morning, "Sure is good I'm here, preacher. I just want you to know that I sacrificed my golf game (fishing trip, overtime at work, etc.) so that I could be at church this morning." My response would be, "It is not a sacrifice not to sin. Forsaking church is sinful" (see Heb. 10:25).

Some believe that their giving is a sacrifice, particularly when their giving gets over and above the tithe. But what do you have that you did not receive? How can your financial gift be a sacrifice if you are simply giving back to God what He already gave you? That is not sacrifice. Your time, your talents, your treasure, all are gifts from God. To give them back to Him can be an act of obedience, but it is not sacrifice (cf. 1 Cor. 4:6-7).

Some see their service as a sacrifice to God. They think along this line: "God, I'm serving you. I'm giving my time and abilities to work for You. I could be doing things for myself. I could be building my nest egg, making more money for my needs, but I'm sacrificing all that to You." Friend, this kind of thinking has nothing to do with New Testament Christianity! The Father doesn't need your so-called sacrifices! He has everything He needs, and if you decide not to work or serve, He will give someone else the privilege of serving in your place. It is not a sacrifice to serve the Lord; it is a privilege. You don't have to, you get to!

God doesn't need your stuff, your service, your good deeds, or your money. He wants *you*! You have nothing to give Him that He needs or wants. *You* are the sacrifice! You are the Isaac! Jesus is the ram caught in the thicket. He wants you to be a *living sacrifice*!

So when the New Testament talks about our sacrifice, it speaks of the offering of ourselves. We are commanded, "Therefore by Him let us continually offer the sacrifice of praise to God, that is, the fruit of our lips, giving thanks to His name" (Heb. 13:15). What is the "sacrifice of praise"? You cannot worship God in spirit and truth if there is unconfessed sin in your life. The "fruit of your lips" is to praise Him with clean hands and a pure heart, coming with thanksgiving in your heart. Your life is to be a life of praise to Him. Others are to see Jesus in you. Consequently, he goes on to say, "But do not forget to do good and to share, for with such sacrifices God is well pleased" (Heb. 13:16). What is it we are to do? We, as individuals, are to be good and to share ourselves, to give Him our life in service. That is the only sacrifice we have that will please Him.

When Paul wrote to the Philippians, he said, "Yes, and if I am being poured out as a drink offering on the sacrifice and service of your faith, I am glad and rejoice with you all" (2:17). A drink offering was a small addition to an Old Testament sacrifice. It was poured out on the fire and went up in an instant. This is what Paul compares his life to! "The sacrifice and service of [their, the Philippians'] faith" was their very lives given to God. Paul closes the letter by saying, "Indeed I have all and abound. I am full, having received from Epaphroditus the things sent from you, a sweet-smelling aroma, an acceptable sacrifice, well pleasing to God" (4:18). The things, in this case, were "an acceptable sacrifice" because they represented the very giving of their lives to God.

If we need further proof, we'll find it in the words of Peter:

> Coming to Him as to a living stone, rejected indeed by men, but chosen by God and precious, *you also*, as living stones, are being built up a spiritual house, a holy priesthood, to offer up spiritual sacrifices acceptable to God through Jesus Christ." (1 Pet. 2:4-5)

It is clear that the sacrifices are the believers who are yielding their lives fully to the lordship of Christ. False religions sacrifice their things; the true blood-bought, redeemed children of the King offer themselves to Him. That is a living sacrifice. Someone has said, "The problem with living sacrifices is that they keep crawling off the altar." Well, Isaac was a living sacrifice precisely because he was removed off the altar! The ram was given by God as the temporary covering for sin. When Jesus became the final sacrifice for us, there was no longer a need for us to stay on the altar. Our sacrifice is not to die, that is what Jesus did! Our sacrifice is to give our lives in His service just as Isaac went on to do.

Paul goes on to describe the type of living sacrifice that we should be: "holy, acceptable to God, which is your reasonable service." What does it mean to be "holy"? To be holy is to be separated unto God, not fleshly or carnal in behavior. It is to be totally conformed to the nature and will of God. It is to be as much like Christ as we can possibly be with the help of the Holy Spirit. Holy carries with it the idea of being "set apart for a special purpose."[3]

We often hear that we should "accept Jesus," normally in reference to being saved. But in reality, we find no such admonition in scripture. We are admonished to "receive" Christ (John 1:11- 13), to "believe" in Christ (John 3:16, 36; 4:41; 5:24; cf. Eph. 2:8-9), to "abide" in Christ (John 8:31; 15:4-10), to "follow" Christ (John 1:43; 8:12; 10:27; 12:26), to "confess" Christ (to surrender or yield to His lordship over our lives [1 John 4:15; cf. Rom. 10:9-10]); but nowhere are we told to "accept" Christ in the scriptures.

---

[3] MacArthur, *The MacArthur New Testament Commentary*, 147.

The word accept is used in the other direction. In talking about our salvation, Paul says (emphasis mine),

> Just as He chose us in Him before the foundation of the world, that we should be holy and without blame before Him in love, having predestined us to adoption as sons by Jesus Christ to Himself, according to the good pleasure of His will, to the praise of the glory of His grace, by which *He made us accepted* in the Beloved. (Eph. 1:4-6)

Clearly, here it is not that we accept Him but rather that He accepts us!

What does it mean to be "acceptable to God"? *Acceptable* simply means "well pleasing." We are to please God in all that we do and in all that we are (cf. 1 Thess. 4:1). We should desire to be as acceptable to God as we can be. Paul says this is "reasonable." This means it is the intelligent thing to do, or the only sensible thing to do. It should be expected in light of the mercies of God. Our lives will be controlled by God or the world. We must choose which it will be. The only reasonable option for us is to give God everything. Abraham is the quintessential example of this mindset as demonstrated in his believing that God would raise his son Isaac from the dead (Heb. 11:19).

This means giving one hundred percent for Jesus. Those of you who play, or have played, on any sports team can imagine the reaction if you went to practice and told the coach, "You are going to be real proud of me. I've decided to make a real sacrifice for the team, you can count on me to give a fifty percent effort to this team." Try that on your boss or your spouse and see what happens! Doesn't make any sense, does it? Then why do we think giving God the leftovers is okay?

If you are going to discover and use your spiritual gifts for the glory of God, the starting place is presenting yourself to Him. It is living the reality of the old hymn "I Surrender All."

> All to Jesus I surrender; All to Him I freely give;
> I will ever love and trust Him, In His presence daily live.
> Refrain: I surrender all, I surrender all;

All to Thee, my blessed Savior, I surrender all.
All to Jesus I surrender; Humbly at His feet I bow,
Worldly pleasures all forsaken; Take me, Jesus, take me now.[4]

If the sentiment of this song is our prayer, we will be well on our way to serving Him effectively through our spiritual gifts.

Proving His Will (v. 2)

"And do not be conformed to this world, but be transformed by the renewing of your mind, that you may prove what is that good and acceptable and perfect will of God."

The next point Paul makes is that after we have presented our bodies to the Lord, our goal is to prove, or accomplish, His will. The word *prove* is δοκιμασία (*dokimazo*) and means "to recognize as genuine after examination, to approve, deem worthy" (ESL). Nothing could be better for you, or those you desire to serve, than for you to be living out the will of God.

In order to know and do the will of God, Paul says that we must not "be conformed to this world." The word *conformed* means "to go along with or to be fashioned after." It is the act of assuming an outward expression that does not come from within. In other words, don't go along with the world's ideas and dictates. We are not to conform to the culture but rather to challenge and confront it with the claims of Christ. Sometimes your worldly associates will tempt you with sin. They may even say that you must "develop a taste for it (sin)." Instead, develop a taste for the things of God. This terminology is referring to the transitory, changeable, unstable things of the world. Don't go after the goals of the world.

In contrast to being "conformed to this world," Paul says we are to be "transformed." To be transformed is to have a radical inner change. This word gives us our English word *metamorphosis*. We

---

[4] Public Domain, *The Hymnal for Worship & Celebration* (Waco, TX: Word Music, 1986), 366.

are changed into something entirely different. The evidence that we are transformed would be summed in that fact that you begin to love what you used to hate and to hate what you used to love. In Romans 8, Paul says,

> There is therefore now no condemnation to those who are in Christ Jesus, who do not walk according to the flesh, but according to the Spirit. For the law of the Spirit of life in Christ Jesus has made me free from the law of sin and death...For whom He foreknew, He also predestined to be conformed to the image of His Son, that He might be the firstborn among many brethren. (Rom. 8:1-2, 29)

We can never live to God's glory in this evil age without this radical change. We are incapable of doing it in our own strength. This change comes only by "the renewing of your mind."

To renew is to change the quality, not the substance. The mind rules us, so its renewal is a new disposition, a new attitude, having the understanding enlightened and having our will bowed to His (cf. Titus 3:3-5; 2 Cor. 4:16, 5:17). Kenneth Wuest says it well:

> Paul therefore says in effect to the saints, "Change your outward expression from that which you had before salvation, an expression which came from your totally depraved nature and was representative of it, to an expression which comes from your regenerated inner being and is representative of it." The saint is to do this by the renewing of his mind. "Renewing" is anakainōsis (ἀνακαίνωσις), which Trench defines as "the gradual conforming of the man more and more to that new spiritual world into which he has been introduced, and in which he now lives and moves; the restoration of the divine image; and in all this so far from being passive, he must be a fellow-worker with God." Thayer defines the word, "a renewal, renovation, complete change for the better." That is, the change of outward expression is dependent upon the renovation, the complete change for the better of the believer's mental process. This is accomplished through the ministry of the indwelling Holy Spirit, who when definitely, and intelligently, and habitually yielded to puts sin out of the believer's life and produces

His own fruit. He does that by controlling the mental processes of the believer. It is the prescription of the apostle. "Habitually be ordering your behavior within the sphere and by means of the Spirit, and you will positively not fulfil the desire of the flesh (evil nature). (Gal. 5:16; WSGNT)

As we renew our minds through the Word of God, we will then be able to discern and do the will of God. We are instructed to "prove what is that good and acceptable and perfect will of God." You demonstrate the will of God by submitting to the lordship of Jesus Christ in every area of your life. God has only one will for you, and you are either in it or you are out of it. The three words given here are not three different kinds or types of the will of God. They are adjectives that describe the will of God for us. It is *good*, meaning that it is for our benefit and blessing. It is *acceptable*, meaning that it is well pleasing to God. And it is, therefore, *perfect* in every respect. If it is good for us and pleasing to God, it must be perfect.

What is critical for us to understand is that we cannot discover the characteristics and operation of the spiritual gifts without first giving ourselves totally over to the lordship of Jesus Christ. We do that by giving ourselves over to the control of the Holy Spirit day by day, moment by moment (Eph. 5:1-20). Once we have given ourselves to Christ as Lord and yielded our minds to His control, seeking to follow His will, we can then begin the important task of properly appraising ourselves for service in His kingdom.

Properly Appraising Ourselves (v. 3)

"For I say, through the grace given to me, to everyone who is among you, not to think of himself more highly than he ought to think, but to think soberly, as God has dealt to each one a measure of faith."

Spiritual evaluations are important and should be done in proportion to our faith. Paul admonishes us, "Examine yourselves as to whether you are in the faith. Test yourselves. Do you not know yourselves, that Jesus Christ is in you? - unless indeed you are disqualified" (2 Cor. 13:5). God has gifted all of us. He has given to each of us "a measure of faith." Everyone has an important part to play in the work of the kingdom through the local church. Paul is emphasizing the need for a proper appraisal or estimation of ourselves so that we will be able to discover and use our gift appropriately.

Paul is able to give this instruction to the church precisely because he is a recipient of the "grace given" to him by God. So he begins with a warning for us in regard to our self-appraisal that we "not...think... more highly than *we* ought to think" about ourselves. In other words, we need to be careful not to give too high an estimate of our own value to the kingdom's work.

We can be easily deceived by thinking too highly of ourselves. The word *think* is φρονέω (*phroneo*) and occurs four times in this verse. In the ancient world, the word was used to refer to a man in his right mind and was often used in wills. The first use of the word *think* is the normal sense, but the phrase *more highly* is actually an emphatic form of the word ὑπερφρονέω (*huperphroneo*) and actually means "arrogant" (DBL), "to be overproud, to have high thoughts" (GEL). Pride has no place in the grace of God. The sin nature, inherited from Adam, all too often carries over, and we give too high an estimation of ourselves. It is a common failing. While the world touts self-esteem, the Bible tells us to "esteem others better than himself" (Phil. 2:3- 4; cf. Rom. 15:1-2, Gal. 6:1-3).

The final use of the word *think* in the verse is "think soberly." This is another strengthened form of the word σωφρονέω (*sophroneo*) and means "to be of sound mind" (ESL) or to "be in right mind, be sober" (SCDBW). So, as believers, we are required to be sensible, or "sober," in making this estimation of ourselves.

How is one to estimate himself? Jesus said, "I am the vine, you are the branches. He who abides in Me, and I in him, bears much fruit; for without Me you can do nothing" (John 15:5). Christ has given us the proper estimation of ourselves: we are nothing; he is everything. In Matthew 19:26, Jesus says, "With men this is impossible, but with God all things are possible." This reminds us of the impossibility of doing anything without God. In and of ourselves, we are nothing.

One who accepts this can become something for God. The one who rejects this notion is doomed to failure and frustration. (This, by the way, rejects the unbiblical theology of "possibility thinking" and the "positive mental attitude" approach of the prosperity gospel crowd.)

Our nation is founded on the principles set forth in the Declaration of Independence, but maybe what we need is a *declaration of dependence*! Any success in serving God will come on the heels of our full and complete dependence on Him as our source of strength (Ps. 18:1-2; 31:2-3; Is. 49:4-5; Phil 4:13).

The phrase "as God has dealt to each one a measure of faith" gives clear indication of a basic truth about spiritual gifts. No one is left out, *every believer has at least one spiritual gift*. In essence, it means that if a man will believe the Word of God and apply what it says about him, if he will readily admit to what he really is (a sinner in need of grace or a saint in need of God), then he will he be able to enter by faith into what he should be in Christ.

We can easily err on the other side by being self-deprecating, thinking less of ourselves than we should. Sometimes this comes across as false humility. Paul says we are to think soberly or sensibly about ourselves (and this certainly applies to the discovery of our gifts). Since each believer has at least one gift, we need to recognize it as from the Lord. An underestimation of our gift causes it to be dishonored and unused. False humility is not an acceptable excuse not to serve God. We must rely on God's grace, utilize our faith, and apply the Word of God.

The issue is meekness. It is the vertical we should be most concerned with, not the horizontal. Moses is a great example of this: "Now the man Moses was very humble, more than all men who were on the face of the earth" (Num. 12:3). Though humble, Moses boldly proclaimed God's instructions and pronounced God's judgments on Pharaoh. It is said that John Knox went to Mary, Queen of Scots, in one of her angriest moods. When warned, he replied, "Why should I be afraid of a queen when I have just spent four hours before God?" When we are low before God, He will put us high before men and use us to further the interests of His kingdom.

You have been chosen by God! You are His servant. He has given you His Spirit and gifted you to serve Him. Jesus declared, "You did not choose Me, but I chose you and appointed you that you should go and bear fruit, and that your fruit should remain, that whatever you ask the Father in My name He may give you" (John 15:16). Therefore, it is not appropriate that you underestimate your ability to serve Him. It has been well said that "God is not nearly as concerned with your ability as He is with your availability."

Taking Our Proper Place in the Body (vv. 4-5)

"For as we have many members in one body, but all the members do not have the same function, so we, being many, are one body in Christ, and individually members of one another."

Having "many members in one body, but all members do not have the same function" plainly reveals the diversity of functions, offices, and gifts within each local church. The idea that any one person has all the gifts is almost ridiculous. This statement could not be any more palpable. We do not have the "same function"; therefore, we have different functions! *Function* is the word πράξις (*praxis*) and means "acting, activity... [a] way of acting, [a] course of action" (BAGD). God has given each of us a different course of action, a different way to serve, so that all the needs of the body might be met.

Therefore, we "are one body in Christ, and individually members of one another." This means that all of us must come together as one. Just like your physical body needs all of its various parts, so the church needs each of its members to function as they were designed by God to function. In short, all the gifts are important, and we need one another. Paul explains this concept in First Corinthians 12:12-27. This passage deserves to be studied carefully by anyone desiring to learn how to serve the Lord through the discovery of their gift. It is also a much-needed study for the leadership of every local church. The key factors from that passage are as follows (verses taken from 1 Corinthians 12):

1. We all have a place of service in the church. "For as the body is one and has many members, but all the members of that one body, being many, are one body, so also is Christ."

2. The church needs us in the particular place God has placed us in order to function properly. "For in fact the body is not one member but many...But now God has set the members, each one of them, in the body just as He pleased. And if they were all one member, where would the body be? But now indeed there are many members, yet one body."

3. We are not useful if we try to take someone else's position. "And the eye cannot say to the hand, 'I have no need of you'; nor again the head to the feet, 'I have no need of you.' No, much rather, those members of the body which seem to be weaker are necessary. And those members of the body which we think to be less honorable, on these we bestow greater honor; and our unpresentable parts have greater modesty, but our presentable parts have no need."

4. Our place of service is designed to benefit and bless others in the church. "But God composed the body, having given greater honor to that part which lacks it, that there should be no schism in the body, but that the members should have the same care for one another."

5. Our spiritual gifts will be directly related to our intended place or function in the body of the local church. "And if one member suffers, all the members suffer with it; or if one member is honored, all the members rejoice with it. Now you are the body of Christ, and members individually."

Some gifts are greater in scope and usefulness, but none are greater in importance. No single gift is the sum total or the whole. All the offices, functions, and/or gifts are necessary for a church to thrive in its service for God. We must find our place and carry out our tasks through the operation of the Holy Spirit and our giftedness. The common thread is *in Christ*.

Grasping the Body Concept

"So we, being many, are one body in Christ" (Rom. 12:5).

The closest worldly illustration to the concept of the "body" is that of *teamwork*. But this word is inadequate to fully explain the *body of Christ* concept. When a person is saved, he enters not only into a new relationship with God but also with God's people. This calls for major adjustments in the new believer's thinking and attitudes. The body's ability to function is tied to the members taking their proper place. What are the differences in the team concept versus the body concept?

Team Concept	Body Concept
Possible for one (or a few) to be superstars	No superstars
Rivalry and competition within	No rivalry or competition
No absolute need for dependence on others	Dependence on others is the key to success
There is a basis for individual decisions	All must submit to the Head (Christ)

Otherwise, the body of Christ as it functions in the mode of a local church is very much like a team. We must work together for the accomplishment of a common goal. The mission of the church is plain. We are to be about the business of prosecuting the Great Commission. We are to evangelize the sinner, edify the saints, and exalt the Savior. I think another thought can be gleaned from the Great Commission, and that is that we must also encourage the society. In order to be effective in "making disciples of all the nations," we must find ways to minister to all the people God puts in our sphere of influence.

What this means is that each member of the church must determine how and where they are best suited to help the team (the local church) accomplish its mission. This begins with discovering your motivational gift and then finding a ministry within the local church to exercise that gift.

4

Basic Truths about Spiritual Gifts

Instructions for discovering and developing your spiritual gift

*Having then gifts differing according to the grace that is
given to us, let us use them: if prophecy, let us prophesy
in proportion to our faith; or ministry, let us use it in our
ministering; he who teaches, in teaching; he who exhorts,
in exhortation; he who gives, with liberality; he who leads,
with diligence; he who shows mercy, with cheerfulness.*
—Romans 12:6-8

In this chapter, we will look at some foundational truths about the spiritual gifts in general and take a look at an overview of the seven motivational gifts. We will also point out some hindrances to the discovery of your gifts, as well the principles you'll need to know to help you discover and develop your gift. In the ensuing chapters, we will break down and explain each of the seven gifts. A survey of the seven motivational gifts is found in Appendix 1.[1]

---

[1] If you are not familiar with the motivational gifts, you might find it helpful to take the survey before reading about the characteristics of the gifts. This could help give you an unbiased result.

Foundational Truths Regarding Spiritual Gifts

1. **Every believer has at least one spiritual gift,** from the list in Romans 12:6-8. It is possible to have more than one; in fact, most believers will find that they have both a primary and secondary gift. God gives the gifts as it pleases Him, but no believer is left out. Since you have the Giver of the gifts indwelling your life, you can operate in any of the gifts, but God will use you more effectively where He has gifted you. Again, we must remember that *your spiritual gift is your motivation for ministry.* Sadly, this may well explain why many professing Christians are on the sidelines watching others. Each one of us needs to get in the game and do something for the kingdom of God. Christianity is not a spectator sport!

2. **Spiritual gifts produce lasting results.** When we operate outside the gifts, we can achieve only temporary results at best. It is God's will that we understand our gift and take part in His divine plan through the local church. You have heard this phrase many times: "Only one life, soon will be past; only what's done for Christ will last." The way the Holy Spirit wants to operate in your life is by being in control. This is what it means to "be filled with the Spirit" (cf. Eph. 5:18-21). You may argue that the Holy Spirit is in control. I do not deny that He is sovereign nor that He can overrule you and do as He pleases. However, it is possible to resist the work of the Holy Spirit (cf. Acts 7:51, Eph. 4:30, 2 Tim. 3:8). Therefore, we must submit to His direction and will if we are to find lasting success in serving Him through the gifts.

3. **The purpose of the gifts is to edify the body of Christ and to perfect it.** The gift is not for your benefit but for you to use to benefit others (cf. Eph. 4:11-13, 1 Cor. 12:7). This is not to say that there will be no benefit to you. There is likely nothing you could do that would enhance your walk with Christ and fellowship with God more than discovering and using your gifts. But the use of your gift is not for you to feel better about

yourself or see yourself as spiritual. It is for you to serve others for Jesus's sake (cf. 2 Cor. 4:5).

4. **Knowing one another's spiritual gifts coordinates and unifies the body of Christ**. The best way to understand yourself and others is through an understanding of the spiritual gifts. There is really no such thing as a personality conflict in the church or among Christians. The Holy Spirit dominates the personality of a Christian, and He is not in conflict with Himself! Joy will be a result of exercising your gift, but the benefit or blessing to you is always a by-product.

5. **Everything we do should be approached on the basis of our spiritual gift**. The Spirit of God is active in every area of our lives. It is a mistake to compartmentalize your life and try to separate your church life from your home life, work, or recreational activity. If you begin to see yourself as God's agent in every situation and circumstance of life, you will be amazed at how God begins to use you for His glory.

Basic Definitions of Each Gift

Paul was very systematic in his presentation of truth. As we look at the seven motivational gifts in Romans 12:6-8, we discover that the seven verses that follow are actually a description of the gifts in order. Verses 9-15 explain the basic concept of each of the gifts. I have heard a number of sermons over the years on one or more of these verses making a general application of them to all believers. In some cases, these generalizations are true, and the concepts can be supported in other places in scripture.

However, it is always best to take scripture in the proper context, and the context of these verses is that they are an explanation of the seven gifts. The connections are not hard to make when you look at them side by side. Here are the basic definitions of each of the gifts from Romans 12:

1. **The gift of prophecy.** This is one who proclaims God's truth (His Word) with authority. To prophesy is to proclaim or preach, not to predict. It is to speak forth, not to foretell. The gift enables the person to declare the claims of God and to demand a response or change of conduct.
   - "Having then gifts differing according to the grace that is given to us, let us use them: if prophecy, let us prophesy in proportion to our faith" (v. 6).
   - "Let love be without hypocrisy. Abhor what is evil. Cling to what is good" (v. 9).

2. **The gift of service (ministry).** This gift is designed to meet the practical needs of others. It is from the same root word as is the word for "deacon."
   - "Or ministry, let us use it in our ministering" (v. 7).
   - "Be kindly affectionate to one another with brotherly love, in honor giving preference to one another" (v. 10).

3. **The gift of teaching.** This gift gives the ability to open the truths of scripture and to clarify that truth without a particular commitment in mind. There is a great desire to discover and share truth. Detailed study and digging out of facts is characteristic of this gift.
   - "He who teaches, in teaching" (v. 7)
   - "Not lagging in diligence, fervent in spirit, serving the Lord" (v. 11)

4. **The gift of exhortation.** This is the gift of encouraging, comforting, and counseling others. This person motivates others to action by admonishing, encouraging, and instructing them. This moves others toward spiritual maturity and increased faith. Usually it is done on a one-to-one basis.
   - "He who exhorts, in exhortation" (v. 8)
   - "Rejoicing in hope, patient in tribulation, continuing steadfastly in prayer" (v. 12)

5. **The gift of giving**. This gift enables one to contribute joyfully and, normally, in abundance to God's work. This is a ministry that manifests the love of Christ. The giving may be to meet individual or ministry needs. This certainly implies giving over and above the tithe.
   - "He who gives, with liberality" (v. 8)
   - "Distributing to the needs of the saints, given to hospitality" (v. 13)

6. **The gift of leading (administration/ruling)**. This is a gift that enables one to organize and put things together. This is a person who is good at finding solutions. They are able to direct others to a common goal.
   - "He who leads, with diligence" (v. 8).
   - "Bless those who persecute you; bless and do not curse" (v. 14).

7. **The gift of mercy**. The gift enables one to sympathize with and to suffer alongside those who fall into affliction or distress. They both care for and share in the needs of others. They are very sensitive and try to see things from God's point of view.
   - "He who shows mercy, with cheerfulness" (v. 8).
   - "Rejoice with those who rejoice, and weep with those who weep" (v. 15).

Let us reemphasize a major point: *everyone has at least one gift.* It is the individual believer's responsibility to determine what their gift is and to use it. However, you should also remember that you have the Giver of the gifts, and therefore, every virtue of the Lord is available to you. One of the reasons for operating in your giftedness is that you encourage others to live godly in areas where they are not gifted in the same manner as you. There are certain aspects of each gift that should be understood and emulated by all.

For example, we are all commanded to tithe. When the person with the gift of giving exercises that gift, it can and often does encourage general faithfulness in giving among others. We are all to be merciful to others. Oftentimes a person with the gift of mercy encourages the sharing of empathy on the part of others through their example.

Some Examples of How the Gifts Work

All of us face the fact that sometimes other Christians behave in ways that do not set a good example. They disappoint other believers and sometimes cause unbelievers to reject the faith. We are all aware of the danger of hypocrisy. Yet the reality is that all of us are hypocritical to one degree or another. Over the years of my pastoral ministry I have always established an open-door policy regarding hypocrites in the church. After all, what better place for a hypocrite to be than the house of the Lord? Nevertheless, we should be ashamed of our hypocrisy and should work to live and speak in ways that honor the Lord and manifest godly behavior (Titus 2:11-15).

Part of the solution to this problem in the church is to better understand how the Holy Spirit motivates us and others through the use of our gifts. If we are using our gifts properly, we can detect issues of sin that may be a hindrance to the spiritual growth and maturity of a congregation.

Think of the situation in Acts 5 when Ananias and Sapphira were caught lying to the Holy Spirit. Peter, using his gift of prophecy, discerned the problem and confronted them with their sin. His goal was to correct the problem and bring them to repentance. If they continued in their sin, their compromise with the world would eventually become a reproach to the church and could even give the enemies of God an excuse for rejecting the gospel message. As we know, they did not repent, and God took their lives. Their sin was exposed, and great fear fell on the rest of the believers.

When Nathan the prophet exposed the sin of King David with Bathsheba, his gift of prophecy brought about true repentance. This, in turn, produced two great psalms on the subject, Psalm 32 and 51.

The point is that when we see problems in the life of a fellow church member, we need to seek the Lord's direction on how we might use our giftedness to bring repentance and reconciliation.

The problems you will tend to notice will be directly related to your gift. For example, if you are a prophet, you would be concerned about things that might demonstrate hypocrisy or compromise. If you are a server, your unease might be related to a failure to show genuine Christian concern through practical acts of kindness. If you are a teacher, your concern would be raised if a situation develops where someone claims their experience trumps scripture. An exhorter would be dismayed at those who show a lack of spiritual maturity.

A giver would be concerned if he thinks that someone is not trusting God in the area of their finances, or that the church is depending too much on how much money they have or don't have rather than trusting God to provide. A lack of setting and achieving goals would be a concern of a leader. One with the gift of mercy would notice if another does not seem to have genuine love for others.

To better understand why others react to certain situations the way they do, it would be helpful to consider several situations where, within a group of seven people, each gift is represented. We will see how each gift might respond and their motivation for doing so.

How the Gifts Would Respond at a Meal Where Someone Dropped the Desert[2]

Prophet: You should have been more careful. (The motivation is to correct the problem.)

Server: I'll clean that up. (The motivation is to meet an obvious practical need.)

Teacher: The reason that fell is that it was unbalanced. (The motivation is to discover why it happened.)

---

[2] The examples used here are based on information gleaned initially from Bill Gothard's *"Institute in Basic Youth Conflicts"* material (1973). Additional information came from a pamphlet provided by the Institute in Basic Life Principles titled *"Understanding Spiritual Gifts."*

Exhorter: It would be better to put the dessert on the table before the meal. (The motive here is to correct the problem for the future.)

Giver: I will purchase another desert. (The motive is to give to meet a tangible need.)

Leader: Let's get some towels and a mop and get this cleaned up. Who can prepare another dessert? (The motive here is to help achieve the immediate goal of the group.)

Mercy: Don't feel bad. It could have happened to anyone. I'm so sorry, I feel terrible for you. (The mercy's motive is to relieve the embarrassment.)

How the Gifts Might Respond to Someone in the Hospital

Prophet: What do you think God is trying to teach through this experience? (The motivation is to correct a potential problem.)

Server: I brought you a gift. I've collected your mail and fed the dog. Is there anything else you need me to do? (The motivation is to meet the patient's practical needs.)

Teacher: I did some research on this illness, and I think I know why this might have happened. (The motivation is to discover why the person is sick and what they might do to get well.)

Exhorter: In the future, you might consider getting a flu shot before you get the flu. But let us consider what has happened and see how we can help others avoid this in the future. (The motive here is to keep this from reoccurring and to prevent others from having the same problem.)

Giver: Does your insurance cover you for this illness? (The motive is to determine if there is a need for financial assistance.)

Leader: Don't worry, I got Jim to teach your Sunday school class, and Sam is handling your usher responsibilities. I called your office and let them know they need to get someone to cover for you this week. (The motive here is help organize the basic needs and responsibilities of the one who is ill.)

Mercy: How are you feeling? I just felt awful when I heard you had to come to the hospital with this illness. I was once sick with this same thing, and I know exactly how you feel. (The motive here is to comfort the sick.)

How the Different Gifts Might Be Used to Form an Ideal Church

Prophet: Well-prepared sermons exposing sin, proclaiming righteousness, and warning of judgment to come.

Server: Providing various ministries to meet the practical needs of both the congregation and the surrounding community.

Teacher: Developing doctrinally sound and in-depth Bible studies, with emphasis on word definitions.

Exhorter: Providing personal counsel and discipleship to help the membership apply scriptural principles for their daily lives.

Giver: Making certain the church has a budget that includes generous support for missions and all the necessary ministries of the church.

Leader: Organizing and leading the various administrative functions of the church so that all will be done decently and in order.

Mercy: Working to ensure ministries are developed to show concern for the feelings of people and that they express properly the loving mercy of God for His people.

Once we begin to see the operation of the gifts and how they affect the way people react to various circumstances in the life of the church, we learn to get along better with others. This can lead to the effective development of ministries in the church that reflect all the gifts and meet a much wider array of needs. There are, however, numerous things that can hinder us from the discovery of our gifts.

Hindrances to Discovering Your Gifts

Failure to Know and Understand God's Purpose and Plan

If we know God has a plan, then we should be able to discern how He intends to work out that plan in our lives. Note what Jesus says,

"The thief does not come except to steal, and to kill, and to destroy. I have come that they may have life, and that they may have it more abundantly" (John 10:10). The enemy wants to destroy God's purpose for your life. He does that by killing your joy, and he kills your joy by stealing the truth from you. That is why is it imperative that we know the will of God and then strive to accomplish it with the help of the Holy Spirit.

Paul understood this, and we see the evidence of it in his prayer for the church at Colosse:

> For this reason we also, since the day we heard it, do not cease to pray for you, and to ask that you may be filled with the knowledge of His will in all wisdom and spiritual understanding; that you may walk worthy of the Lord, fully pleasing Him, being fruitful in every good work and increasing in the knowledge of God; strengthened with all might, according to His glorious power, for all patience and longsuffering with joy; giving thanks to the Father who has qualified us to be partakers of the inheritance of the saints in the light. He has delivered us from the power of darkness and conveyed us into the kingdom of the Son of His love, in whom we have redemption through His blood, the forgiveness of sins. (Col. 1:9-14; cf. Jer. 29:10-14)

You will notice that Paul prayed that they would know God's "will," have the "wisdom" to carry it out, and then be blessed with "spiritual understanding" in the process. In other words, he prayed that they would know the what, how, and why of God's will. This would lead them to walk with God, to please Him, and to be fruitful in good works (perhaps he has in mind here the faithful exercise of their gifts). As they did this, they would be "increasing in the knowledge of God." There is a difference in knowing God's will and knowing God! You only get to know God by doing His will (cf. Matt. 7:21-23; John 3:21, 7:17; Titus 1:16; 1 John 2:4).

Rejection of What We Know Is God's Plan or Will

James tells us we must submit ourselves to God:

> But He gives more grace. Therefore He says: "God resists the proud, But gives grace to the humble." Therefore submit to God. Resist the devil and he will flee from you. Draw near to God and He will draw near to you. Cleanse your hands, you sinners; and purify your hearts, you double-minded. (James 4:6-8)

If we fail to follow this instruction and do all that we clearly know is God's will, then we will not be in a position to discover our gift. Jesus said that if we loved Him, we would obey Him (John 14:15).

A Lack of Commitment

Dr. Sam Cathey says, "We serve under sealed orders." This means that we must go and do as He commands us. God's will is not cafeteria-style where we pick and choose what we like and reject the rest. We are to do all He commands us to do. This was the example of Paul's life. Scripture shows us that Paul was content, consistent, and confident.

> Not that I speak in regard to need, for I have learned in whatever state I am, to be content: I know how to be abased, and I know how to abound. Everywhere and in all things I have learned both to be full and to be hungry, both to abound and to suffer need. I can do all things through Christ who strengthens me. (Phil. 4:11-13)

The major area in the lack of commitment comes in relation to the local church. The impact of this on the discovery of spiritual gifts cannot be overstated because the local church is the very place where the gifts are designed to operate. Carelessness about our duty to church is a sure way to fail in our spiritual gift. We must be faithful in our attendance, with our tithes, talents, and time. Since the gifts are designed to be used through the local church, we must find our place of service in the church (Heb. 10:24-26). The idea that you can have your own personal, private relationship with God fully apart from the local church is foreign to scripture!

Unresolved Spiritual Problems

Moral problems and bad relationships must be dealt with before spiritual gifts can be discovered or used. You must be right with God. If there is unconfessed sin, hostility, bitterness, or an unforgiving spirit, it will break your fellowship with God and hinder your understanding of His will. If we are to know and effectively use our gifts, we must die to sin and self and then determine to serve God (Col. 3:5-17; cf. Rom. 2:4-11, Acts 8:21-23). The gifts of Romans 12 cannot be understood until the moral conflicts and spiritual requirements of Romans 1-11 are dealt with.

Failure to Walk in the Spirit

> I say then: Walk in the Spirit, and you shall not fulfill the lust of the flesh. For the flesh lusts against the Spirit, and the Spirit against the flesh; and these are contrary to one another, so that you do not do the things that you wish. (Gal. 5:16-17)

This is a corollary to unresolved spiritual problems. It is likely that if we are not walking in the Spirit, we will have been remiss in resolving our spiritual problems and repenting of our sin.

Walking in the Spirit will make us aware of things we need to reconcile or resolve. If we are in tune with the Spirit, He will be doing His work of conviction in our hearts on a regular basis (John 16:7-11). When this happens, we are ready for Him to reveal to us where and how we should use our gifts.

Over concern with the Gifts of Others

In First Corinthians 3:4-6, Paul teaches us that we are simply a part of God's overall plan. We cannot try to imitate someone else's motivational gift as that will obscure our own gift. Romans 12:3 tells us to take our place; therefore, we are not to be covetous or jealous of others' gifts. Rejoice in your gift and do not resent the gifts of others.

As we use our spiritual gifts, we confirm them in our own life while coming to see the need for others' gifts. If we fail to understand the operation of the gifts, we may become easily frustrated. Needs that are overlooked by those with other gifts arise. Rather than frustrating us, this should cause us to see the opportunity for service that God has given us, confirming our own gift and encouraging others to meet the needs that they see through their gifts.

Elevating Experience over Scripture

While experience certainly needs to be considered in understanding how we are gifted, we must always submit our opinions, ideas, and experiences to the authority of scripture. Just the fact that an experience took place does not mean it is of God or that it validates your possession of a particular gift. The best means for discovery of your gift is to become thoroughly immersed in what God teaches you through the Word about the gifts. This is the first principle in the discovery of your gifts.

Lack of Concern for the Needs of Others

You will fail in discovering and using your gift if you have no genuine concern for the needs of others. The New Testament is filled with "one another" commands. In his discussion of spiritual gifts in First Corinthians 12, Paul says, "That there should be no schism in the body, but that the members should have the same care for one another" (v. 25). He told the Galatians that "through love we should serve one another" (5:13). To the Ephesians, he said, "And be kind to one another, tenderhearted, forgiving one another, even as God in Christ forgave you" (4:32; cf. Col. 3:13; 1 Thess. 3:12; 4:18; 5:11; Heb. 10:24).

Peter gave this instruction in direct relation to the spiritual gifts:

> And above all things have fervent love for one another, for love will cover a multitude of sins. Be hospitable to one another without

grumbling. As each one has received a gift, minister it to one another, as good stewards of the manifold grace of God. (1 Pet. 4:8-10)

I believe that if one is genuinely saved, the Holy Spirit will create a desire in the heart to serve others for Jesus' sake (2 Cor. 4:5). If you have little or no concern for the needs of others, then perhaps your greatest concern should be for the salvation of your own soul!

Principles for Discovery of Your Gift

The right attitude toward spiritual gifts will be essential in discovering your gift. You must be motivated to find your spiritual motivation! You must also be willing to use your gift and to develop it when you discover it. Keep these attitudes in mind:

Know the Gifts by Personal Study of God's Word

This is a key to living the Christian life in general. Ignorance is not a good excuse not to serve God. Paul made this clear when he said, "Now concerning spiritual gifts, brethren, I do not want you to be ignorant" (1 Cor. 12:1). Whatever you do in the Christian life, it should be done with a great deal of desire and effort. We should take our faith seriously and have a great desire to serve the One who has given His all for us (2 Tim. 2:15, 2 Pet. 1:10).

Be willing to accept with joy the revelation of the Holy Spirit to you as it relates to your gift.

You should be thankful for your gift (1 Cor. 12:7). God is not nearly as interested in your *opinion* as He is your *obedience*! The only way to achieve lasting results and, consequently, lasting joy is to follow the Lord's will for your life. That means using the gifts He has given you and doing it His way, not your way.

Dissatisfaction in life is a problem that will defeat you regardless of your understanding of the gifts. Many people think that God has somehow erred in their case. With John the Baptist, we need to take the position, "He must increase, but I must decrease" (John 3:30).

Be active in serving the Lord!

Do not allow yourself to be idle. Get busy serving the Lord. Do something for the Lord even if you are not yet sure what your gift is. We recall that this was Paul's admonition as he laid the foundation for our understanding of the gifts:

> I beseech you therefore, brethren, by the mercies of God, that you present your bodies a living sacrifice, holy, acceptable to God, which is your reasonable service. And do not be conformed to this world, but be transformed by the renewing of your mind, that you may prove what is that good and acceptable and perfect will of God. (Rom. 12:1-2)

If you are unsure of your gift, then pick your personal favorite, what you believe is the gift through which you could most faithfully serve God. Then get to work finding a ministry in your local church to use that gift. If it turns out that the gift you have chosen is not your gift, the Spirit will quickly reveal that to you. At that point, you can try another gift. Trial and error is a method you can use because all the gifts are needed, and there are only seven. You'll eventually discover what you are gifted to do.

Develop a deep desire for God's best in your life.

> "But seek first the kingdom of God and His righteousness, and all these things shall be added to you" (Matt. 6:33). "Delight yourself also in the Lord, And He shall give you the desires of your heart" (Ps. 37:4).

It is critical that you sell out to Jesus. We've all heard, and perhaps used, the phrase, "What would Jesus do?" It seems that there are many who know the question, but few seem to have the answer. As we study the Word and grow in our walk with Christ, seeking His best, the natural result of that will be to know our gift so that we can serve Him better.

Be willing to accept godly counsel from others, especially those who know you.

There is much wisdom in seeking godly counsel (Prov. 11:14; 15:22; 24:6). This is especially true if you are unsure of your gift. Ask someone (preferably a very mature believer who understands the gifts) close to you to give you an honest appraisal. If you are the one asked to appraise someone else's life to help them discover their gift, consider it an honor and then be honest with them.

Don't confuse the motivational gifts with the ministry gifts or the manifestation gifts, which God produces as a result of using spiritual gifts.

The concentration of your study on the gifts should begin with knowing the seven primary motivational gifts from Romans 12:6-8. We will devote the next seven chapters to explaining and revealing those seven gifts. When your focus is there, everything else you need to know will fall into place as you walk in the Spirit, seeking God's best for your life.

Finally, and most important of all, submit yourself to the lordship of Jesus Christ in every area of your life.

The blessings of God come on the basis of obedience to His Word and will. "Then He said to them all, 'If anyone desires to come after Me, let him deny himself, and take up his cross daily, and follow Me' (Luke 9:23). The old hymn "Trust and Obey" (John Sammis 1887) would be a good one to consider as we yield to the lordship of Christ and seek to know our giftedness.

When we walk with the Lord in the light of His Word, What a glory He sheds on our way! While we do His good will, He abides with us still, And with all who will trust and obey.
Refrain: Trust and obey, for there's no other way
To be happy in Jesus, but to trust and obey.

Not a burden we bear, not a sorrow we share, But our toil He doth richly repay; Not a grief or a loss, not a frown nor a cross, But is blessed if we trust and obey.

But we never can prove the delights of His love Until all on the altar we lay; For the favor He shows, and the joy He bestows Are for them who will trust and obey.

Then in fellowship sweet we will sit at His feet, Or we'll walk by His side in the way; What He says we will do, where He sends we will go; Never fear, only trust and obey.[3]

---

[3] Public Domain, *The Hymnal for Worship & Celebration* (Waco, TX: Word Music, 1986), 349.

5

The Gift of Prophecy

Preaching the Word to help people gain a clear conscience

Having then gifts differing according to the grace that is given to us, let us use them: if prophecy, let us prophesy in proportion to our faith.
—Romans 12:6

Let love be without hypocrisy. Abhor what is evil. Cling to what is good.
—Romans 12:9

The gift of prophecy is given to one who proclaims God's truth (His Word) with authority. Prophecy is properly to forth-tell, not to foretell.[1] Rightly understood, this gift never claims to bring any new revelation, but only to apply the inerrant revelation found in the Bible. The gift enables a person to declare the claims of God and, normally, to demand a response or change of conduct. The prophet

---

[1] It is true that the Old Testament prophets, and sometimes the New Testament prophets, along with the prophetic authors of scripture, did foretell when they gave the Word of God. But what they were doing was simply speaking the Word given to them by God. This was how we received the inspired canon of scripture (cf. 2 Tim. 3:16, 2 Pet. 1:20-21). The canon of scripture is closed, and there are no more future details to be revealed. Thus, when we speak of prophecy now, we strictly refer to the speaking forth of God's Word or preaching the Bible.

is one who wants to see a visible response to the message preached. His goal is to see changed lives, to see the transforming work of the Holy Spirit come to full fruition in the life of those he teaches. (It should be noted that the term *prophet* can be misleading to some. In this work, the word will be used to refer to an individual who has the spiritual gift of prophecy and who preaches God's Word, not someone who lays claim to an unbiblical office or who attempts to predict the future.)

The motivation of this gift is to reveal unrighteous motives or actions in men by presentation and proclamation of God's truth. Vincent says, "Prophecy in the New Testament, as in the Old, the prominent idea is not prediction, but the inspired delivery of warning, exhortation, instruction, judging, and making manifest the secrets of the heart" (wsGNT).

The word in Greek is προφητεια (*propheteia*) and means "the gift of expounding scripture, of speaking and preaching" (GEL). *Prophēteia* "denotes a. ability to declare the divine will, b. proclamation, and c. prophetic office" (TDNTA).

According to Vine, this has to do with "speaking forth the mind and counsels of God." In describing the work of the prophets, Vine says,

> The purpose of their ministry was to edify, to comfort, and to encourage the believers, 1 Cor. 14:3, while its effect upon unbelievers was to show that the secrets of a man's heart are known to God, to convict of sin, and to constrain to worship, vv. 24,25. (vine)

Our scriptural guidelines are found in the text that says that one is to prophesy "according to the proportion of faith." Meyer comments,

> Those who prophesy are to interpret divine revelation according to the strength, clearness, fervor, and other qualities of the faith bestowed upon them; so that the character and mode of their speaking are conformed to the rules and limits which are implied in the proportion of their individual degree of faith. (wsGNT)

This phrase refers both to the grace of faith given to us by God and to the body of faith or doctrine as revealed in the Word. The prophet's words must never contradict scripture. Anyone who claims the gift of prophecy yet whose words have no basis or foundation in scripture should be considered a "false prophet," of whom Jesus said to beware (Matt. 7:15).

According to Romans 12:6 and 9, a prophet must exercise the following:

- Preach according to the faith (the Word of God)
- Have love without hypocrisy
- Hate evil
- Hold fast to that which is good

Paul understood the importance of overcoming hypocrisy. The Lord Jesus often mentioned the sin of hypocrisy and leveled the charge at the religious leadership of Israel on numerous occasions (cf. Matt. 15:7, 16:3, 22:13, 23:1-39). Those who preach the Word of God must be free from hypocrisy. Integrity is greatly needed in the pulpits of our churches.

Paul also knew that the church needed to know right from wrong and truth from error. They would need to understand the difference between good and evil. Therefore, hating evil and loving good is the proper mark of a prophet. The prophet knows that righteousness is not up for a vote. It is determined by "what saith the Lord." So the prophet loves the Word of God. He hates what God hates (sin), and he loves what God loves (righteousness and holiness).

That is why the prophet does not hesitate to call sin what it is. It is sin, and God hates it. He does not back down from mentioning that which is abhorrent to God. The prophet Isaiah warns us, "Woe to those who call evil good, and good evil; Who put darkness for light, and light for darkness; Who put bitter for sweet, and sweet for bitter!" (Isa. 5:20).

The Basic Characteristics of the Gift of Prophecy

The basic characteristics of one with the gift of prophecy are detailed below. (It should be noted that one may not have every single one of these characteristics listed, but they will likely manifest most of them.)

1. A need to express thoughts and ideas verbally. Prophets[2] are very persuasive in speech (Acts 2:14, 3:12, 4:8, 11:4). The best biblical example of this gift is Peter, and he often demonstrated his prophetic gift. If we follow Peter through the book of Acts, we find him following a similar pattern as when he was walking with Jesus on the dusty roads of Judea.

When the disciples were getting organized at the outset of the church, it was Peter who expressed himself clearly and succinctly. In Acts 2:14, we read, "But Peter, standing up with the eleven, raised his voice and said to them, 'Men of Judea and all who dwell in Jerusalem, let this be known to you, and heed my words.'"

Peter was the one to take the lead in making explanations for the actions and words of the early disciples. After a lame man was healed, the people were quite amazed. Peter responded with this, "Men of Israel, why do you marvel at this? Or why look so intently at us, as though by our own power or godliness we had made this man walk?" (Acts 3:12).

When Peter and John were arrested and questioned in Jerusalem for preaching and healing others, it was Peter, filled with the Holy Spirit, who spoke up and gave a defense. Prophets have a hard time keeping quiet. They have a need to express themselves. This is motivated by the Holy Spirit who works through men to give explanation to the miraculous nature of God (Acts 4:8f).

In Acts 11, it was Peter who spoke up to defend the taking of the gospel to the Gentiles. It was critical to the founding of the church

---

[2] I use the term prophet only as a reference to someone who has the spiritual gift of prophecy, and no other meaning is implied or intended.

that a strong spokesman be raised up to make clear that the call of the Great Commission was to all people.

2. A tendency to make quick judgments. As a general rule, prophets can discern and draw conclusions quickly. All one has to do is follow Peter through the Gospels and see how often he expressed snap decisions. If the quick judgment is a result of the motivating work of the Holy Spirit, it can be a very good thing. Sometimes decisiveness is needed. The so-called gift of discernment is something that is really a part of the gift of prophecy (see point 3 below).

Note in the following scriptures the way Peter often made quick judgments:

- And Peter answered Him and said, "Lord, if it is You, command me to come to You on the water." (Matt. 14:28)
- Then Peter answered and said to Him, "Explain this parable to us." (Matt. 15:15)
- Simon Peter answered and said, "You are the Christ, the Son of the living God." (Matt. 6:16)
- Then Peter took Him aside and began to rebuke Him, saying, "Far be it from You, Lord; this shall not happen to You!" (Matt. 16:22)
- Then Peter answered and said to Jesus, "Lord, it is good for us to be here; if You wish, let us make here three tabernacles: one for You, one for Moses, and one for Elijah." (Matt. 17:4)
- Then Peter answered and said to Him, "See, we have left all and followed You. Therefore what shall we have?" (Matt. 19:27)
- Then Jesus said to the twelve, "'Do you also want to go away?" But Simon Peter answered, "Lord, to whom shall we go? You have the words of eternal life. Also we have come to believe and know that You are the Christ, the Son of the Living God." (John 6:67-69)
- Then He came to Simon Peter. And Peter said to Him, "Lord, are You washing my feet?" (John 13:6)

You will notice that in some cases, Peter's quick assessment and expression was right on target. There were a few times when he missed it big-time and probably should have remained quiet. But even in those times, he was expressing something the others probably were thinking.

3. The ability to sense when someone or something is not what it appears. The one with the gift of prophecy can *discern* right and wrong effectively, and normally does so immediately. They will react strongly to any perception of dishonesty. Such was the case with Peter when he dealt with Ananias and Sapphira in Acts 5:1-10.

Peter, either through his prophetic gift or divine revelation from the Lord, knew that Ananias and Sapphira had sold property and that they had "kept back part of the proceeds." Apparently, they made a show bringing a portion to the apostles but indicated they were giving all they had received. Peter questioned the motive:

> But Peter said, "Ananias, why has Satan filled your heart to lie to the Holy Spirit and keep back part of the price of the land for yourself? While it remained, was it not your own? And after it was sold, was it not in your own control? Why have you conceived this thing in your heart? You have not lied to men but to God."

Peter repeated this event a few hours later with the wife of Ananias. Again, Peter discerned a lack of truthfulness and accused her of lying to the Holy Spirit. Peter's gift allowed him to be sensitive to the sin problem and to declare judgment. The best outcome would have been repentance on the part of this couple, but since they did not repent, they became an example.

4. Very impulsive. Those with the gift of prophecy often make quick decisions, whether right or wrong. This is the example of Peter in his discussion with the Lord about whether or not Jesus should wash his feet or all of him (John 13:6-10).

> Then He (Jesus) came to Simon Peter. And Peter said to Him, "Lord, are You washing my feet?" Jesus answered and said to him, "What I am doing you do not understand now, but you will know after this."

This would have been a good time for Peter to curtail his impulsive nature, but he acts in accordance with his gift, albeit an abuse of the gift. Peter said to Him, "You shall never wash my feet!" Jesus answered him, "If I do not wash you, you have no part with Me." Simon Peter said to Him, "Lord, not my feet only, but also *my* hands and *my* head!" Jesus said to him, "He who is bathed needs only to wash *his* feet, but is completely clean; and you are clean, but not all of you."

The event is, to some degree, comical. Peter's initial impulsive reaction is a form of false humility: "Lord, you cannot wash my feet. That is beneath your dignity." Then, after the Lord informs him of the importance of the act, Peter jumps to the other side of the fence and with a prideful tone asks that the Lord get all of him in the washing! In both cases, he responded impulsively.

There is another case of impulsiveness that reflects more positively on Peter and the gift of prophecy. Perhaps it would be better to label this characteristic of the gift decisiveness or boldness. When Peter and John were arrested in Acts 4 for preaching the gospel, Peter, being confronted by the high priest and other rulers, acted impulsively.

But his quick answer to their questions was both bold and decisive. He upheld the truth in a time of crisis and distress. The boldness of Peter and John, coupled with the undeniable fact that they had healed a man, left their detractors with few options.

Unable to further punish or jail them, the Sanhedrin commanded them to cease speaking and teaching in the name of Jesus. Boldly and impulsively, Peter says, "Whether it is right in the sight of God to listen to you more than to God, you judge. For we cannot but speak the things which we have seen and heard" (Acts 4:19-20; cf. vv. 1-22).

5. Very open and direct about everything. The individual with the gift of prophecy is often painfully direct, even with close friends. It is wise not to ask one with the gift of prophecy what they think unless you really want to know. They will tell you clearly what they think and why. Sometimes we need someone to be direct with us, to tell us the truth even when we don't want to hear it.

In the early days of my commitment to serve the Lord and surrender to full-time vocational ministry, I was struggling with a few issues in my life. I needed someone to confront me over these things. It wasn't that I was unaware that some of my actions were sinful; I just didn't have my life in full surrender to the Lord. Some of my brothers in Christ had the courage to be open and direct with me. They risked my friendship to be obedient to God in challenging me. I am grateful that they loved me and the Lord enough to say, "What are you doing?"

Their motives were right in line with the motive of one with this gift: to reveal unrighteous motives through the teaching of God's truth. The result in my life was conviction. Through these men, the Holy Spirit spoke to me. It was a process, and God used these fellow believers to conform me more closely to the image of Christ.

Peter was so bold that he was even very open and direct with the Lord. Notice the event in Mark 8 where Jesus "began to teach them that the Son of Man must suffer many things, and be rejected by the elders and chief priests and scribes, and be killed, and after three days rise again. He spoke this word openly." But what Jesus spoke did not sit well with Peter. The idea of Jesus suffering and being killed was not what Peter had in mind for Jesus. I think he missed completely the fact that Jesus had promised that the resurrection would follow. So Peter demonstrated this characteristic of the gift: "And Peter took Him aside and began to rebuke Him" (Mark 8:31-32).

Let us keep in mind that Peter's motive was to protect the Lord, he did not want to see any harm or evil come to Him. He expressed his thoughts that were of his concern for Jesus. We do not see the others being that direct with the Lord, though they surely must have thought the same thing.

6. Grieves over sin. As is plainly stated in the explanation of the gift in Romans 12:9, the one with the gift of prophecy abhors what is evil and clings to what is good. Sin bothers the prophet, whether it is his own sin or that of others. In consequence of this, he deeply desires to see real repentance.

Repentance may be the most missing element in the presentation of the gospel today. Without true repentance, there can be no real salvation. Peter clearly understood this, and it is demonstrated in his early preaching. When preaching to the crowds on the day of Pentecost, he preached, "Repent, and let every one of you be baptized in the name of Jesus Christ for the remission of sins; and you shall receive the gift of the Holy Spirit" (Acts 2:38). Just a few days later, he once again emphasized the need for repentance, saying, "Repent therefore and be converted, that your sins may be blotted out, so that times of refreshing may come from the presence of the Lord" (Acts 3:19).

7. Strives for outward evidences of inward conviction. The one with the gift of prophecy is never content to just lay the instruction of the Lord out before the people and let it go. He is looking for an outward response, an evidence that the convicting power of the Holy Spirit has both penetrated and moved the heart of the hearer. He knows that when the Word is presented in power, the Holy Spirit will bring conviction of sin, righteousness, and judgment to come (cf. John 16:7-11).

The prophet is looking for some outward evidence, a volitional act that indicates the change needed has been wrought by the Spirit. Inward conviction is only the starting point. The prophet understands that true belief results in changed behavior. To put it another way, belief predicates behavior, and behavior demonstrates belief.

The apostle Paul demonstrates what the prophet is looking for in his comment on prophecy (meaning, the preaching of the Word):

> But if all prophesy, and an unbeliever or an uninformed person comes in, he is convinced by all, he is convicted by all. And thus the secrets of his heart are revealed; and so, falling down on his face, he will worship God and report that God is truly among you. (1 Cor. 14:24-25)

Definitively, Paul assumed that the preached Word would effect a noticeable change in the lives of those who heard and believed.

8. Places a high emphasis on authority and truth. The prophet bases his convictions on the Bible and, therefore, is very bold (John 6:67-69; 1 Pet. 2:2; 2 Pet. 1:19-21). Dr. Sam Cathey once made the statement, "You can be dogmatic if you are right." When it comes to biblical doctrine, you can have pure doctrine. In other words, it is possible to get it right, and the prophet is the type of person who desires to do just that. Of course, this requires diligent study of the Word and discipline in one's personal walk of faith, but those things are characteristic of true prophets.

The prophet is not the type to make it up as he goes. His authority is based on the Word of God, and his desire is for "truth in the inward parts" (Ps. 51:6). Peter often expressed this emphasis on authority and truth. At one point, the crowds were beginning to turn away from the demands that came from following Jesus. In John 6, we find Jesus questioning the disciples. "Then Jesus said to the twelve, 'Do you also want to go away?'" Impulsive but bold and accurate, "Simon Peter answered Him, 'Lord, to whom shall we go? You have the words of eternal life. Also we have come to believe and know that You are the Christ, the Son of the living God'" (John 6:67-69).

Peter would later write this instruction to all believers: "As newborn babes, desire the pure milk of the word, that you may grow thereby" (1 Pet. 2:2). He knew that an authoritative standard was essential, lest the faith became littered with subjective opinions and the shifting sands of man's religious conceptions rather than the objective foundation of the Word of God.

When Peter came to refer to the authority and truth upon which he founded his ministry, he was very clear that the Christian faith is not about human opinions. He said,

> And so we have the prophetic word confirmed, which you do well to heed as a light that shines in a dark place, until the day dawns and the morning star rises in your hearts; knowing this

first, that no prophecy of Scripture is of any private interpretation, for prophecy never came by the will of man, but holy men of God spoke as they were moved by the Holy Spirit. (2 Pet. 1:19-21)

9. Very concerned about the reputation of God and Christianity

(2 Peter 3). A prophet will be deeply hurt whenever there is a falsification, aberration, deception, or distortion of the Lord's person or the Christian faith. Much of what parades under the banner of evangelical Christianity fails to show a genuine concern for sound doctrine, and consequently it defames the reputation of the Lord and the church.

Some may have a relatively correct doctrinal position in that they know what the Bible teaches, but they have no evangelical zeal. Others are very zealous. They are out telling people how to get right with God, but their testimony is a lie because they have no soundness in the things of God. They are "evangelical" but not "Christian" in their doctrine.

Peter expressed this characteristic of prophecy in Second Peter 3. In an effort to remind his readers of an important biblical truth, he said,

> Knowing this first: that scoffers will come in the last days, walking according to their own lusts, and saying, "Where is the promise of His coming? For since the fathers fell asleep, all things continue as they were from the beginning of creation." (vv. 3-4)

He was deeply concerned with an attack that would scoff at God's reputation. Just as it was in Noah's day, the people scoffed. For decades, Noah had declared that the world would be flooded, and so it was. Peter continued,

> For this they willfully forget: that by the word of God the heavens were of old, and the earth standing out of water and in the water, by which the world that then existed perished, being flooded with water. (vv. 5-6)

Peter went on to apply the same concern to the promised judgment of fire that will come on the earth. Peter was declaring that God's reputation and that of the Christian faith was proven unequivocally by God's faithfulness to His past promises.

Since we know these things, Peter surmises that we should call people to repentance and that we should be ever vigilant in living lives marked by "holy conduct and godliness." Any attack on the veracity of

> The Lord is not slack concerning His promise, as some count slackness, but is longsuffering toward us, not willing that any should perish but that all should come to repentance. But the day of the Lord will come as a thief in the night, in which the heavens will pass away with a great noise, and the elements will melt with fervent heat; both the earth and the works that are in it will be burned up.
>
> (2 Peter 3:9-10)

God's reputation will draw an immediate response from the prophet. Peter concludes his second letter by referring to this particular attack on God's reputation as "the error of the wicked."

10. Willing to suffer for what is right. The prophet is so certain, so confident in his convictions, that he is always willing to suffer if that becomes necessary in standing up for what is right. The prophet is always inclined to do what is right simply because it is right, and for no other reason. The prophet is typically the one to be challenged because he is on the forefront, leading the charge against heresy and error.

Preachers sometimes shy away from preaching the whole truth lest they offend someone. I recall that in seminary, one of my professors suggested that one ought not to preach against premarital sex because the singles in the church might be offended. Statistics were given to show what number of singles in a given congregation might be involved in this ungodly lifestyle. The warning was that if you were to preach against the sin, then those committing it might leave the church.

My gift of prophecy abhorred this suggestion. I offered an alternative view. Using the same statistics, I said I would lift up the ones who were not committing the sin as an example of godliness and encourage the others to repent and get right with God. This is not a comment on my courage in class; it is simply an illustration of how the Holy Spirit works through the gift of prophecy. I wasn't being courageous; I was just reacting through the motivational gift the Spirit has given to me. The prophet abhors evil and clings to what is good. If he suffers for standing up for the truth, so be it.

In Acts 5:29-42, Peter and John are beaten for preaching in Jesus's name, but they do not cease to do so. They had been severely threatened in chapter 4, but they made it clear that obedience to God trumped any ordinance or concern of man. Later in Acts 12, James is killed and Peter is imprisoned. The rest of the book Acts speaks of the persecution of the church and the apostles. Church history is filled with the stories of the martyrs. Many of those who suffered were gifted with prophecy.

Peter writes about suffering in First Peter 3 and 4. As a prophet, he knew what it was to suffer and was willing to do so. He was therefore an excellent choice for the Holy Spirit to use to encourage others along the lines of the suffering that will come your way if you choose to live a holy life of separation to the things of God.

11. Knows how to define truth. Because the prophet's convictions are critical to his work of revealing unrighteous motives, it is essential that he have the spiritual maturity to know right from wrong. Prophets are generally very spiritually mature, serious-minded, and given to skillfulness in the Word of God.

A good definition of *spiritual maturity* can be gleaned from Hebrews 5:11-14. The writer wants to discuss the deeper things of the Christian life. He seems frustrated at the inability of his readers to mature in the faith. He says,

> Of whom we have much to say, and hard to explain, since you have become dull of hearing. For though by this time you ought to be teachers, you need someone to teach you again the first principles of the oracles of God; and you have come to need milk and not solid food. For everyone who partakes only of milk is unskilled in

the word of righteousness, for he is a babe. But solid food belongs to those who are of full age, that is, those who by reason of use have their senses exercised to discern both good and evil. (Heb. 5:11-14)

His reference to "full age" is a reference to maturity, to growing up in the things of God. The evidence that one has reached this level of growth is the ability to use their own "senses" to "discern both good and evil." In other words, the prophet knows the right thing to do in any given situation. He has reached the point of spiritual maturity so that he knows what he should do. In consequence of this, he is able to instruct others in correct conduct.

Misunderstandings and Misuses of the Gift of Prophecy

Our goal in these chapters on the individual gifts is to assist pastors and church members in understanding, knowing, and developing their motivational gifts. The characteristics discussed above—and with each subsequent gift in the ensuing chapters— are given to help one analyze what their gift may be and to understand how others with the gift may act.

We have already made the point that we do not believe there is really any such thing as a "personality conflict" among true believers. Usually, the inability to get along, to develop unity within the church for the cause of the kingdom, is more directly related to misunderstandings of the operations of the gifts. If human personalities are allowed to rise to the top and become the driving force behind our work for the Lord, then we are operating in the flesh. It is no wonder conflict exists in such circumstances.

If we walk in the Spirit and emphasize the work of ministry through the exercise of our spiritual giftedness, then we can better understand why fellow believers act the way they do. As we look at each of the gifts, we will list various misunderstandings and misuses of the gift. Careful study of this will reduce conflict in the church and lend itself to a greater usefulness in the service of our Lord.

Misuses or misunderstandings regarding the gift of prophecy may produce the following circumstances:

1. May cause the person to come off as arrogant or harsh. The prophet often exposes sin as the first step in restoration (Gal. 6:1). Since the Bible is clear on the need for church discipline, it is normally the prophet who will be first to see this need and address it. Sometimes people react with statements such as, "Who does he think he is?" or "It's none of his business" or "No one is perfect." While we could address the error in each of these reactions, the point is that the prophet is normally just responding as the Holy Spirit has motivated him.

Is it the business of the church if a believer, particularly one who is member of that fellowship, is living in sin? According to the Word of God, it is (cf. Matt. 18:15- 20; 1 Cor. 5:1-7; Gal. 6:1-10). Since the very motive of a prophet is to reveal unrighteous motives, it should not surprise us when they rise up to speak against even the appearance of evil. Church discipline is neglected to the shame of the modern church. I have a phrase about church discipline: "It never works - when you don't do it."

Another consideration is that, sometimes, a prophet's confidence is mistaken for arrogance. You can't preach the unchanging, pure, and unadulterated gospel unless you are confident that you know the truth. This confidence is given by the Holy Spirit to bring conviction to the hearers of the prophet. While prophets should be careful not to allow their personal mannerisms to appear prideful, those who hear the prophet should not be quick to make the accusation of arrogance. The bottom line will always be related to the prophet's fidelity to the truth of the Word.

2. Desires results and resents it if they do not come. Prophets will be upset when they have preached or spoken the truth, and there is no visible response or change of behavior. To desire results is a good thing; to resent the fact that the results are not apparent is not so good. Prophets should remember that sometimes the Spirit is doing a work through the gift that will take time.

It is best if the response to the conviction of the Holy Spirit is immediate. But experience and the teaching of scripture combine to tell us that God's timing is not always according to our own wishes. I have witnessed people get under conviction, and it would be days, weeks, or months before they finally responded to what God was doing.

3. May be viewed as intolerant and impatient. The prophet views his ministry as urgent, and so the appearance of being impatient is very possible. Most of the time, the prophet is simply declaring the truth with boldness and conviction. My friend Pastor Dan Spencer once commented in a sermon, "I'm not mad. I'm just fired up." It's important to know the difference. Paul reminds us that we are not to despise the preaching of God's Word. "Do not despise prophecies" (1 Thess. 5:20).

The word *despise* is *exoutheneo* and means "despise, treat with contempt, look down on, ridicule" (DBL). It is the same word that was used to describe how Herod and his "men of war" treated Jesus when He was brought before him for trial (Luke 23:11). We are called upon by Paul not to ridicule, scoff, or ignore the truth when preached with conviction.

4. Often does not appear to care for the person but seems only concerned with perfection. The prophet is motivated by the Holy Spirit to tell the truth wherever he sees the need for correction in someone's life. He is willing to risk the love and friendship of someone to tell them the truth. While it may seem the prophet is looking for perfection, he is really looking for correction (cf. 2 Tim. 3:16-17).

I believe prophets care greatly about people. Of course, they should always be "speaking the truth in love" (Eph. 4:15). They should recall Paul's admonition:

> And though I have *the gift of prophecy*, and understand all mysteries and all knowledge, and though I have all faith, so that I could remove mountains, but have not love, I am nothing. (1 Cor. 13:2)

The importance of this was revealed to me in conversation many years ago with my evangelist friend Joel Horne. Dr. Horne had heard me say on several occasions, since I was his pastor at the time, something along the lines of, "I don't care what you think. This is what God says." He lovingly corrected my thinking. He said, "Tom, of course, you care what people think. Otherwise, you wouldn't be in the ministry. You care *more* about what God thinks, but you do care what people think."

Of course, Dr. Horne was correct, and I'm grateful for his timely and godly admonition. In consequence of that, I began to change the way I phrased it. In fact, I have learned that one of the best methods of evangelism is to use a survey where you find out what another person thinks and believes about the important issues of life and death. Once you care enough to know where they are, you will be much better able to share the gospel with them!

For some, this won't change the perception. Prophets do deeply want to see change, and they will appear sometimes to be calling for perfection. But if we are honest, we know that in reality, that is the goal we should set. "Therefore you shall be perfect, just as your Father in heaven is perfect" (Matt. 5:48). The balance between caring for people and telling them the truth they need to hear is often delicate. But remember, truth without love is harshness while love without truth is mere sentimentalism.

5. May appear overbearing but often is simply seeking a commitment. Prophets will press hard for response and will come on strong, sometimes to the point of being overbearing. The prophet can temper his gift and remain more faithful to the call of God if he will keep ever before him the fact that Jesus loved sinners and he is to love them too. The one who is confronted by the prophet should keep in mind that the only pathway to a life blessed by God is through obedience, and this is the motivation of the prophet—to help one to full and complete trust and obedience in the things of God.

6. Becomes distressed over the abuse of authority. It has been rightly said that "authority should produce tenderness not tyranny." While a prophet can be prone to abuse authority, he should be upset with himself or any other person who abuses it. The need for protection for pastors and counselors, many of whom have the gift of prophecy, has never been greater. Prophets must guard their ministries and not allow themselves to fall into potentially compromising situations.

The greatest abuse of authority in the life of the church generally revolves around pastors or counselors taking advantage of counselees. It is wise for any prophet not to counsel members of the opposite sex unless their spouse is present or the spouse of the counselee is present.

7. Refuses to be coy or evasive. Therefore, the prophet will be honest to a fault. If you ask a prophet whether or not they like your tie or your dress, you should be prepared to receive an honest answer! If they don't like it, they will probably tell you. A fellow prophet once told me that if I would continue wearing the sport coat I had on, it would come back into style one day!

People whose feelings are easily hurt will be more likely to be offended by a prophet, but normally it is for your own good that the Holy Spirit motivates the prophet to speak truth into your life. When it comes to matters of physical appearance, the consequences may not always be so high; but when it comes to matters of morality or obedience to the things of God, the stakes are very high.

Peter understood this, and it is demonstrated in his response to Jesus when the Lord first called him to follow Him. Peter was instructed to let down his nets for a catch of fish. They had toiled all night with no results. But Peter obeyed the Lord, and a great number of fish were caught. It was miraculous. "When Simon Peter saw it, he fell down at Jesus' knees, saying, 'Depart from me, for I am a sinful man, O Lord!'" (Luke 5:8). Peter made no attempt to be coy or evasive about who he was. He readily admitted his sinfulness and unworthiness to follow Jesus.

8. Finds it easy to condemn self when he fails. A prophet's desire to preach and obey the truth will bring much condemnation when the prophet is the one to fail. Prophets can be very hard on themselves. When they bring a stinging word from God, it would be helpful to remember that they have likely already applied it to themselves. I have preached myself under conviction on more than one occasion.

It is also possible for a prophet to cut off others, and sometimes quickly, for their failures. But we should remember that the gospel we preach, while strong against sin, is the very gospel that has the answer for sin - forgiveness through the cleansing blood of Jesus! True repentance will always result in the forgiveness of the Lord (cf. Mark 16:7).

Bible Characters Who Illustrate the Gift

Peter best illustrates the gift of prophecy. He was the spokesman for the disciples and was the leading preacher during the early days of the church. His boldness was a great blessing to the establishment of the New Testament church. Paul also clearly had the gift of prophecy as evidenced by his straightforward preaching, ministry, and writing. As you go through the characteristics and the misunderstandings of the gift, you can see Peter in each of them.

The Old Testament prophets also serve as biblical examples of the gift, though sometimes their work had a different context than that of the New Testament gift of prophecy.

Bible Verses That Explain the Gift

There are a host of verses that refer to the gift of prophecy. For the one who believes they have this gift, the study of these sections and verses will be indispensable (cf. 1 Cor. 12:10; 13:2; 14:1-3, 6, 22, 24-25; 2 Pet. 1:20-21; 1 Thess. 5:20; Eph. 4:11-16; 2 Tim. 4:1-5).

It is difficult to rank the gifts in importance. We have seen that all the gifts are important and that every believer is gifted to serve. Like the parts of a body are all important to the effective function of life, so are all the gifts needed for the greatest effectiveness of the church. But it does seem clear that prophecy is the greatest of the gifts. Paul commands the pursuit of love above all things, commends the spiritual gifts, and then puts the gift of prophecy in the place of prominence (1 Cor. 14:1-3).

The charge to preach given by Paul to Timothy is a clear look at how the gift of prophecy is designed to work. Paul said,

> I charge you therefore before God and the Lord Jesus Christ, who will judge the living and the dead at His appearing and His kingdom: Preach the word! Be ready in season and out of season. Convince, rebuke, exhort, with all longsuffering and teaching. For the time will come when they will not endure sound doctrine, but according to their own desires, because they have itching ears, they will heap up for themselves teachers; and they will turn their ears away from the truth, and be turned aside to fables. But you be watchful in all things, endure afflictions, do the work of an evangelist, fulfill your ministry. (2 Tim. 4:1-5)

How Jesus Demonstrated the Gift of Prophecy

Jesus is not only the Giver of the gifts. In His exemplary life on earth, He was the quintessential example of each of the seven motivational gifts. To be a Christian is to be like Christ. This could not be more evident than when it comes to the spiritual gifts. Whatever your gift, you can look to the example of Jesus in the Gospels as your model of how to best glorify God through the development and use of your gifts.

In the case of the gift of prophecy, we can look to Jesus as our model and guide. If we study His life and how He preached, we will be better able to minister in the gift of prophecy. There is no question that Jesus had a prophetic ministry. We refer to Him as Prophet, Priest, and King, and so He was.

Jesus began His ministry by preaching and doing so in a very prophetic manner. The first word of the very first sermon was *repent*. "From that time Jesus began to preach and to say, 'Repent, for the kingdom of heaven is at hand'" (Matt. 4:17). That He was a prophet was recognized by all who encountered His ministry. "And when He had come into Jerusalem, all the city was moved, saying, 'Who is this?' So the multitudes said, 'This is Jesus, the prophet from Nazareth of Galilee'" (Matt. 21:10-11). "Then fear came upon all, and they glorified God, saying, 'A great prophet has risen up among us;' and, 'God has visited His people'" (Luke 7:16).

When Jesus confronted the woman at the well of Sychar in John 4, He gave a perfect example of how the spiritual gift of prophecy works. He certainly demonstrated care and compassion for the woman, but He was not negligent to point out unapologetically the changes she needed to make in life. He called to her to repentance and corrected her faulty view of doctrine. In the end, He called upon her to worship Him in spirit and truth.

Conclusion

The gift of prophecy is listed first because Paul understood that it was the most important and foundational to the others. A solid foundation in revealed truth through the Word of God is the first line of defense in understanding and using any of the motivational gifts. A prophetic ministry in the church is absolutely necessary. It is the method by which the Holy Spirit holds us accountable, convicts us of sin, warns us of judgment, encourages us to live righteously, and sets us apart for the work of the ministry (Eph. 4:11-16). Every believer will be blessed by understanding this gift and expressing gratefulness for the ministry of those gifted with prophecy whom God has placed in their lives.

6

The Gift of Service

*Serving others for Jesus's sake, meeting practical
needs to free others for ministry*

Or ministry, let us use it in our ministering.
—Romans 12:7

*Be kindly affectionate to one another with brotherly
love, in honor giving preference to one another.*
—Romans 12:10

The gift of service, or ministry, is designed to meet the practical
needs of others, often to free them for other areas of ministry. The
word is διακονία (*diakonia*), "a service or ministry." It is primarily the
idea of ministering to the personal needs of others but, by extension,
can include any service need in the life of the local church. The literal
meaning of the word is to "wait on a table." The root word is the same
for that translated, *deacon*.

The definition of the word *diakonia*, which occurs some thirty-
four times in the New Testament, is "service, ministering, especially
of those who execute the commands of others." As the word is used
in New Testament, it refers to "the ministration of those who render
to others the offices of Christian affection especially those who help

meet needs by either collecting or distributing of charities; the office of the deacon in the church; the service of those who prepare and present food" (ESL).

Kenneth Wuest says of the word, "It is a wise man who stays within the sphere of service for which God the Holy Spirit has fitted him, and does not invade some other field of service for which he is not fitted" (WSGNT). Paul's reminder that we do not all have the same function is a telling expression of this truth (Rom. 12:4; cf. 1 Cor. 12).

Kittle points out that this is "a labor of love" or "any discharge of service in genuine love." Further describing the word, Kittle says, "A decisive point for understanding the concept is that early Christianity learned to regard and describe as διακονία all significant activity for the edification of the community (Eph. 4:11 ff.), a distinction being made according to the mode of operation" (TDNT).

The scriptural guidelines given in our text say simply that one is to exercise the gift of service by serving! Literally the text reads, "Or ministry, let us use it in our ministering." The KJV says, "Let us wait on our ministering," which is an amplification of the Greek. It literally translates "in service." We are to minister with ministry. This gift is primarily directed toward people and meeting their practical needs.

Further, verse 10 says that the servers should "be kindly affectionate to one another with brotherly love, in honor giving preference to one another."

According to Romans 12:7 and 10, a server must do the following:

- Serve in a ministry
- Be willing to lovingly serve others
- Be willing to give others the credit for the work accomplished

To serve in a ministry means to be involved in serving others through a ministry of the local church. While this could include working at the local soup kitchen or rescue mission, if that were a ministry of the church or one supported by the church, it necessarily includes being involved in service to and through the local church.

Paul says that servers must "be kindly affectionate to one another with brotherly love." This is willing and loving service to others. The word translated "kindly affectionate" is the word φιλόστοργος (*philostorgos*) and means "loving or devoted." The idea behind the word is the love of belonging in the context of a family setting. The people served gain a sense of belonging to the fellowship because of the gracious ministry provided to them. The word for "brotherly love" is φιλαδελφία (*philadelphia*), which literally refers to the love of brothers or sisters but came to refer to the idea of cherishing fellow believers as brethren; hence, the reference to the church as the family of God (ESL).

The second part of the guideline in verse 10 reveals that the server should be willing to give to others the credit, or honor, for whatever ministry is accomplished. *Giving preference* is the word προηγεομαι (*proegeomai*), which means "to go before and lead" (ESL) and is used here in our text in the sense of taking the lead in showing deference one to another, "in honour preferring one another" (KJV). The ESV correctly translates it as "outdo one another in showing honor."

The Basic Characteristics of the Gift of Service

It is important to recall that as we discuss the characteristics of each gift, you may not necessarily have all of them. You will; however, notice a definite tendency toward most of them.

1. An ability to recognize personal needs and a desire to meet them. The server does not normally need to be told of needs. They will rarely say, "If I had only known." In fact, you know someone has the gift of service if they come to your house and see dirty dishes in your sink and begin to wash them without asking. The idea is that they see a need and are motivated to meet the need.

Paul knew that Timothy would provide this kind of ministry to the Philippian believers. He also knew that Timothy would serve the apostle himself by returning and giving him a full report of the state of the church. Paul says (emphasis mine),

> But I trust in the Lord Jesus to send Timothy to you shortly, that I also may be encouraged when I know your state. For I have no one like-minded, *who will sincerely care for your state.* For all seek their own, not the things which are of Christ Jesus." (Phil. 2:19-21)

2. A joy in serving when it frees others to do more important things. This is a simple motivation. The server knows that those who preach, teach, counsel, and lead have very important roles. They are willing to take the lower place and get their hands dirty, so to speak, so that others are able to do the critical and important things of ministry. Paul had been freed to do his ministry through the personal service of Timothy. He reminded the Philippians, "But you know his proven character, that as a son with his father he served with me in the gospel. Therefore I hope to send him at once, as soon as I see how it goes with me" (Phil. 2:22-23).

3. Very diligent and will do more than is necessary. This is often at disregard to personal comfort. Working in this way, the server may use up all their energy and exhaust themselves, but they understand the work must be done, and they want to do it correctly and quickly. Epaphroditus is a great example of this. He was another man with the gift of service who was apparently a member of the church at Philippi. The church as a whole was a serving church, and they sent Epaphroditus to minister to Paul.

Epaphroditus had a heart for his fellow believers back at Philippi. Paul speaks of him fondly (emphasis mine),

> Yet I considered it necessary to send to you Epaphroditus, my brother, fellow worker, and fellow soldier, but your messenger and *the one who ministered to my need*; since he was longing for you all, and was distressed because you had heard that he was sick. *For indeed he was sick almost unto death*; but God had mercy on him, and not only on him but on me also, lest I should have sorrow upon sorrow. Therefore I sent him the more eagerly, that when you see

him again you may rejoice, and I may be less sorrowful. Receive him therefore in the Lord with all gladness, and hold such men in esteem; *because for the work of Christ he came close to death*, not regarding his life, to supply what was lacking in your service toward me. (Phil. 2:25-30)

It is obvious that Epaphroditus was the kind of man who did more than expected, was extremely perseverant, and was so to his own detriment. The church could greatly benefit in our day from such serving saints doing the work of the ministry not for personal gain but for the glory of the Lord and the good of the church.

4. A difficulty in saying no. While this is characteristic of the server, it can disrupt personal priorities by creating a variety of involvements and cause the server to get sidetracked. Prophets are good at saying, "What part of *no* do you not understand?" But generally, those with the gift of service have a great deal of difficulty in saying no. Again, we could look to Epaphroditus as an example.

5. A desire to be appreciated for what they do but does not require or request public fanfare or applause. We should keep our eyes out for servers and give them a pat on the back for their wonderful service to others. We do not need to go overboard and put their names on the church marquee.

Phoebe is a tremendous example of this particular trait. Paul says of her (emphasis mine),

> I commend to you Phoebe our sister, who is a servant of the church in Cenchrea, that you may receive her in the Lord in a manner worthy of the saints, and assist her in whatever business she has need of you; *for indeed she has been a helper of many* and of myself also. (Rom. 16:1-2)

Paul simply commends her service to himself and other saints but also tells the Romans to receive and assist her.

6. An appreciation for instructions that are clear; however, does not like red tape and unnecessary restrictions. When requested, servers are very adept at getting a service project underway and completed. Once given general direction on what needs to be done, they don't want to have to jump through a lot of administrative hoops to get the job done. Servers are apt to move ahead even without instructions but do appreciate a solid and workable plan.

They will often use personal funds if necessary in order to get a job done correctly and to avoid the red tape sometimes required in cumbersome church business settings. (First and Second Timothy contain both praise and instruction, more so than to any of Paul's other assistants in the ministry, demonstrating that Timothy likely had the gift of service).

7. Does not delegate but would rather do the job themselves. Sometimes servers will not ask what needs to be done but will just begin doing whatever they see needs doing. The following example is not typical of Martha's attitude but does indicate that she had the gift of service.

When Martha approaches Jesus in this first instance, she is upset that Mary isn't helping her (emphasis mine):

> But Martha was *distracted with much serving*, and she approached Him and said, "Lord, do You not care that my sister has left me to serve alone? Therefore tell her to help me." And Jesus answered and said to her, "Martha, Martha, you are worried and troubled about many things. But one thing is needed, and Mary has chosen that good part, which will not be taken away from her." (Luke 10:40-42)

But the next time we find Martha preparing a meal, she is no longer concerned with what her sister is doing. She is just serving, doing what she was motivated by the Holy Spirit to do.

> There they made Him a supper; and Martha served, but Lazarus was one of those who sat at the table with Him. Then Mary took a pound of very costly oil of spikenard, anointed the feet of Jesus,

and wiped His feet with her hair. And the house was filled with the fragrance of the oil. (John 12:2-3)

8. Prefers short-range over long-range projects. Servers like to see a job through to completion and tend to prefer short-range tasks that can be completed in a minimum of time. Where long-range projects require the help of servers, it is wise to have someone with the gift of administration overseeing the project to keep it on track. This may be the reason for Paul's pointed instruction to Timothy to "give attention" to certain matters and then to "continue in them" in his letter to him (1 Tim. 4:13-16).

9. May feel inadequate for spiritual leadership. While this is characteristic of the gift of service, it need not be a drawback to spiritual leadership. Timothy was a server. It is likely that he was also a gifted teacher. Paul admonished him, "Let no one despise your youth, but be an example to the believers in word, in conduct, in love, in spirit, in faith, in purity" (1 Tim. 4:12).

Misunderstandings and Misuses of the Gift of Service

1. May appear insensitive or impatient with others. Servers are generally hard workers, and they will stay at a task until it is completed. I believe it would be fair to say that they do the job right the first time, without cutting corners, because they don't want to have to do it again. They will work tirelessly at times and can become impatient with people who don't share their same work ethic. They may be especially frustrated with the lack of stamina shown by others.

If you've ever hung around the fellowship hall at church to help clean up after the social was over, then it's likely that you have the gift of service. Thank God for those true servants who are willing to get their hands dirty and get the job done.

2. May come across as pushy and as desiring to exclude others. Sometimes the server just wants to get the job done effectively and professionally, but in the process, they may appear pushy. They sometimes want to do it themselves so that it will be done right. If others do not have the same diligence in the task, they may want to cut them off and go alone. Patience is needed, and the server should always seek the Lord's will and guidance and behave with grace toward others.

3. Will neglect their personal and family's needs to help others. This is a common misuse of the gift of service. It is akin to the wife of the plumber who can't get her sink unstopped because the plumber is always fixing someone else's plumbing. Servers derive great joy out of helping others, but they should take care of their personal needs and put their families first when necessary.

4. May be hurt by ingratitude on the part of those helped. When the people you help are ungrateful, it can be painful to the heart of the server. While not looking for fanfare, they do desire at least a simple recognition on occasion. Over the years, I have trained many deacons to serve the church through taking care of the church's benevolence ministry. It is a sad commentary on human nature that more often than not, those who are helped through a benevolent act rarely return to the church to say thank-you.

Sometimes those who are helped, when they are not church members already, will promise to come to church. That would constitute a degree of appreciation, now wouldn't it? Yet it is rare that the promise is fulfilled.

Servers must always remember that they are serving the Lord and that their ministry should be done "heartily, as to the Lord, and not to men" (Col. 3:23). If they do not keep this in mind, it may cause them to run ahead of God and to seek the approval of men rather than God.

5. A tendency to wear oneself out physically. Servers should in particular consider the need for that seventh day of rest. In the process of wearing out physically, it is also possible for the server to be so busy meeting practical needs of others that they neglect their own spiritual disciplines. They would do well to remember the old adage, "If you are too busy to pray and read your Bible, then you are too busy!"

There is a time and place for stepping in and rendering unrequested help, but discernment and being sensitive to the leading of the Holy Spirit are important in this regard. On the other hand, they can be taken advantage of all too easily.

6. May become easily sidetracked. Let's remember that this concept is a misuse of the gift and something that needs to be corrected. What happens is that in the midst of doing one thing, the server notices another task that has some degree of urgency to it. They leave what they started and pick up in another area. I am particularly bad about this when I go out to tackle a project on my home or yard. Sometimes I get so sidetracked I can't remember the first job I started doing!

Apparently there was some danger of this in Timothy's life, and so Paul reminded him,

> *Be diligent* to come to me quickly...Only Luke is with me. Get Mark and *bring him* with you, for he is useful to me for ministry. And Tychicus I have sent to Ephesus. *Bring the cloak* that I left with Carpus at Troas when you come— *and the books*, especially the parchments...*Do your utmost* to come before winter...The Lord Jesus Christ be with your spirit. Grace be with you. Amen. (2 Tim. 4:9-16, 21-22)

7. Will sometimes try to go around proper authorities to get a job done. Because a server is generally well equipped to know how to do a service job or willing to find out how, they are not interested in permission but rather accomplishment. They sometimes operate by the saying "It's better to get forgiveness than to ask permission." "They'll thank us when we are through" is sometimes the idea, but operating under proper godly authority is always the best course of action. We know that the end does not justify the means.

8. May neglect more important spiritual needs to take care of physical needs. We alluded to this under number five above. There is always a danger, even with other gifts, to assume that our service or ministry, whatever it might be, is so important that it must take priority over our spiritual disciplines. When our growth in the grace and knowledge of the Lord wanes, then it is time for serious reflection on our priorities. You will never be the most effective in your ministry of service to others unless you are daily walking with the Master you profess to serve.

Bible Characters Who Illustrate the Gift of Service

Timothy is one of the best demonstrators of the gift of service, but it is also important to note that he had the gift of teaching (1 Tim. 4:13-16; 2 Tim. 2:2). Martha is another example of this gift of service, as are Epaphroditus (Phil. 2) and Pheobe (Rom. 16). Studying the lives of these biblical characters will provide valuable assistance for the one with the gift of service. This will, in turn, enable them to become more effective in this most essential area of ministry to the local church.

Bible Verses That Explain the Gift of Service

Acts 6:1-7 points out the great need for servers in the early church. Most scholars believe that the passage in Acts 6 refers to the calling of the first deacons who served the church. If they were not the first deacons, they were certainly precursors to them. This is, of course, where we get the word for *deacon*. *Deacons are to serve by meeting practical needs*, primarily in the life of the church they have been called to serve. Since the word originally meant "to wait on tables," this is the idea behind the term. Therefore, it is appropriate that deacons serve the Lord's Supper, that they take up the offering, and that they serve the church in other ways, such as door greeters and ushers. But there is much more to it than that.

Deacons should determine what the needs of the body are and find ways to meet them. The visiting of, caring for, and assisting with the elderly, the sick, widows, and orphans - along with taking care of the benevolence ministries of the church - seem to be the general direction of the New Testament on their duties. Of course, there is far more instruction in the Bible on what kind of men they are to be rather than on what they are to do.

Here are some general biblical references to service:

- Of angels: Matthew 4:11, Mark 1:13, Hebrews 1:13
- Instructions to serve: Matthew 25:31-46 (in reference to the judgment of the nations at the beginning of the millennium); Galatians 5:13; Luke 17:7-10, 22:24-20; John 12:26-27; 1 Peter 4:10-11
- Examples of service: Matthew 8:15, 27:55; Luke 8:3; John 12:2; Romans 15:25; Hebrews 6:10

Note: This word, *diakonia*, is also used in connection with other spheres of service. The duties of preaching, teaching, and attending to other spiritual needs are certainly considered in the New Testament to be a service or ministry. The gift of service distinguishes itself by relating to the meeting of practical or physical needs. To meet spiritual needs is also a "service" but does not imply the gift. The best way that I have of personally serving is through the exercise of my gift, which happens to be prophecy. You serve best by exercising your gift, whatever it happens to be. In the following verses, you can see the application of the biblical word *diakonia* to the general ministry of a servant of the Lord: Acts 20:24; 2 Corinthians 4:1, 6:3, 11:8; 1 Timothy 1:12; 2 Timothy 4:5.

How Jesus Demonstrated the Gift of Service

Perhaps the greatest example of Jesus demonstrating the gift of service is in His washing of the disciples' feet in John 13. He saw a practical need, was motivated to meet it, and in the process, taught a valuable lesson to all of us regarding meeting needs. In fact, as we see Jesus operating in this gift, we realize that all of us have a ministry. Servers are sometimes used by the Holy Spirit simply to set the example for the rest of us. The things that set Jesus apart in the area of service seem to be humility and compassion. Both are elements of service that should be considered a priority by anyone who has this gift.

The server should note some of the instructions of the Lord regarding service (emphasis mine):

> Just as the Son of Man did not come to be served, *but to serve*, and to give His life a ransom for many (Matt. 20:28, Mark 10:45)

> Blessed are those servants whom the master, when he comes, will find watching. Assuredly, I say to you that *he will gird himself* and have them sit down to eat, *and will come and serve them.* (Luke 12:37)

Conclusion

One of the most compelling statements Jesus gave about service is found in the following passage (emphasis mine):

> And which of you, having a servant plowing or tending sheep, will say to him when he has come in from the field, "Come at once and sit down to eat"? But will he not rather say to him, "Prepare something for my supper, and gird yourself and serve me till I have eaten and drunk, and afterward you will eat and drink"? Does he thank that servant because he did the things that were commanded him? I think not. So likewise you, when you have done all those things which you are commanded, say, "*We are unprofitable servants. We have done what was our duty to do.*" (Luke 17:7-10)

Our service to the Lord will not gain us entrance into heaven. When we serve the Lord, we are doing that which was our duty to do. But what a great privilege it is to serve the Lord. As you serve the Lord—and in particular, if you have the gift of service—I pray that you will serve Him with gladness (Ps. 100)!

7

The Gift of Teaching

Teaching God's Word to clarify truth and validate information

He who teaches, in teaching.
—Romans 12:7

Not lagging in diligence, fervent in spirit, serving the Lord
—Romans 12:11

The gift of teaching gives one the ability to open the truths of scripture and to clarify that truth without necessarily having a particular commitment in mind. There is a great desire in the heart of the teacher to discover and share the truth with others. Detailed study and digging out of facts is characteristic of this gift.

The motivation behind this gift is to clarify truth by searching it out, validating it, and presenting it to others. Barnhouse says, "Such a gift exacts much study and consumes much time over the course of years. Yet, I believe that many could teach if they were willing to pay the price."[1] There is a price to pay if one is to be effective in teaching God's Word. But to the one so gifted by the Holy Spirit, it is a natural characteristic given graciously by God.

---

[1] Donald Grey Barnhouse, *Romans Vol. IV: God's Discipline* (Grand Rapids: Wm. B. Eerdmans Publishing Co., 1964), 48-49

The gift of teaching is uncomplicated and direct. The two words used in verse 7 are διδάσκων (*didaskon*), "teaches," a verb that refers to the act of teaching; and διδασκαλία (*didaskalia*), "teaching," a noun that can refer to that which is taught or to the act of teaching.

The definition of *teaching* is simply "teaching, instruction... that which is taught, doctrine" (ESL). The primary emphasis would be the imparting of correct doctrine to others.

Kittle refers to the usage of the word in teaching technical skills. He points out that "the decisive point is that systematic instruction is given" (TDNT). This requires that the teacher must research the subject carefully and present it systematically. As this relates to a teacher of the Word of God, it would involve careful exegesis with historical backgrounds and precise analysis of scriptural categories and words.

According to Romans 12:11, a teacher has three primary responsibilities:

- To be diligent in his work.
- To be fervent in the spirit.
- To serve the Lord; doing all as unto Jesus.

"Not lagging in diligence" is of absolute importance to the teacher. The word *lagging* is οκνηρος (*okneros*), which has the idea of being lazy, troublesome, or irksome. The word is defined as "sluggish, slothful, backward" (ESL). The "diligence" required of a teacher leaves no room for backing down or slothfulness. *Diligence* is from "*spoude* ('haste'), *spoudazo* means 'to make haste' or transitively 'to hurry something on,' then 'to treat seriously or respectfully'" (TDNTA).

Hard work alone, though, is not enough for the teacher's success in communicating effectively the timeless truths of the Word. The teacher must also be "fervent in spirit," from ζεω (*zeo*), which literally means to "show enthusiasm, have great fervor" (DBL). John MacArthur says, "Whereas diligence pertains mainly to action, being fervent in spirit pertains to attitude...The idea here is...to produce the energy necessary to get the work done."[2]

Much in the church today fails for lack of commitment. It would seem that the church is plagued with ignorance and indifference. If the average church member were to be asked if they agreed with that assessment, some would likely respond by saying, "I don't know, and I don't care!" The church is in need of teachers who will diligently and fervently take on the important task of teaching nonbelievers the gospel and believers the doctrines by which they might live the abundant life they were called to live (cf. Gal. 6:9).[3]

Finally, the teacher is admonished to remember that they, through their ministry of teaching, are "serving the Lord." Serving here is doing so as a true servant, a *doulos*, literally "as a slave." As MacArthur points out, "This has to do with perspective and priority."[4] The teaching must be in submission to the Holy Spirit, and all that is taught must be in accord with God's Word.

The Basic Characteristics of the Gift of Teaching

1. A deep love for the Word of God with a burden to know and teach it. One might wish that all of God's people had a deep love for the Word of God. This characteristic is evident in the teacher, and one of the reasons is so that they might communicate to the church the importance of the Word.

A favorite passage of anyone with the gift of teaching should be Psalm 119, the glorious passage that extols the many timeless virtues and values of the Word. The guidelines from Romans 12:11 indicate that the life of a teacher will be marked by "diligence." This diligence is the essence of the heart of a lover of God's Word as Psalm 119

---

[2] MacArthur, *The MacArthur New Testament Commentary*, 190.

[3] Apollos is an example of a teacher whom the scripture says was "fervent in spirit, he spoke and taught accurately the things of the Lord, though he knew only the baptism of John" (Acts 18:25).

[4] MacArthur, *The MacArthur New Testament Commentary*, 191.

says, "They also do no iniquity; They walk in His ways. You have commanded us To keep Your precepts *diligently*" (vv. 3-4; cf. vv. 25-32).

Of course, the love of God's Word is replete through the entire Psalm:

- "And I will delight myself in Your commandments, Which I love" (v. 47);
- "Oh, how I love Your law! It is my meditation all the day" (v. 97)
- "I hate the double-minded, But I love Your law" (v. 113)
- "Therefore I love Your commandments More than gold, yes, than fine gold!" (v. 127)
- "Your word is very pure; Therefore Your servant loves it" (v. 140)
- "Great peace have those who love Your law, And nothing causes them to stumble" (v. 165).

The burden for others to know the Word is evident in the life and ministry of a teacher. There will always be a deep desire to communicate the Word to others, and especially to fellow believers. Paul's letters to Timothy are filled with references to teaching and doctrine. As Paul sensed that his ministry was coming to an end, he urged Timothy to take the truth of the Word and communicate that truth to others. "And the things that you have heard from me among many witnesses, commit these to faithful men who will be able to teach others also" (2 Tim. 2:2).

Paul would go on encourage Timothy's diligence in the matter of "rightly dividing the word of truth" (2 Tim. 2:15). That the apostle loved the Word is evident in his charge to Timothy in chapters 3 and 4 of his second letter to Timothy. In essence, Paul said to Timothy that he must become a thorough Bible man (2 Tim. 3:10-17) and that he must establish a thorough Bible ministry (2 Tim. 4:1-8).

The work and role of the pastor-teacher is clearly set forth in Second Timothy 3:10-4:8. I believe this passage could be applied to any man or woman with the gift of teaching. First, a teacher must be a thorough Bible man or woman (2 Tim. 3:10-17); that is, they must have a deep and growing knowledge of the Word of God, coupled with a personal walk with God. It should go without saying that a belief in the infallibility and inerrancy of scripture and its authority over faith and practice is foundational. Second, a teacher must have a thorough Bible ministry (2 Tim. 4:1- 8), one that is based on biblical principles.

2. Tends to be introverted but normally will be self-disciplined.
You may recall teachers from your days in school who were outgoing with strong personalities. They were energetic and communicated knowledge to you in ways that caused you to sit up and listen. But if the truth be told, the teachers from whom you learned the most might not have had the showiest personalities. Good teachers in the realm of the Christian disciplines are not necessarily outgoing. They more often tend to be somewhat introverted.

Those with the gift of teaching, however, are normally very self-disciplined. If you read through the Pastoral Epistles, you find that this must have been true of the apostle Paul. For example, he said to the Corinthians, "But I discipline my body and bring it into subjection, lest, when I have preached to others, I myself should become disqualified" (1 Cor. 9:27).

Let us not forget that it is Paul who calls for the exercise of "diligence" in the ministry of the teacher.

3. A high view of the gift of teaching. The teacher feels that this gift is vital to the church and foundational to the other gifts. Let there be no question—the gift of teaching is critical to the life of the church. As Robert L. Thomas says, "Teaching, or its product, doctrine, is the essence of Christianity." He goes on to point out that references in the Gospels to Jesus' teaching ministry outnumber those to His preaching ministry by about one-third. Jesus is referred to as "teacher" between forty-five and fifty times. Acts mentions teaching or doctrine some twenty times, and the epistles have around sixty references to these two words.[5]

Thomas goes on to say, "Teaching is the lifeblood of the Christian faith because without doctrine Christianity is nonexistent." We might do well to remember that teaching is a part of the Great Commission (Matt. 28:19-20). The task of evangelism is incomplete without the addition of discipleship through teaching. The lack of sound biblical exposition in the teaching ministry of the church is surely a cause of the low level of living among many professing Christians.

So what does the gift of teaching really embody to the church? Thomas says, "It consists of an ability to grasp, arrange, and present revealed truth effectively and in an organized manner so that recipients have an enhanced understanding of the Scripture under consideration." Such teaching leaves the hearers "with a better comprehension of [that] particular part of the Bible than what they had before hearing the lesson."[6] It is hard to imagine anything that could be of greater importance to the church in the times that we find ourselves.

John Calvin had a high view of teaching and accords significant import to the office:

> Let him who excels in teaching know that the end is, that the Church may be really instructed; and let him study this one thing, that he may render the Church more informed by his teaching.[7]

Would to God that we had a "more informed" flock of worshipers!

4. An extremely heavy emphasis on accuracy. Accuracy is important to the teacher, especially as it relates to word definitions, biblical meanings, and historical backgrounds. We are reminded of the

---

[5] Robert L. Thomas, *Understanding Spiritual Gifts* (Grand Rapids: Kregel Publications, 1978), 194.
[6] Ibid.
[7] John Calvin, *Calvin's Commentaries: Romans*, trans. by John Owen (Grand Rapids: Baker Book House, 1996), 462.

significance Luke placed on getting the facts correct. There is no doubt that he intended his books, Luke and Acts, to be accurate renderings of the information he shared. Speaking to Theophilus, the original recipient of these books, Luke said (emphasis mine), "That you may know *the certainty of those things* in which you were *instructed*" (cf. Luke 1:1-4, Acts 1:1-3).

If we take the Great Commission as our standard, and we should, let us recall the exact nature of the instruction Jesus gave: "teaching them to observe all things that I have commanded you." The word "all" is significant. If we are to be taught to "observe all things," then accuracy in the teaching of those things is paramount. Failure to carefully study and know the meaning of words has led to many a false view of what the scripture actually says.

In Hebrews, we find a passage of scripture that is very important to our understanding of the need for emphasis on accuracy. In this passage, we are told that those who have been believers, who have been under the preaching and teaching of the Word of God, should aspire to be teachers. We know they are well taught in the things of God because they are called "holy brethren" (Heb. 3:1). They have been instructed not to drift away from the things they had heard, not to harden their hearts and fall into unbelief and rebellion. They have been instructed to be *diligent* in regard to the Word and bold in coming to the throne of grace for help from the Lord (cf. Heb. 2, 3, 4).

Then in chapter 5, we read, "For though by this time you ought to be teachers" (Heb. 5:11). But sadly, they were "unskilled

An Example of the Need for Accuracy....

We recall that after the resurrection Jesus said to Mary Magdalen, "Do not cling to Me." But the writers of the King James Version translated it, "Touch Me not." The word is hapto and means "to fasten oneself to, to adhere to, cling to" (ESL). The idea has been fostered that while in His resurrection body no one could even touch Him. Other texts conflict with this stating plainly that Jesus invited others to "touch" Him, to see that His resurrection body was real. A teacher will demand that words be accurately defined and used in the presentation of truth to God's people.

in the word of righteousness" (v. 13). The word for *unskilled* is *apeiros*, with the basic meaning of "inexperienced." It is the negative version of the word *peirao*, which means to "act...'to attempt,' 'to strive,' 'to make an effort'" (TDNT). The passage is about spiritual maturity. In order for believers to grow to "full age," to have the ability to "discern both good and evil" (v. 14), faithful and accurate Bible teaching is a necessity.

5. A need to validate other's statements. A person with the gift of teaching will be very alert to false teachers. He will check out others and often will give his own qualifications, assuming others will see this as necessary. In short, this person expects exactness out of others in relation to truth. We have a marvelous example of this in the teaching of Paul and Silas at Berea. Having come under intense scrutiny and forced to flee Thessalonica, they came to the synagogue of the Jews at Berea. Luke reports (emphasis mine),

> These were more fair-minded than those in Thessalonica, in that they *received the word with all readiness*, and *searched the Scriptures daily to find out whether these things were so.* (Acts 17:11)

They went right back to the Old Testament to check out the teaching, whether it was accurate or not. Upon discovery of the correctness of the teaching, "many of them believed" (v. 12).

6. Enjoys reading and research of facts, loves to study. The person with the gift of teaching will be very thorough, often gathering many facts and much background information. They will present them in an orderly and systematic manner. Sometimes there is greater delight in researching the facts than in presenting them.

Teachers sometimes enjoy giving those details that have not been noticed by others. We mentioned Luke earlier, and we find that in the Gospel of Luke and the book of Acts, he gave very precise details, citing names, titles, places, and circumstances; more so than other writers of the New Testament (cf. Luke 1:1-4).

7. Has a tendency to demand contextual proof. In other words, he will be satisfied only with the use of biblical stories and illustrations, finding it difficult to make wider, practical applications. Teachers will see a danger in using personal experience to serve as a foundation for truth. Rather than taking experiences and looking for a proof text from scripture, they will start with scripture. Only if an experience matches what the Word says will they consider using it.

Experience should never be elevated above scripture! The fact that something happened does not validate that it is of God. All our experiences must be seen in light of God's truth, and that truth should never be overlooked or ignored. Paul warns us of this problem when he cautions us to be careful as to how we build on the foundation of God's Word, reminding us that our work will be revealed by fire at the judgment seat of Christ (cf. 1 Cor. 3:10-17).

Misunderstandings and Misuses of the Gift of Teaching

1. May appear more interested in accuracy of the text than in practical application of the truth. The teacher is perfectly content to give the facts and walk away without demanding or even requesting any response. (This is a primary difference with the gift of prophecy.) As long as the teacher feels he has been accurate with the text, he may ignore practical application of any kind.

Teachers shy away from illustrations that are not biblical, that is, those which are "outside of scripture." But the saints down through the ages have provided us countless illustrations of how biblical truth works itself out in the lives of believers (and sometimes unbelievers). In fact, we have only to look around us in the church and society where we live to find excellent examples of how biblical principles operate.

Teachers need to work to make sure that their correct doctrine has proper application to the hearers.

2. There is a tendency to rely more on head knowledge, or the research of others, than on the Holy Spirit. It can be easy to depend on the work of others to interpret scripture rather than on the work and ministry of the Holy Spirit. The digging out of facts and validation of truth is important and, depending on respected resources, is certainly acceptable. But there needs to be an exceptional dependence on the Holy Spirit for direction and motivation as well.

If a teacher is challenged regarding either the correctness or accuracy of his facts, he will likely not receive the charge of error lightly. But his normal reaction will be to retrace his steps to determine where or if he might have gone in the wrong direction. Of course, he will be likely to use this same approach in helping others whom he believes may have missed the mark.

The good news is that those gifted with teaching want to get the facts correct. I have umpired youth and high school baseball for over forty years. In the early years, the rule of thumb in the umpiring business was to stick with your call. Even if you had some doubt as to the correctness of the call, you made it; and once the call was made, that was the way it was. Fortunately, as the game of baseball has changed, so has the approach to umpiring. The new rule of thumb is "get the call right." This may mean getting together with your partner to see what he saw or to discuss the rule in question. I think the game has improved with this change in philosophy.

Teachers should adopt the same philosophy, to get it right by "rightly dividing the Word of truth." And the best way to get it right is to study hard and lean on the Holy Spirit for guidance and direction (cf. John 14:26-27; 16:13-15).

3. It is easy to become proud of one's knowledge. A faithful and accurate Bible teacher is a blessing to the church. But when a teacher becomes proud of their knowledge, they lose the ability to effectively communicate that knowledge to others. It may appear to others that truth seems more important than the persons involved in the teaching ministry. Paul's warning is appropriate (emphasis mine): "Now concerning things offered to idols: We know that we all have knowledge. *Knowledge puffs up*, but love edifies" (1 Cor. 8:1). We should always attempt to speak "the truth in love" (Eph. 4:15).

On the other hand, those of us who sit under the teaching of gifted men and women who know the Word should not be too quick to assume pride on their part. Most teachers and preachers do their work with confidence, and that should not be mistaken for arrogance.

The fact is, the teacher often knows something you don't, which is why you need to be taught in the first place! While they may seem to want to impress you with their knowledge, it could be that the Holy Spirit is simply using them to grow you up into Christ, into a more mature believer.

I remember one of the dear saints of the Lord who sat under my teaching in a previous pastorate. She was a learner and was very much a Berean, one who searched the scriptures daily. One evening, she came up to me after the service, and her eyes were aglow with excitement. She said, "I got it!" She was a referring to a particularly tough area of doctrine that I had been teaching. Trusting the Spirit of the Lord, studying the Word on her own, she came to each service looking to be taught the truth. May her tribe increase!

She went on to say, "Where were you fifty years ago? I needed your teaching fifty years ago. Where were you?" I said, "Ma'am, I wasn't born fifty years ago." Obviously, this was an event earlier in my ministry! It was a compliment to my teaching, but I was only presenting the truth of scripture as led by the Spirit of God. The Spirit had manifested a "word of knowledge" in the life of this dear saint.

To the teachers reading this, I encourage you to teach the things of the Lord with confidence. Study hard, know your facts, and present them with courage and conviction, for the glory of God and the good of the church (cf. 2 Cor. 3:12; 10:1-2; Eph. 6:19-20; 1 Thess. 2:2).

4. May tend to bog down in details and give information that is more extensive than necessary. If this bores the listeners, they may miss the point of the teaching. Details may also appear to be a way of flaunting their knowledge, making them appear arrogant. I have learned that it is not necessary to say everything you know on a given subject or text of scripture.

Another note to those of us sitting under the teacher is that, generally speaking, the teacher has worked hard to dig out the facts and wants others to have the truth. This is the Holy Spirit working in the life of the teacher to help you discern biblical knowledge you might not otherwise receive. The teacher will give his/her life to the task of teaching.

5. May tend to let truth get out of balance. A proper balance in all preaching and teaching ministries of the church is important. If the emphasis on a doctrine ignores its moral setting, then the result can amount to heresy. For example, if one teaches evangelism, the facts of the gospel one needs to believe to be saved, without the corresponding moral value of love for lost souls, then the resulting witness can come across as harsh.

This is why Paul admonishes us, "But, speaking the truth in love, may grow up in all things into Him who is the head—Christ" (Eph. 4:15). If we teach the doctrinal truth of the law without the moral understanding of grace, we will again find ourselves imbalanced and off track.

Bible Characters Who Illustrate the Gift of Teaching

Luke demonstrates the gift of teaching as well as anyone in the New Testament. The books of Luke and Acts (both authored by Luke) demonstrate Luke's gift of teaching (cf. Luke 1:1-4; Acts 1:1-3).

We should also note that Timothy had the gift of teaching (1 Tim. 4:13-16; 2 Tim. 2:2). Obviously, Paul had this gift as well as he was the one who originally taught Timothy and, by all rights, functioned as the primary teacher of the early church. If you read the Pastoral Epistles, Paul's instructions to Timothy and Titus, you realize that teaching was, and is, foundational to the operation of the church. It is an error to get the doing ahead of the knowing! The phrase "Do something even if it's wrong" is not a good one for the church.

There is a need for wisdom and understanding to correctly apply the truth (or knowledge) that we have (cf. Col. 1:9-14). But the starting point is knowledge of the truth, and that is where the one gifted with teaching becomes such a valuable resource to the life of the church. Robert Thomas makes a great assessment: "Teaching is the lifeblood of the Christian faith...without doctrine a person knows nothing of what to believe in or how to obey. Doctrine is the rock-bottom line, and teaching is the God-chosen method for transmitting that doctrine."[8]

We might recall that in the context of the main passage on spiritual gifts, Romans 12:1-15, we are told of the importance of "renewing the mind" in relation to knowing and doing the will of God (see v. 2). The best way to renew the mind is to saturate it with the teaching of God's Word.

> *The phrase "Do something even if it's wrong," is not a good one for the church.*

Bible Verses That Explain the Gift of Teaching

The command to teach is given clearly as we have mentioned. Teaching is an integral part of the Great Commission (Matt. 28:19-20). Jesus quickly set the example for what He wanted His newly commissioned church to do. In giving the Great Commission, He said that in addition to making disciples and baptizing those new converts into the church, we are to teach the new believers "to observe all things that I have commanded you." This is exactly what He did on the road to Emmaus with the two disciples He encountered.

"And beginning at Moses and all the Prophets, He expounded to them in all the Scriptures the things concerning Himself" (Luke 24:27; cf. Luke 24:13-34). The Emmaus road disciples clearly received the message and realized that Jesus had "opened the scriptures to [them]." This is the objective, the mission of every New Testament church, to teach the whole counsel of God!

---

[8] Thomas, *Understanding Spiritual Gifts*, 194.

In fact, when Paul gathered the elders of the church at Ephesus together in Acts 20, he reminded them that his ministry there had been to teach the entire message of the gospel. He said, "For I have not shunned to declare to you the whole counsel of God" (Acts 20:27). He went to instruct them to follow through with the same standard, commending them "to the word of His grace, which is able to build you up" (v. 32).

Paul further commended the importance of teaching in the church in addressing the church at Colosse (emphasis mine):

> Let the word of Christ dwell in you richly in all wisdom, *teaching* and admonishing one another in psalms and hymns and spiritual songs, singing with grace in your hearts to the Lord." (Col. 3:16)

The noun form of the word *teaching* is often translated "doctrine." The importance of doctrine is made clear throughout the Bible. The verses are almost too numerous to list (cf. Mark 1:27; John 7:16-17; Acts 2:42; 5:28; Rom. 6:17; 16:17; Eph. 4:12-16; 1 Tim. 1:3, 10; 4:6-16; 5:17; 6:1-5; 2 Tim. 3:10, 16; 4:2- 3; Titus 1:9; 2:1, 7.)

The Bible makes a plea for the fact that, in some sense, all believers are teachers. We recall the passage mentioned earlier in reference to the characteristic of accuracy in the ministry of the teacher that says we all "ought to be teachers" (Heb. 5:11). I have often said that every believer needs to be careful about their behavior, both words and actions, because there are always little eyes watching and little ears listening. And this is true whether you have small children or grandchildren around you in your home or not. They are in your church and at most of the other places you go.

We teach with our actions more clearly than with our words on some occasions. Spiritual maturity is not just for the "super spiritual," whoever they may be. We are all supposed to be growing in Christlikeness, growing up into the Head, even Christ, growing to spiritual maturity (Eph. 4:14-16, Heb. 5:11-14).

This makes the ministry of the teacher even more important in the life of the church. Teachers are, in reality, teaching every member of the church how to be a good teacher to others. They may not have the gift of teaching, but they are communicating every day, either positively or negatively, the gospel of Christ.

How Jesus Demonstrated the Gift of Teaching

We have already alluded to many of the passages that refer to Jesus as the ultimate Teacher. If you have this gift as your primary Holy Spirit motivation for ministry, you would do well to make a serious study of the Gospels. There, it will be easy to see how Jesus employed the gift of teaching. Jesus was called "the Teacher," and there is no question that was a very high priority for His time here on earth.

One lesson we learn from the Teacher is that He always practiced what He preached. He walked the talk. In this way, He is the supreme example for all of us who have been called and motivated by the Spirit to teach others.

One of the most significant teaching events of Jesus's life here on earth was the *Sermon on the Mount*. It is a very typical account of Jesus's teaching method. Jesus was indeed the greatest teacher of all (cf. Matt. 5-7; 7:28-29; 13:54; 19:16; 22:24-40; John 3:2; 7:46; 13:13; Luke 20:21).

Conclusion

There is a caution in James 3:1 that we should be careful with this gift. If you have it, then by all means use it. If you don't, stay away from teaching, in the sense of the classroom instruction of other believers! "My brethren, let not many of you become teachers, knowing that we shall receive a stricter judgment" (Jas. 3:1). There is a very real sense in which those of us who have been called to teach others bear a heavier and greater burden. We should not shy away from it, if it is indeed the call of God, but we need to make certain that we are called to teach before taking on the role.

The church needs teachers. The emphasis within the church on Sunday School and Bible study ministry, and in particular, the growth of such ministries, has driven many to the conclusion that teachers must be recruited and new units started. I think the statistics regarding growth in numbers for such actions can be verified. But sadly, this ignores the instruction from James.

It would be better to have fewer (and perhaps larger) classes with genuinely called and Spirit-motivated teachers than many classes who end up with a teacher who is not gifted to teach. Can you imagine the call for doctors going out, and many responding to the call, having never graduated from medical school? You get the idea, I'm sure.

Jerry Vines says it well:

> I read a book once which said that anybody can teach Sunday School. I do not believe this is true. There is a definite *spiritual gift* of teaching...Thank God for wonderful, Spirit-filled teachers. What a blessing these gifted individuals are. They explain the word of God in a powerful way to those who listen and hear.[9]

It is hard to overemphasize the importance of teaching to the church, and the emphasis needs to be renewed and revived in our day. The Bible is clear that the most important function of a church's pastor is to teach the Word of God. In fact, pastors, or elders, are required to teach. They do not necessarily have to "preach" (prophesy), but they must teach.

> A bishop then must be blameless, the husband of one wife, temperate, sober-minded, of good behavior, hospitable, able to teach. (1 Tim. 3:2)
>
> For a Bishop must be...as a steward of God...holding fast the faithful word as he has been taught, that he may be able, by sound doctrine, both to exhort and convict those who contradict. (Titus 1:7, 9)

This is the pastor-teachers primary responsibility. They are gifts to the church for this very purpose:

---

[9] Jerry Vines, *Spirit Life* (Nashville: Broadman & Holman Publishers, 1998), 120-121.

And He Himself gave some to be apostles, some prophets, some evangelists, and some pastors and teachers, for the equipping of the saints for the work of ministry, for the edifying of the body of Christ, till we all come to the unity of the faith and of the knowledge of the Son of God, to a perfect man, to the measure of the stature of the fullness of Christ; that we should no longer be children, tossed to and fro and carried about with every wind of doctrine, by the trickery of men, in the cunning craftiness of deceitful plotting. (Eph. 4:11-14)

Ultimately, they will be judged on this basis (cf. 2 Tim. 4:1-5).

8

The Gift of Exhortation

Encouraging God's people, promoting spiritual maturity

He who exhorts, in exhortation.
—Romans 12:8

Rejoicing in hope, patient in tribulation
continuing steadfastly in prayer.
—Romans 12:12

The motivation of this gift is to strengthen the faith and character of others by urging them to adopt some course of action in accord with God's Word. The exhorter can discern what someone needs to do in order to get their life on track for the future. They realize that failure is a part of our lives and that all people are sinners. But they also know that repentance leads to forgiveness. Once forgiveness comes, the goal is to stay on track in one's walk of faith.

The word *exhortation*, translated in Greek, is παρακαλέω (*parakaleo*) from *para* ("to the side") and *kaleo* ("to call"). Thus, it literally means "to call to one's side." It is the act of encouraging and comforting another, often urging them to a particular course of action. Strong's says it means "to console, to encourage and strengthen by consolation, to comfort" (ESL).

According to W. E. Vine's definition, the word is described as "to admonish, exhort, to urge one to pursue some course of conduct (always prospective, looking to the future, in contrast to the meaning of comfort, which is retrospective, having to do with trial experienced)" (VINE). Another definition says "to encourage and strengthen by consolation" (JHT).

Vine, I believe, is most correct when he notes that the word is *prospective* rather than *retrospective*. The idea is moving someone toward a goal, of getting them on the straight and narrow path, not so much the idea of comforting them related to a past event or difficulty (which is the motivation of one with the gift of mercy). This is not to say there is no comfort in the process. What could ultimately be more comforting than to know that you are able to "prove what is that good and acceptable and perfect will of God?" (Rom. 12.2).

The meaning of the word can be clearly understood when we look at the context in which it is used in Paul's appeal to the Corinthians to join their brethren from Macedonia in giving to the offering that was being collected for the poor in Jerusalem. He says that the Macedonian believers were "imploring us with much urgency that we would receive the gift and the fellowship of the ministering to the saints" (2 Cor. 8:4). The word *imploring* is the word *parakaleo*, "to entreat," and here has distinct reference to a future course of action that is being encouraged.

Then, in verse 6, Paul uses the word to encourage Titus as he goes to Corinth to seek their participation in the offering. Again, the context shows the emphasis on exhorting others to take a positive course of action, leading to spiritual growth or maturity.

According to Romans 12:8, an exhorter should be consistently about the business of exhorting others, "he who exhorts, in exhortation" (v. 8). Here, both the verb and noun form of the word are used for emphasis. After all, what good is a spiritual gift that goes unused?

Romans 12:12 indicates three responsibilities for the one with the gift of exhortation:

- To rejoice in hope

- To endure in tribulation (to be patient)
- To persist in prayer

Since the work of an exhorter is always prospective, that is, forward-looking, the need for rejoicing in hope should be obvious. You cannot give people hope for the future if you don't have it for yourself. The exhorter knows that there is always hope with God. Exhorters would rely on the sentiment of Psalm 16:9: "Therefore my heart is glad, and my glory rejoices; My flesh also will rest in hope."

The second responsibility has to do with the important exercise of patience. Telling people how they can mature spiritually usually includes the pointing out of sin, for which there is need of repentance. In such cases, lifestyle changes will doubtless be required. This doesn't always sit well with some of God's sainted millions. Helping people grow in Christlikeness is hard and, sometimes, disappointing work. Patience is required for success.

In all likelihood, there was no one who understood this more than the apostle Paul. He commented on this in two of his letters. He mentioned the reputation of the Thessalonian church: "So that we ourselves boast of you among the churches of God for your patience and faith in all your persecutions and tribulations that you endure" (2 Thess. 1:4). Although this church was spiritually mature, the process of growth to maturity had its share of trouble.

To the Corinthians, Paul writes, "But in all things we commend ourselves as ministers of God: in much patience, in tribulations, in needs, in distresses" (2 Cor. 6:4). The task of bringing the Corinthian church to spiritual maturity was one of the most daunting tasks that Paul had during his ministry. To say that Paul was an exhorter of the Corinthians would be a vast understatement. From his experience with that church, he fully grasped the fact that exhorters would need to be able to endure patiently under stressful times of ministry.

There is a sense in which everyone called to vocational ministry is an exhorter. While it is not my primary motivational gift, I do find that it is important, particularly as a pastor, to understand the gift and how it works. I am grateful for my wife, Victoria, who is an exhorter.

She has been able, on numerous occasions, to suggest a course of action for some beleaguered believer and then to recommend a course of patience on my part in bringing certain individuals and churches to spiritual maturity.

The apostle John, who was no stranger to this task of bringing people to spiritual maturity, had this to say as he sat to compose the words of the book of Revelation:

> I, John, both your brother and companion in the tribulation and kingdom and patience of Jesus Christ, was on the island that is called Patmos for the word of God and for the testimony of Jesus Christ. (Rev. 1:9)

The third responsibility listed in Romans 12:12 is that of continued steadfastness in prayer. Ultimately, the person whom the exhorter is helping must turn to God for both guidance and growth, not to mention the fact that the exhorter will need God's help in giving the best of godly advice and admonition to others. They will often need to depend on God to change hearts before progress will be made toward the goals they have in mind for those they serve with their gift.

The Basic Characteristics of the Gift of Exhortation

1. Motivated to see people develop to their full spiritual maturity. Exhorters make excellent mentors. Mentoring is a discipline that should be developed in the church, and we need those who are willing to work one-on-one with others. If you are going to take people to full spiritual maturity, you are going to have to invest in their lives.

Paul had tremendous responsibilities for mission work, church planting, oversight of previous churches established, and writing specific instructions for the churches (which eventually became a large part of the New Testament), and yet he found time to invest individually in the lives of a large number of people.

This, of course, was the very example of Jesus. While He constantly had multitudes of people demanding His time, He nevertheless spent time focused on mentoring the disciples and His closest followers (cf. John 6).

Paul explains the lengths he was willing to go to invest in others (emphasis mine):

> But it is good to be zealous in a good thing always, and not only when I am present with you. My little children, *for whom I labor in birth again until Christ is formed in you*, I would like to be present with you now and to change my tone; for I have doubts about you. (Gal. 4:18-20)

There are two critical things we find in Paul's statement to the Galatians. First, bringing them to spiritual maturity ("until Christ is formed in you") was to him like raising a child. It is that important! Just as you would pour yourself into teaching and training your own children, so should you invest in the lives that God brings your way for discipleship.

Second, we can take from Paul's tone that he was very concerned about their failure to grow in grace. It was personal to him that at least some of the Galatian church members had drifted away from the truth since Paul left to minister elsewhere. He was having doubts about their relationship with Christ, literally about their very salvation. Exhorters are particularly motivated in this way. They care about spiritual maturity because that is the one thing that gives greatest evidence to one's salvation.

The personal, one-on-one aspect of this is confirmed by Paul when he spoke of his preaching of Jesus to the Colossian church (emphasis mine):

> Him we preach, *warning every man* and *teaching every man* in all wisdom, that we may *present every man* perfect in Christ Jesus. To this end I also labor, striving according to His working which works in me mightily. (Col. 1:28-29)

2. Can identify people's problems and relate to them. One of the reasons people struggle so often with habits and sins that they can't seem to overcome is that they never really deal with the root problem or sin. Perhaps you have struggled repeatedly with sin issues or bad habits. You have gone to the altar, you have repented—perchance even in sackcloth and ashes!—but alas, you go and do it again. I suggest persistence and continuing repentance as proper.

Could it be, however, that you are repenting of the symptom rather than the root cause of the problem? Exhorters have the ability to discern where a person is in their spiritual growth and to see the root sins that may be the cause of their problems.

There are three primary root sins that lie behind all that we do that offends God. Those sins are unbelief, rebellion, and pride. All other sins could be grouped as subsets of those three (cf. Jude 5-7). It is not my purpose in this volume to deal with all the specific aspect of how exhorters exhort, but it is important that exhorters understand the real cause of a sin problem. Their ability to get to the root sin and suggest a path to repentance and recovery is very important to the spiritual maturity of any congregation.

An area where exhorters can be a great blessing to the church is in regard to learning to accept people where they are and then move them in a godly direction. We should not be surprised when lost people act lost. Nor should we be surprised when the spiritually immature act in immature ways.

The Christian life is, to a great degree, progressive. Paul expressed this in First Corinthians:

> For though I am free from all men, I have made myself a servant to all, that I might win the more; and to the Jews I became as a Jew, that I might win Jews; to those who are under the law, as under the law, that I might win those who are under the law; to those who are without law, as without law (not being without law toward God, but under law toward Christ), that I might win those who are without law; to the weak I became as weak, that I might win the weak. I have become all things to all men, that I might by all means save some. Now this I do for the gospel's sake, that I may be partaker of it with you. (1 Cor. 9:19-23)

There is no issue here with Paul compromising the gospel or making allowance for sinful behavior. He is simply saying that he would do whatever necessary within the bounds of the faith to reach individuals. Paul had a keen insight, or discernment, regarding spiritual growth. Don't you think it is true that most problems you try to help another person with, you have been in a similar situation before yourself?

Paul was well aware of where the Corinthians were in their walk with the Lord; exhorters have a way of seeing through false faith: "And I, brethren, could not speak to you as to spiritual people but as to carnal, as to babes in Christ" (1 Cor. 3:1). Paul was not creating a second category of Christians, as in spiritual ones and carnal ones. He was simply saying that some of them were behaving in immature ways and that they needed to grow in their faith.

> ### ROOT SINS
> -The root sins are unbelief, rebellion, and pride (cf. Jude 5-7). You sin because either...
> 1) You don't believe God (Jude 5; cf. Heb.3; 1 Cor. 10:1-10); or
> 2) You believe God but are in rebellion to His commands (Jude 6; cf. Heb.3:8, 15, 18); or
> 3) You are filled with pride (Jude 7; Prov.8:13; 16:18)
> -If you deal with and repent of the root of your problem you can gain resolution to your trouble. This is the primary ministry of an Exhorter, to assist others in recognizing root sins and repenting from them.

I think most pastors would agree that we need to be more faithful in building disciples in the church. Mentoring people one-on-one or in small groups is essential to the spiritual health of any congregation. That means we need to discover who the exhorters are and get them trained to build up the church (cf. Eph. 4:11-16).

Often, guilt is a big factor for keeping people from growing in the grace of the Lord and in their expressions of faith. It must be dealt with so the exhorter has to relate to the need and speak forthrightly to it. Exhorters have a great responsibility in helping people gain a clear conscience so that they can use their own spiritual gifts more effectively (cf. 1 Tim. 1:18-20).

3. Knows how to minister to the person or problem. Exhorters can give precise steps of action in encouraging spiritual maturity. As a general rule, they are solution oriented, and they are convinced that they have the answers to lead others on a journey of spiritual growth. In consequence of this, they dislike meetings, details, and organizational structure. Their watchword is, "Let's get on with it." Such is the example of Paul in instructing Timothy: "Flee also youthful lusts; but pursue righteousness, faith, love, peace with those who call on the Lord out of a pure heart. But avoid foolish and ignorant disputes, knowing that they generate strife." (2 Tim. 2:22-23)

4. Believes in the principles and precepts of God's Word and, from experience, can demonstrate these principles. The exhorter knows how to visualize spiritual advancement for people and uses this to motivate them to action. This is known as a cause-and-effect sequence, where both scripture and experience are used to discover these underlying life principles. But let us give a word of warning in this regard. Experience is never to be elevated over scripture! Something is not right just because you had an experience. All our experiences must be brought under the authority of scripture. Where our experience lines up under God's Word, then the experience becomes a "teacher" to our faith.

In counseling people who are not spiritually mature, or who are dealing with the negative fallout of a lifestyle in contradiction to the Word of God, I often ask the following question: "Do you want the blessings of God in your life?" If they do, then they are at a good starting point for the exhorter to show them the roadway of repentance and the highway of holiness.

Paul's writings are filled with these principles, such as, "Flee sexual immorality or you sin against your own body" (cf. 1 Cor. 6:15-20), "Be not unequally yoked or you will destroy your spiritual life" (cf. 2 Cor. 6:14-18), and "Don't be conformed to the world or you will not be able to follow the will of the Lord" (cf. Rom. 12:1-2).

This means that if you are an exhorter, you must become thoroughly familiar with the Word of God, especially the writings of Paul. You must know these scriptures so that you can see how they apply to the lives of those God leads you to instruct (cf. 2 Tim. 2:15).

5. Prefers to deal with people on a one-to-one basis. Normally, this means meeting with them face-to-face to determine their response and to ensure a positive result. Paul knew that being with a person was the best way to disciple them. I'm grateful that you are reading this book. The fact that you have reached this point indicates a true desire to develop not only your gift but to discover how all the gifts work in the life of the church. I greatly enjoy writing, and the ability to convey these truths in this manner is a great blessing to my heart.

But my real love is to preach and teach this material. An exhorter's real love would be to take the material and share one-on-one, face-to-face, with someone they are trying to help grow in spiritual maturity. No one understood this better than Paul (emphasis mine): "But we, brethren, having been taken away from you for a short time in presence, not in heart, *endeavored more eagerly to see your face with great desire*" (1 Thess. 2:17). He would also add that he was "night and day praying exceedingly that we may *see your face* and perfect what is lacking in your faith" (1 Thess. 3:10).

Personal conferences were common with Paul. He spoke often of his meetings with Timothy: "Greatly desiring to see you, being mindful of your tears, that I may be filled with joy" (2 Tim. 1:4). He reminded the believers in Thessalonica, "As you know how we exhorted, and comforted, and charged every one of you, *as a father does his own children*, that you would walk worthy of God who calls you into His own kingdom and glory" (1 Thess. 2:11-12).

6. Has a desire to be transparent, open, and honest. Often exhorters are able to do their ministry out of the trials and experiences they have been through themselves. They are willing to sacrifice their own reputation if sharing their story can help someone else get the victory. Sometimes they are honest to a fault. Their openness often creates an opportunity to get a wider hearing for the message of salvation.

Exhorters will often be found working in a prison ministry or homeless shelter, or reaching out to addicts or the disenfranchised. Paul was not ashamed to call himself "the chief of sinners" (1 Tim. 1:15; cf. Phil. 3:1-11). The exhorter shares his or her struggles with sin, not to brag on their sinfulness but to brag on the power of the blood of Christ that not only provided forgiveness but the power to overcome the most painful and powerful of sinful addictions.

7. A desire for harmony between Christian individuals and groups. Exhorters know that differences of opinion can be a roadblock to effective ministry. When church members can't get along with one another, it damages the reputation of the church and hampers the church's effectiveness in carrying out the Great Commission. One great hindrance to the attainment of spiritual maturity is the display of self-centered motives, often with some type of desire to control things in the church, if not the whole church.

Exhorters want to see believers reconciled. Paul demonstrates this in his appeal to two women in the church at Philippi whose division had created a serious threat to the spiritual health of the church. So much so that Paul "implored" them "to be of the same mind" (cf. Phil 4:2-7). The word used in Philippians 4:2, which is translated "implore," is *parakaleo*, "to exhort"! Paul had already given the Philippian church a general instruction in this regard (emphasis mine):

> Fulfill my joy by being like-minded, having the same love, being of one accord, of one mind. Let nothing be done through selfish ambition or conceit, but in lowliness of mind *let each esteem others better than himself.* Let each of you look out not only for his own interests, but also for the interests of others. (Phil. 2:2-4)

Paul fully understood that harmony or peace is never to be sought at any cost! *We must never sacrifice purity on the altar of unity!* We should never weaken or water down our doctrine just for sake of unity (cf. 1 Cor. 3:3-4, Eph. 4:1-6, Phil. 2:2). In fact, it is our doctrine that provides the platform from which our unity is built. Paul said that we are to "endeavor to keep the unity of the faith."

We might do well to remember that union and unity are not the same. I once heard Dr. Sam Cathey use this illustration: "If you take two cats and tie their tails together and then throw them over a clothesline you will have union, but you will not have unity!" Neither he nor I are suggesting that you try the experiment. We trust that you can use your sanctified imagination to realize what a mess that would be.

The sad thing is that often such a picture is exactly the one you would see in a church, where two people or more have decided to be united but not to be in unity. They fight like cats and dogs against one another but have no energy left to take on the real enemies of God and His precious bride, the church. May God forgive us, and may He raise up many exhorters to lead us to spiritual maturity and true unity in Christ.

Misunderstandings and Misuses
of the Gift of Exhortation

1. May oversimplify problems. Experience and success in counseling may cause the exhorter to fail to listen clearly and thus neglect to sense the direction of the Holy Spirit. To oversimplify may cause the exhorter to give bad advice. "He who answers a matter before he hears it, It is folly and shame to him" (Prov. 18:13).

Whether you are an exhorter or not, it is good to learn to listen to people and not give an answer before you know what the question is! I have learned that an effective method for evangelism is to take the approach of simply having a gospel conversation. My desire and intent to is witness, to share the gospel, but first I need to know what the person whom I am talking to believes. I will share more detail on this evangelistic approach in chapter 13, "The Relationship of Evangelism to Spiritual Gifts."

But this is true in the church as well. Sometimes we are more judgmental than we are willing to admit. I'm not making excuses for open and blatant sin. But the way people act and speak, and the situations they get themselves into, often with inappropriate and sometimes sinful attitudes and motivations, do have a history. Do you know what the person whom you look down upon is dealing with? They may be in the wrong, but at least you could have some understanding, Jesus did (cf. John 8:1-11)!

May I say that when we oversimplify people's problems, or perhaps just because we have a history of doing so, it is no wonder that people will not open up to us and share their hearts with us. When they believe they are going to get the hammer, they are less likely to be open and honest. If they are not open and honest, then we, as exhorters particularly, are behind the eight ball when it comes to helping them. I can't recommend a proper path to spiritual maturity if I don't fully understand what has gotten them into the current mess they are in.

I recommend that exhorters find a way to ask a series of questions to learn the spiritual condition of the person and the special circumstances they may be dealing with. Then remember that condemnation is the work of the Holy Spirit through conviction (John 16:7-11). Shall we hold them accountable? Yes. But let us do so while we are speaking the truth in love.

2. May seem to be overconfident or proud. Since the exhorter knows the steps of action he or she proposes will work (because they are based on tried-and-true biblical precepts the exhorter has observed to work over and over in the past), he may give the impression of being more concerned with projects than people.

In marriage counseling, I have said to couples experiencing marital distress, "I can give you a 100 percent guarantee of success." That's a tall claim, but it will be true if I apply the principles of Scripture and give the couple biblical steps to reconciliation. If they will follow the prescription, take the medicine, if you will, then I know their problem can be resolved. The Holy Spirit has promised, and He is faithful.

In consequence of this confidence in the things of God, sometimes prophets and exhorters get a bad name unnecessarily. Usually, they really do care and want the best for the people they are trying to help. This is why misuse number one above must be taken seriously by any counselor, whether prophet, teacher, or exhorter by spiritual gift.

3. May settle for outward conformity rather than true inward change. This is a clear misuse of the gift. What the exhorter should be looking for is true spiritual maturity. The evidence of spiritual maturity is the ability of someone to learn to make godly decisions about life on their own. To know the difference in right and wrong, truth and error. A great rule of thumb for the exhorter in this regard would be the instruction found in Hebrews (emphasis mine):

> Of whom we have much to say, and hard to explain, since you have become dull of hearing. For though by this time you ought to be teachers, you need someone to teach you again the first principles of the oracles of God; and you have come to need milk and not solid food. For everyone who partakes only of milk is unskilled in the word of righteousness, for he is a babe. But solid food belongs to those who are of full age, that is, *those who by reason of use have their senses exercised to discern both good and evil.* (Heb. 5:11-14)

The clear direction of the passage is that for one to become spiritually mature, they must know how to apply the Bible to every situation and circumstance of life. *Full age* or *spiritual maturity* is defined then as "being able to know the right thing to do or say in any given situation." That is the goal that every exhorter should have for those whom they are attempting to help.

4. Spends a great deal of time sharing and talking with those they are helping. Exhorters will invest themselves in others, sometimes spending a tremendous amount of time with them. This can cause resentments to surface in the family if the exhorter is not careful to put their family first. One of the many issues pastors and other full-time ministry staff face is the demands that people make on them for their time. Those called to serve reason that this is what God has called them to do; and this, therefore, gets the priority.

Before God called you to any specific form or level of ministry, He called you to be faithful in your commitments. While your relationship to God Himself should be the highest priority, your next commitment is to your family, your spouse, and children. We read with saddened hearts the many reports of pastors and church staff who, in essence, offer their families on the altar of "good ministry" or "hard work for the Lord."

One of the best things a pastor, church worker, teacher, or exhorter can do is set a good and godly example by having a model marriage and faithful and obedient children. You will find no one more important to your spiritual health and maturity than your own family. If you fail them while serving others, you will have failed.

Another important warning at this juncture is that of having some protections in place for counseling. Most of the work of an exhorter is done one-on-one. But protections must be put in place. A good general rule of thumb, particularly for laymen and women who have this gift is for men to counsel men and women to counsel women. If an exhorter is particularly gifted or enabled to do marriage or family counseling, then either a man or woman could counsel a couple.

> *You will find no one more important to your spiritual health and maturity than your own family. If you fail them while serving others you will have failed.*

In those very rare circumstances where a pastor or church counselor needs to counsel a member of the opposite sex, then they should have their spouse present (and perhaps the spouse of the counselee, if they have one). In unusual circumstances, one might consider a second counselor to assist. The main point is that one-on-one counseling with a member of the opposite sex is never acceptable. Nor would it be acceptable to counsel a child without the child's parent present. I am not suggesting that single people cannot counsel others, but I am saying that they should not counsel someone of the opposite sex absent these important protections.

5. May sometimes appear too factual or unsympathetic. In reality, most of the time, the exhorter hurts when others hurt. The difference is they don't generally express it in the same way a person gifted with mercy would.

Another problem is that exhorters who misuse the gift by being unsympathetic tend to give up on people who don't respond as quickly as they would like. They may move on to greener pastures and create disillusionment on the part of those given up on. The true Christian faith is a process; it is growth in grace. We are encouraged to be patient in scripture, and this is one of the clear guidelines for an exhorter: "patient in tribulation."

Paul, who was the consummate exhorter, often reminded his readers of the patience of the Lord toward us and admonished us to have that same level of patience with others (cf. Rom. 15:4-5, Col. 1:11). Patience is a fruit of the Spirit (Gal. 5:22-23). Paul encouraged Timothy to "pursue...patience" (1 Tim. 6:11). James exhorts us to "let patience have its perfect work, that you be perfect and complete, lacking nothing" (James 1:4).

This problem can also lead to the setting of unrealistic goals. For example, while we might all agree that reading the Bible through in three months could be helpful to one's storehouse of knowledge, it may be a project that will cause discouragement when the counselee fails to achieve the goal.

6. May tend to avoid heavy doctrinal teaching that does not have immediate practical application. The result of this emphasis can be an imbalance of teaching, which will eventually show up as doctrinal error in the advice of the exhorter. The teacher will be bothered if the exhorter takes scripture out of context to make application to daily living that does not actually apply.

Bible Characters Who Illustrate the Gift of Exhortation

As demonstrated in the basic characteristics, Paul is perhaps the greatest New Testament example of an exhorter. But Barnabas may be an even more important example, for surely he was Paul's teacher in this area. Barnabas's name means "son of encouragement." In Acts 4:35-37, we see his name explained and how he encouraged the apostles. Of course, the term *encouragement* is the same word as *exhorter (parakaleo)*.

We meet Barnabas again in Acts 9:27 as he becomes Paul's exhorter and apparently gave him precise steps of action to convince the church at Jerusalem of his spiritual maturity. In Acts 11:22-24, Barnabas is sent to exhort the believers as far away as Antioch. He then seeks out Paul and brings him to Antioch, where they both minister as exhorters! Note that it is here believers are first called Christians.

In Acts 13:2-5, Paul and Barnabas set out on their first missionary journey. Barnabas was still in the role of mentoring Paul and bringing him to full spiritual maturity. In Acts 15:36- 41, Paul refused to take John Mark, who had turned back on the first journey. Barnabas chose to take him, no doubt outlining the steps for his return to spiritual maturity. Though the situation with John Mark caused a brief division between Barnabas and Paul, in the end it created another opportunity for Barnabas to use his gift. That he was successful with bringing John Mark to repentance and full spiritual maturity is proven in the fact that Paul reconciled with John Mark (2 Tim. 4:11).

Bible Verses That Explain the Gift of Exhortation

A guideline for the exhorter is to rejoice in hope. Note that we are to exhort one another with words of hope over our Lord's return (cf. Heb. 10:24-25; 1 Thess. 4:18; every chapter in First Thessalonians ends with a reference to the Lord's return with a note of hope and/ or rejoicing).

The ministry of exhortation is spoken of in several places in scripture (emphasis mine):

> Now then, we are ambassadors for Christ, as though God were pleading through us: *we implore you* on Christ's behalf, be reconciled to God. (2 Cor. 5:20)

I *urged* Titus, and sent our brother with him. Did Titus take advantage of you? Did we not walk in the same spirit? Did we not walk in the same steps? (2 Cor. 12:18)

I *appeal* to you for my son Onesimus, whom I have begotten while in my chains. (Philem. 10)

Whom I have sent to you for this very purpose, that you may know our affairs, and that he may *comfort* your hearts. (Eph. 6:22)

How Jesus Demonstrated the Gift of Exhortation

Anyone with the gift of exhortation should study carefully the life and ministry of Jesus with a particular note on the interest He took in individuals. He certainly preached to the crowds, but the greatest impact He had was in dealing with people one-on-one. Sometimes He did that while many others were looking on and listening, but you cannot fail to see how Jesus was our greatest example of exhortation.

We could begin by going through the Gospels and pulling out all the examples of Jesus explaining the parables to His disciples, of His instructing them and taking them away to quiet places for training. I am only scratching the surface here, but just think of all the individuals, or small groups, that Jesus gave His time and attention to, including the following:

- Andrew, Philip and Nathaniel (John 1)
- Nicodemus (John 3)
- The woman at the well (John 4)
- The lame man (John 5)
- The woman caught in adultery (John 8)
- The blind man (John 9)
- Mary, Martha, and Lazarus (John 11)
- The disciples (John 13)
- Mary Magdalene and Thomas (John 20)
- Peter (John 21)
- The rich young ruler (Matthew 19)

- The paralyzed man (Luke 5)
- The centurion (Luke 7)
- A demon-possessed boy (Luke 9)
- A woman with an infirm spirit (Luke 13)
- Ten lepers (Luke 17)
- Zacchaeus (Luke 19)

Jesus taught about exhortation as well (emphasis mine):

> Blessed are those who mourn, For they shall be *comforted*. (Matt. 5:4)

> And with many other *exhortations* he preached to the people. (Luke 3:18)

Simeon referred to Jesus as the "consolation of Israel," meaning the "exhorter" (Luke 2:25). Jesus is our wonderful Counselor and the greatest example of the gift of exhortation.

Conclusion

Let's remember the importance of exhorters to the life of the church. Not everyone likes to be instructed, especially when that instruction is specific to our lifestyle and failures to live as we should. It would seem that some in the church think biblical counseling is an option. It is not! Recall the admonishment of Paul: "Now we exhort you, brethren, warn those who are unruly, comfort the fainthearted, uphold the weak, be patient with all" (1 Thess. 5:14).

Counseling should be available from the church. Counselors should be trained. I recommend that anyone with a counseling ministry, whether they have the primary gift of exhortation or not, to read *Introduction to Biblical Counseling*, edited by John F. MacArthur Jr. and Wayne Mack (Dallas: Word Publishing, 1994). A myriad of resources are listed in that book which will prove helpful to any biblical counselor.

A Textbook Case of Exhortation

Many years ago, young man, a Christian believer, who was attending the church I pastored at the time, came and revealed he was having marriage problems. I suggested he bring his wife in so that I could counsel the two of them (it usually takes two to tango!). He said he didn't think she would come, but he would ask. As he thought, she refused, so I asked if it would be all right if I came to their home to see them. The husband said we'd give it a try, but he wasn't sure she would listen.

One night after church, I followed him and his children home, and we came into the home. I had never met his wife prior to this. She was sitting on the end of a couch curled in the fetal position. A small lamp was the only light in the room. I took a seat opposite the wife and the husband in a chair nearby. He introduced me to his wife, but she never looked up, never spoke one word. I was there for about an hour.

I looked at the young man and said, "It's worse than you said." (I did not need my college or seminary education to figure this out!) I tried to assess the situation better and asked him a number of questions. The house was a mess, really beyond words to describe. It was one of those scenes that you never forget. Now, mind you, the place did not smell bad, it was not dirty, and it was not invested with pests, it was just a mess. It was as if no cared about the home.

So I asked him this, calling him by name, "Are you willing to do whatever it will take to save this marriage?" He answered in the affirmative. I said, "I don't believe you. I don't think you have what it takes to turn this around, but if you want to try, I will give you counsel. You can start by getting this house cleaned up and put back in order." I gave him a few specific suggestions, reasoned with him about why his wife might be in the condition she was in, and we made an appointment for him to come in for counsel. And then I left.

I counseled him on how to turn his marriage around by focusing on his problems and correcting them, repenting and trusting God, then learning to love his wife by serving her. The things I told him were simple biblical principles. A few Sundays later, his wife appeared in church with him. They sat on the pew about five feet apart, but she was there. The next week, she returned; and they were a little closer on the pew, but not touching. The third week, there they sat, he with his arm around her shoulder.

That Sunday, as the invitation started, she nearly ran down the aisle. She said, "I want to be saved." I shared the plan of salvation with her, and she was gloriously and marvelously saved. Her husband followed, and they joined the church. She was baptized the next Sunday. As you can imagine, I was curious as to what brought about this change.

You recall that the husband said he wasn't sure whether she would listen. The night I had been in their home, there was no evidence that she had heard a thing I said. So I asked her, "What made the change? Why did you come today to be saved?" She replied, "Do you remember the night you came to our home and what you asked my husband?" I said, "I'll never forget it." "Well," she said, "you said you did not believe him, and quite frankly, I didn't believe him either." So I asked, "What happened?" She responded, "It's really quite simple. He actually began to do what you were telling him to do. When I asked him why, he said it was because of his relationship with Jesus. I saw him change. I knew that if he could change that much, I needed what he had!"

Friend, this is what the exhorter has been motivated by God to do: to bring the sinner hope that the blessings of God will come when they commit to grow in the grace and knowledge of their Lord and Savior, Jesus Christ.

9

The Gift of Giving

Meeting the needs of ministry, using resources
to advance kingdom causes

He who gives, with liberality.
—Romans 12:8

Distributing to the needs of the saints, given to hospitality.
—Romans 12:13

The gift of giving enables one to contribute joyfully and often in abundance to God's work. This is a ministry designed to manifest the love of Christ. The giving may be to meet individual or ministry needs. The aspect of giving that is typical of one with the motivating gift of giving certainly implies giving over and above the tithe.

The word is μεταδίδωμι (*metadidomi*) and is a strengthened form of the normal word for giving, *didomi*. The prefix to the word, *meta*, means "with," so the literal meaning would be "to give with." The dictionary definition is "share, impart by contributing to needs" (DBL).

We can note the meaning of the word more clearly by seeing how it is used in the New Testament. John the Baptist instructed his hearers that they might "bear fruit worthy of repentance" through sacrificial giving. "He answered and said to them, 'He who has two tunics, let him give to him who has none; and he who has food, let him do likewise'" (Luke 3:11). The word *give* is from *metadidomi*.

Paul used the word to express his desire to "give" spiritual gifts to the church: "For I long to see you, that I may impart to you some spiritual gift, so that you may be established" (Rom. 1:11). Here, the word is translated in a way where we get the correct impact: *impart*.

John MacArthur says,

> In his letter to Ephesus he [Paul] makes clear that, whether or not a believer has the gift of giving, he is to have the spirit of generosity that characterizes this gift. Every Christian should "labor, performing with his own hands what is good, in order that he may have something to share [*metadidomi*] with him who has need" (Eph. 4:28).[1]

W. E. Vine says the word means "to give a share of, impart... as distinct from giving." He goes on to mention that Paul, in writing to the Thessalonian church (1 Thess. 2:8f), "speaks of himself and his fellow-missionaries as having been well pleased to impart to the converts both God's Gospel and their own souls (i.e., so sharing those with them to spend themselves and spend out their lives for them)" (VINE).

The motivation of the gift of giving is to further and enhance the ministry of an individual or church by sharing personal assets with that ministry. The idea behind this motivational gift is never giving in order to get or be recognized. The purpose is to help a ministry move forward in accomplishing its God-given task or to free a minister to do the Lord's work unhindered.

The guidelines for the gift are found in our two primary verses in Romans 12:8 and 13. According to those verses, there are three guidelines or responsibilities in relation to the gift:

- Giving is to be done with "liberality."
- Giving is a "distribution to the needs of the saints."
- Giving is marked by "hospitality."

---

[1] MacArthur, *Romans 9-16*, 175.

One of the best definitions I have read regarding the spiritual gift of giving is by Darrell W. Robinson: "The gift of giving is the God-given ability to earn money and give generously beyond the tithe to the right things at the right times to support God's work."[2]

The old King James Version uses the word simplicity, which gives a good sense of the word as being unaffected by outside influence. It is perhaps better translated "liberality" (NAS, NKJV). If there is one place that a believer should be liberal, it is in his giving. The word comes from the Greek ἁπλότης (*haplotes*), "simplicity, sincerity, unaffectedness" (VINE). Thayer says it is "singleness, simplicity, sincerity, mental honesty; the virtue of one who is free from pretense and dissimulation" (JHT). This kind of giving is done without public display or fanfare. There is no ulterior motive involved; it is the idea of sincere, generous, and heartfelt giving.

> "The gift of giving is the God-given ability to earn money and give generously beyond the tithe to the right things at the right times to support God's work."
> —Darrell W. Robinson

"Distributing to the needs of the saints," be they individuals, churches, or other ministries, carries with it the idea prevalent in scripture regarding the attitude of all givers doing so freely and willingly. The NAS translates the word *contributing*. It comes from the word κοινωνέω (*koinoneo*), which is where we get the word *fellowship*. The idea is to share in or with someone, a partnership of sorts.

A good example of the partnership in giving concept is that of the Macedonian churches who gave to support the ministry of the apostle Paul. The generosity of the Philippian church is expressed in Philippians 4:10-20, where Paul thanks them that they "shared" in meeting his needs. The word for *shared* is actually a strengthened form of the word *distributing* found in our text.

Paul instructs those who are "rich in this present age...to do good, that they be...ready to give, willing to share" (1 Tim. 6:17-18).

---

[2] Darrell W. Robinson, *Incredibly Gifted* (Grand Rapids: Eerdmans Printing, 2002), 148.

The idea of "ready to give" indicates generosity. The word *share* is *koinonikos*, again with idea of fellowship or sharing in common. The one motivated by the Holy Spirit with the gift of giving will be the one to set the example and be the first to share in the needs that are presented to the church.

"Given to hospitality" is a clear mark of the gift of giving. Some see hospitality as a separate gift from that of giving. But in the context of Romans 12, it seems clear that hospitality is a subset of giving. Who would be more hospitable than a giver?

The word is φιλόξενος (*philoxenos*), which literally means "love of strangers." Jesus certainly considered this concept a high virtue, referring to it often in His parables and making mention of it when it was practiced for and around Him. Of course, all believers are urged to behave as givers who provide hospitality. In fact, pastors are required to demonstrate hospitality (1 Tim. 3:2, Tit. 1:8).

All believers are admonished by Peter to "be hospitable to one another without grumbling" (1 Pet. 4:9). In reality, this is an outworking of the love that believers should show toward one another (1 Pet. 4:8). So it is clear Peter believes that hospitality is primarily for the meeting of the needs of fellow believers "to one another." What is interesting is that the dual commands of "fervent love for one another" and being "hospitable to one another" are found in connection to Peter's admonition for each believer to use his or her spiritual gift in ministry "to one another" (1 Pet. 4:10-11).

This makes a very important point about the whole concept of spiritual gifts in the life and work of the local church. The gifts are given for the edification of the church. The design is that we show our love for one another by the exercise of our gifts. In this way, God is most glorified, and the church has its greatest impact on the culture around it.

As we consider the characteristics of the gift of giving, let us recall the fundamental foundation of giving. God Himself is the greatest giver of all! We have nothing that we did not receive (1 Cor. 4:7). Donald G. Barnhouse reminds us that "under grace we realize that everything we have belongs to the Lord."

Nonetheless, it is hard to discuss giving without getting on the nerves of a good many people who are regular church attenders. But the issue is more than just giving; it is stewardship. Those with the gift of giving are motivated to lead the way for the rest of us.

Jerry Vines says it well: "All of us are supposed to give. The Bible teaches that we should give to the Lord one tenth of our income (the tithe) and give offerings on top of that." The "on top" part is what we might refer to as grace giving. Those with the spiritual gift of giving are truly grace givers.

Vines goes on to say, "This is a touchy subject with a lot of Christians."[3] But this is where the Holy Spirit comes and gifts some of the members with the gift of giving. They sense and know the financial needs of the church and can set the tone for others to learn that giving is, in reality, the pathway to the blessings of God.

We should be careful to note that we are in no way talking about the methodology of the Word of Faith movement or the prosperity gospel teachers. God's blessings come in direct proportion to our obedience. If we are obedient in the area of our money, God will pour out blessings that we will not have room enough to store. The passage that tells us of this is found in Malachi 3 and makes it clear that the blessings God grants are not primarily financial blessings.

Every church should learn to operate on the motto "Tell the people, trust the Lord." In other words, it is more than acceptable for the financial needs of the church to be shared with the membership. But we should never trust human ability. The best example of giving in the New Testament, that of the Macedonian believers, was clearly something they did under the guidance and direction of the Holy Spirit (cf. 2 Cor. 8-9).

Thank God for faithful church members who have been blessed with the gift of giving!

---

[3] Vines, *Spirit Life,* 138.

The Basic Characteristics of the Gift of Giving

1. The ability to discern and make wise investments. The motivation of givers is to use all of their assets to advance the cause of Christ. They have a supernatural ability to invest wisely, both in the matter of earning income and in the matter of distributing those funds to meet needs in the church. They are able to differentiate between good and bad investments. Darrell Robinson says,

> Persons with the gift of giving have an uncanny, creative ability to invest, earn money, and gain property. They always have a desire to give and participate in what God is doing by giving money to support His kingdom…They are usually good managers, well-organized, and private.[4]

Matthew said much about the wise use of money, more so than any of the other Gospel writers (cf. Matt. 6:19-20; 25:14-30). While he was simply recording the teaching of Jesus on the subject, it was obvious that the teaching made an impact on Matthew personally.

2. The need for reassurance that his decisions are in accordance with God's will. Because of this, the giver will first give himself to the Lord as Paul indicated was characteristic of the Macedonian believers. While he extols their virtues in the giving of the offering, he points out, "But they first gave themselves to the Lord, and then to us by the will of God" (2 Cor. 8:5).

The lordship of Jesus Christ is a very important factor in all spiritual gifts, but especially so here. A giver will not respond well, or quickly, to high-pressure appeals. They will take time to pray and, as needed, to investigate the validity of the need.

3. Frugal and content. The giver not only wants to save money but to get the best buy. They will tend to buy quality gifts that will last because they are motivated by value. Matthew demonstrates this as

---

[4] Robinson, *Incredibly Gifted*, 149.

he is the only one who records "the treasures" at Christ's birth, the price of Mary's ointment, and the value of Joseph's tomb (Matt 2:11; 26:6-11; 27:57-60).

As a rule, they are content with such things as they have and are willing to sacrifice to meet the needs of others. Contentment is a virtue that has to be learned, but it can be learned, and givers are often the ones who best demonstrate that (cf. Phil. 4:11-13). In fact, Paul demonstrates that contentment is the foundation of consistency and confidence in the things of God.

4. Ability to see needs others never see, or needs that are not obvious. It is not unusual for a giver to be prompted by the Lord to give even when the need is not urgent or particularly noticeable. Great joy comes when it is discovered that the gift was actually an answer to prayer. They are generally sensitive to others and the Holy Spirit in this regard. They are often compassionate people who care deeply that the evangelistic efforts of the church are properly funded.

When Paul was addressing the Corinthians to encourage them to give in a manner similar to the Macedonians, he reminded them that "God is able to make all grace abound toward you, that you, always having all sufficiency in all things, may have an abundance for every good work." He knew that he could act on God's direction in giving because God would be faithful to provide. The nature of God is to give. Paul says of the Lord, "He has dispersed abroad, He has given to the poor; His righteousness endures forever."

He then goes on to remind them of the fact that the beneficiaries in this giving would glorify God and rejoice in the answer to their prayers for their financial needs.

> While, through the proof of this ministry, they glorify God for the obedience of your confession to the gospel of Christ, and for your liberal sharing with them and all men, and by their prayer for you, who long for you because of the exceeding grace of God in you. (Cf. 2 Cor. 9:8-15).

5. Gives only to effective ministries, which will be revealed to the giver by God. As stated earlier, the giver will resent pressure tactics. In the early days of the church, prayer and preaching motivated the people to give. We read,

> And when they had prayed, the place where they were assembled together was shaken; and they were all filled with the Holy Spirit, and they spoke the word of God with boldness. (Acts 4:31)

Then we read in verses 32-37 that the givers began to come forward and took care of all the needs! Ananias and Sapphira missed the opportunity, but the others who gave realized through their demise that they were giving to a powerful organization (cf. Acts 4:31ff; 5:11).

6. Gives to motivate others to give. Sometimes the giver will give on a matching-gift basis. Barnabas was used mightily by the Lord in Acts 4 to encourage generosity on the part of many. Paul used the giving of other churches to encourage the Corinthian church to give (cf. 1 Cor. 16:1- 2; 2 Cor. 8-9).

7. Often have the desire to give secretly. As the giver looks to the Lord for direction, he wants the receiver to look to the Lord for provision. Matthew 6:1-4 discusses this principle in detail. Future reward from God is more important than praise from men today. But the giver wants to be a part of what he gives to. He wants to feel a personal involvement with the person or ministry. (Paul's many discussions about giving and its results in his ministry show the personal-involvement aspect so prevalent with this gift.)

8. Concern over the effect their giving will have. The giver recognizes the destructiveness of the love of money (1 Tim 6:6-10). Therefore, he will avoid giving that would tempt the recipient to become dependent or slothful. When someone with the gift of giving is involved in the distribution of benevolence funds, they normally will not give cash because of the negative effect that could have. This is good policy for benevolence committees and church staff to follow.[5]

Misunderstandings and Misuses of the Gift of Giving

1. May appear to be materialistic, showy, or impressive to others. While being wealthy is not a requirement to have the gift, it is true that many who do have it are financially in very good condition. There is nothing wrong with this. It is a misuse of the gift to be showy or to flaunt one's wealth. It is wrong to give the impression that one is spiritually superior because they have been blessed financially. This would be prideful and would negate the positive aspects of the gift.

On the other hand, it is a misunderstanding for others to assume that someone is materialistic just because they have nice things. Since it is characteristic for them to give secretly, others will not know how much they give. There is nothing wrong with having money. The problem comes in having the wrong attitude toward money.

Givers must guard against hoarding resources for themselves. Giving always depends on a proper fear of the Lord, which was the reason for the tithe.

> You shall truly tithe all the increase of your grain that the field produces year by year. And you shall eat before the Lord your God, in the place where He chooses to make His name abide, the tithe of your grain and your new wine and your oil, of the firstborn of your herds and your flocks, *that you may learn to fear the Lord your God always.* (Deut. 14:22-23, emphasis mine)

---

[5] Dealing with benevolence in the church is always a difficult task. People with the gift of giving are often best suited for this task. Deacons should be involved as well, and many times a church will have deacons with this gift. For a detailed summary of the work of deacons and others in the church with regard to mercy ministries, I highly recommend Alexander Strauch's *Minister of Mercy: The New Testament Deacon* (Littleton: Lewis and Roth Publishers, 1992).

2. May be accused of attempting to control people with money. It is characteristic of givers to give a gift other than cash to see that the funds are used wisely. While this may appear controlling to some, it is generally just the giver carrying out their God-given motivation. This stems from the characteristic concern over the effect their giving might have on the recipient (see number 8 above).

There are many individuals who have misused the gift of giving by using their money to attempt to control the pastor and/or the church. Such individuals are troublemakers for the church. They will complain about the way every dollar is spent. Pastors and other church leaders should be very careful about receiving money from individuals in the church lest they turn around and try to use the gift as leverage to get their way.

I recall numerous examples of this over the course of my ministry, but one such event stands out. An individual had given the church a significant financial gift many years before I became the pastor. At the time the gift was given, it was set up in a trust account and was more than the annual budget of the church at the time. The giver received a tax donation for his gift but had drawn up a legal agreement placing himself in control of the funds.

Over the years, this man used the interest on the money to fund his pet ministry project in the church. His own family members and some close friends benefitted from the funds more than anyone else. While there were some checks and balances in the agreement, they were largely ignored. After all, since he gave the money, he should be able to control it, right? No, it was wrong. The man eventually moved away and later died, but before leaving, he left one of his close friends in charge of the money. This caused significant grief in the life of the church and was clearly a misuse of the gift of giving.

3. May neglect family in giving. Family is important, and givers should set the example in providing for their own. Scripture is clear about the necessity of each believer taking care of their own family as a priority (cf. 1 Tim. 5:8). If they do not, their neglect of the family may cause the family to react negatively to the generosity they display toward others.

4. Danger of measuring spirituality by assets. Judas may be an example of this. Money does not mean you are right with God. The story of Job's friends clearly illustrates the danger of this mentality. Consequently, "health and wealth" theology must be rejected on the basis of God's Word.

5. May become proud of their generosity, causing people to focus their attention away from the Lord. It is a misuse of the gift to lead people to depend on another person rather than the Lord. Not only can this create a level of pride in the giver, but it can also attract others with wrong motives. It is important to keep people ahead of projects and to make sure that giving is based on legitimate need, whether ministry or benevolence related.

One issue that givers face is that there are always more needs than any one person can meet. Discernment as to where financial support would be most effective and appreciated takes prayer, investigation, and wisdom. Ill feelings can come from those whose project or need is turned down. This can create jealousy among some and can even lead to bitterness as the giver may be wrongly accused of trying to gain control over things in the church.

Sometimes the best solution is to keep the giving and giver secret. But regardless, the church, or individual recipient, should appreciate all gifts given and see to it that the funds are used wisely and in the manner they were intended to be used.

6. Pride may be apparent when testifying, but generally, the giver just wants to share his victories and help others rejoice too. Some of the greatest victories I have seen in the life of the church have been related to reaching or exceeding goals that have been set for various ministry needs or mission endeavors. There have been times when a need was expressed, and the people openly and quickly gave. It is a misunderstanding of the gift to be too quick to level the charge of pride at those who are able and willing to give.

I remember an evening service in which the church I served at the time had a pastor from another country present in the service. He shared about some of the needs of his congregation. The church was in an inner-city location, and they had a leaky roof. The Spirit led us to take an offering to repair the church's roof. With a crowd of only about two hundred people $8,000 was raised! Those with the gift of giving led the way, some challenging others to give. There was great rejoicing. The following year, I went on a mission trip to minister with this pastor in his church and saw the fruit that had resulted from our church's investment.

7. If pressured, they may appear stingy. It is important to let God motivate the giver. All the same, givers should not reject an opportunity for the single cause of a pressured appeal. While the giver may appear stingy at times to others, there is, on the other hand, the danger that the giver may become offended when others do not give in the same measure that they do.

It should be remembered as well that some givers have been stung when taken advantage of by charlatans. It becomes hard for them to regain trust, but this they must do if they are going to continue to be used by the Lord with their gift.

Bible Characters Who Illustrate the Gift of Giving

Matthew, a tax collector by trade, demonstrates this gift extremely well, which is discernable from the emphasis given to the subject in his Gospel. As mentioned already, Matthew included more counsel on the wise use of money than the other Gospel writers. He is the only one who records Jesus's comments about giving in secret from the Sermon on the Mount (Matt. 6:1-4). Matthew detailed the value of gifts given. He also recorded Jesus's parables on the foolishness and rebellious attitude of those who would misuse the resources given them by God (Matt. 19:16-26; 21:33- 46; 25:14-30).

It would appear from Luke's comments about the call of Matthew that he was a wealthy man. Luke says, "So he left all, rose up, and followed Him" (Luke 5:28). The fact that "he left all" indicates that Matthew had great wealth to leave behind. We are further convinced by the fact that Matthew gave a significant feast for Jesus and invited a large number of his tax-collector friends. This is the activity of a wealthy man.

Matthew is the one who records the parable of the laborers where the generosity of the landowner, who paid the same wage to his workers regardless of the number of hours they worked, is recognized (Matt. 20:1-16). In a similar parable, Matthew is the only one to record Christ's condemnation of a man who was forgiven much but failed to forgive a small debt owed him (Matt. 18:23-35). Anyone with the gift of giving should seriously study the Gospel of Matthew.

Other notable individuals who demonstrated the gift of giving are Zacchaeus (Luke 19:1-10), the poor widow (Luke 21:1-4), Barnabas (Acts 4), and Joanna and Susanna, who represented a number of women who used their resources to support the Lord's work while He ministered on earth (Luke 8:1-3).

Bible Verses That Explain the Gift of Giving

The Bible has a great deal to say about giving and money, sometimes to the dismay of once-in-a-while churchgoers and occasional Bible readers. I recall one Sunday that one of my members excitedly reported to me that his neighbor, whom he had been inviting, was present, dropping his kids off in the children's department for Sunday School at that very moment. Then he said, "Please tell me tell that you are not preaching about money today." Much to his chagrin, it was the Sunday of our annual stewardship emphasis!

Apparently, this man had made it clear that every time he went to church, all the preacher talked about was money. I suspect he was exaggerating, don't you? But the truth is, there are many preachers, churches, and ministries, especially the prosperity gospel proponents, who take the Bible's message on money and use it as a club to beat the bucks out of reluctant givers. They make promises of earthly rewards that are a serious misconstruction of the truth. In fact, most such promises are just downright lies, gimmicks to seduce the unsuspecting into parting with their hard-earned dollars.

If there is anything we should learn from the Bible, it is that "God loves a cheerful giver." In his commendation of the gracious giving of the Macedonian churches, and in an effort to get the Corinthians to follow suit, Paul says,

> So let each one give as he purposes in his heart, not grudgingly or of necessity; for God loves a cheerful giver. And God is able to make all grace abound toward you, that you, always having all sufficiency in all things, may have an abundance for every good work. (2 Cor. 9:7-8)

God's plan for giving is supernatural, something that can't really be explained in human terms. I have often said that if one is obedient with the tithe, they will find that 90 percent will buy more than 100 percent! God has a way of getting His cut. Unfortunately, though, many of the appeals for money in church don't ring true to the biblical message. The reason for biblical stewardship is not that you need to meet a need, regardless of how legitimate that need might be, but so that you might demonstrate your complete trust in God!

The root problem with a failure to give to the Lord's work through the local church is unbelief. The prophet Malachi plainly says,

> "Will a man rob God? Yet you have robbed Me! But you say, 'In what way have we robbed You?' In tithes and offerings. You are cursed with a curse, For you have robbed Me, Even this whole nation. Bring all the tithes into the storehouse, That there may be food in My house, And try Me now in this," Says the Lord of hosts, "If I will not open for you the windows of heaven And pour out for you such blessing That there will not be room enough to receive it." (Mal. 3:8-10; cf. Prov. 11:4; Eccl. 2:21-22; 5:14-16; Matt. 6:19-21; 1 Tim. 6:7)

If we believed God, then we would readily be obedient in our stewardship, not just in what we give to the Lord's work but in how we use all of our money. As this relates to the gift of giving, we can see how God uses givers to teach the rest of the church how to maximize their funds for the greatest blessings and most effective support of the Lord's men and work. The truth is, giving is not an obligation—it is a privilege!

The Bible has numerous commands related to giving, a sampling of which can be found in the following: Leviticus 27:30, Psalm 24:1, Matthew 23:23, Malachi 3:8-12, Numbers 18:28, and Deuteronomy 14:22-23. Instructions about how to give are found in First Corinthians 16:1-2, 2 Corinthians 8-9, and Matthew 6:1-4.

How Jesus Demonstrated the Gift of Giving

Jesus's comments about giving include the following, which should be studied by anyone who believes they have the gift of giving:

- One should concentrate on heavenly treasure (Matt. 6:19-20).
- It is better to give than receive (Acts 20:35).
- He approved of generosity (Mark 14:6).
- He said materialism can defeat you (Mark 10:23).
- He taught that you can't live on material things only (Luke 12:15).
- There is danger in greed (Luke 12:15).
- We are accountable for our use of money (Luke 12:20).
- Your motives in using money are important (Matt. 6:1-2, 33).
- You should not worry (Matt. 6:25-34).
- You should help others (Luke 10:35).

The reality is that Jesus was the greatest giver who ever lived. He gave everything, including His very life, leaving the glory of heaven to come and die for us and provide us with the greatest treasure of all, eternal life through a relationship with Him (cf. Heb. 2).

Conclusion

You have heard this phrase before: "He is no fool who gives away that which he cannot keep in order to gain that which he cannot lose!"

The statement is credited to the missionary Jim Elliott, who lost his life on the mission field. He literally gave away that which he could not keep, his life (not to mention his material possessions). In the process, he gained that which he could not lose: eternal life.

In Luke 12, Jesus taught a parable about a rich man whose crops had come in plentifully. In fact, his harvest was so great that he did not have room to store it. He made the choice to pull down his barns and build bigger ones. Self-satisfied, he said to himself, "Soul, you have many goods laid up for many years. Take your ease, eat, drink, and be merry." But God had a message for this miser, "Fool! This night, your soul will required of you. Then whose will those things be which you have provided?" Jesus gave the moral to the story: "So is he who lays up treasure for himself, and is not rich toward God" (Luke 12:13-21).

The one with the gift of giving has settled in their heart that all they have is a gift from God and, in a very real sense, it all belongs to God. They understand that the Bible teaches that we are stewards of God's money that He has, in reality, simply loaned it to them. All that we have we have received from Him. When we give all of our things back to Him, we experience a great freedom and will be on our way to learning the true joy of grace giving!

10

The Gift of Leading

Making ministry more effective through excellence

He who leads, with diligence.
—Romans 12:8

Bless those who persecute you, bless and do not curse.
—Romans 12:13

The gift of leading is sometimes referred to as the gift of ruling or the gift of administration. It is a gift that enables one to organize and put things together for the accomplishment of goals and objectives. The person with this gift is one who is a solution finder. They are able to direct others to a common goal.

The *motivation* behind this gift is to advance the cause of Christ (especially in the local church) by administrating, organizing, and leading others to achieve common goals and objectives. The gift is defined as follows:

> The special God-given ability to recognize the gifts of others, enlist and engage them in ministry. Those who possess this gift have the ability to organize and manage people, resources, and time for

effective ministry. They have the ability to coordinate details and execute the plans of leadership.[1]

I had the privilege, for the last nine years of my military career, to serve as a reserve chaplain in the US Air Force. Like any good organization, the Air Force has some core values that serve as the touchstone for every mission and operational activity of the service. Those values are *integrity, service before self,* and, *excellence in all we do.* I have found these values to be effective, productive, and biblical. In all the churches I have served in recent years, I have used these core values as a foundation for the church staff in its efforts to lead ministry in the local church.

While all the members of the staff do not necessarily have this gift, it is generally a good idea to have one or more people with this gift in positions of leadership, both on the staff and in whatever type of organizational structure a church has.

The word translated "leads" is the word προιστημι (*proistemi*) from *histemi*—"to stand," with the prefix *pro* ("before"), so it literally it means "to stand before." One of the ministry gifts is that of "governments" or "administrations" (1 Cor. 12:28). This refers, of course, to the administrative areas of leadership that a church needs. People with the gift of leading are the best candidates to fill the administrative and governing positions in the church.

The word used in First Corinthians 12:28 is a nautical term used of "steering the ship." The noun form of the word is translated "helmsman." The idea is that the church needs godly leaders who can guide the church through the dangerous waters that are sure to come. Any sailor who has spent time at sea understands that, at some point, he will face rough waters and storms. Every church will have its difficult days. None should want to see the church run aground on the rocks of false doctrine, unbelief, rebellion, pride, or some of the many other hard circumstances that will inevitably arise.

---

[1] Robinson, *Incredibly Gifted*, 143.

The one with the gift of leading is charged with a great responsibility. There is an essential need for consistency in leadership. An interesting use of the word is found in Titus 3:8 and 14. Twice Paul uses the word that is there translated "maintain." He says that we should be "careful to *maintain* good works" and that we should "learn to *maintain* good works." It would seem to imply that the leadership of the church should consistently lead the church to accomplish the good works we have been called to do, not the least of which is evangelism (see chapter 13).

The word is used to describe directly the leadership of elders or pastors. "Let the elders who *rule* well be counted worthy of double honor, especially those who labor in the word and doctrine" (1 Tim. 5:17, emphasis mine). This is in perfect harmony with the definition of the word that means "lit., 'to stand before,' hence, to lead, attend to (indicating care and diligence), is translated to rule… with reference to the local church" (VINE). Thayer says it means "to set or place before; to set over; to be over, to superintend, preside over; to be a protector or guardian" (JHT). The idea then is clear that this is "referring to anyone placed in a position of authority or superintendence" (WSGNT). Barnhouse says it carries "the idea of government and administration…the gift of management of the affairs of the church."[2]

According to Romans 12:8 and 14, there are three definite concepts regarding leadership in the church:

- One should lead with "diligence."
- You must learn to bless those who persecute you.
- You must not curse those who refuse to follow.

Romans 12:8 says the one who leads should do so with "diligence." The word itself means "haste, with haste; earnestness, diligence… earnestness in accomplishing, promoting, or striving after anything; to give all diligence" (ESL). Wuest says, "The idea of making haste,

---

[2] Barnhouse, *God's Discipline*, 56.

being eager, giving diligence, and putting forth effort are in the word. The word speaks of intense effort and determination" (wsgnt).

Good leadership is certainly not an easy thing. Leading others takes a toll on the emotions and energy of even the very best leaders. There is a need for discipline and full faith and trust in the Lord if one is going to lead God's people. The concept of haste in the word "precludes procrastination and idleness."[3]

The instruction in verse 14 may seem a little odd. But since the other verses are so clear in their descriptions of the other gifts, there is no question that Paul meant this verse in relation to the gift of leading.

He says, "Bless those who persecute you." The reality is that leaders are not always going to be well received by others. In fact, though the leader is operating within his/her gift in telling others what to do, that is still often resented. You cannot be a leader and not be shot at on occasion. Leaders must learn to handle criticism, or they will likely end up becoming a quitter.

This resistance to retaliation goes against the grain of nature. Not only are leaders not to retaliate, they are to bless. This discipline is needed desperately in the church today. Surely this is leading like Jesus, for He is the One who commanded us to love our enemies. There is nothing easy about it.

This is not to say that we should allow others to run over us and hold the church back from the direction God has clearly given. But when our leadership is resisted, as best we can, we are to "bless those who persecute" us. To bless someone doesn't mean to agree with them or give in to them. It means to treat them as if they were your friend in spite of their negative reaction to you.

The fact that the admonition is given twice is interesting. Paul goes on to say, "Bless and do not curse." I believe this has to do with producing tenderness in the heart of those in authority. The warning is not to overreact to those who rebel. While remaining firm in what is right, do what you can to help others, even the rebellious, be

---

[3] MacArthur, *Romans 9-16*, 177.

happy and spiritually prosperous. This, of course, does not mean we disregard the need for church discipline.

The bottom line is that we must try to be the kind of leaders whom people will follow. We should attempt to pull rather than push. Being demanding is sometimes necessary to get the job done, but leadership should be exercised in a servant style manner (1 Pet. 5:1-5).

One of the principles that leaders need to understand is suffering. If you are going to organize others to accomplish goals, you must be sensitive to their needs, recognizing that they may not have the same agenda as you.

The Basic Characteristics of the Gift of Leading

As we look at the characteristics of the gift of leading, we will find that Nehemiah is a tremendous biblical example of this gift. We will refer to numerous passages in the book of Nehemiah to support our case for those concepts that best exemplify this gift.

1. An ability to see the big picture, to visualize the final result and make long-range plans (Neh. 1:2-3; 2:5). Nehemiah visualized the goal of removing the "great distress and reproach" of God's people due to the breakdown of the walls and the society in Jerusalem. To say that he was a man of vision is almost an understatement. Like Nehemiah, those with the gift of leadership are able to see what needs to be done and to visualize what the end result will look like, which leads us to the second characteristic.

2. An ability to set goals, breaking down long-range plans into achievable tasks. They can put together an organization (Neh. 3:1-32). If we study Nehemiah chapter 3, we note the amazing approach that Nehemiah took to effectively organize the work of the people. The organization was simple and yet perfectly fit the need of the hour. He assigned many separate groups to work on specific smaller sections of the wall needing repair. The important mission of getting the wall up around the city was not taken in one big single project but divided up for steady progress. I'm thinking that some of our Department of Transportation folks and road builders today could learn some valuable lessons from Nehemiah!

3. An ability to determine the necessary resources and the knowledge to acquire them (Neh. 1-2). Nehemiah quickly and accurately assessed what would be needed to get the project accomplished. Good leaders will not easily be sidetracked. The materials needed for the project were determined based on the report Nehemiah had received. We cannot overlook the place of faith and prayer in Nehemiah's work, which we will emphasize in point 5 below. But what is clear is that those with the gift of leading are able to determine what will be needed to accomplish a ministry task.

This may explain why those with the gift of service and those with the gift of leading butt heads on occasion. Note that Nehemiah set a specific time, wrote letters to prepare and provide for the needs of the project, and got proper permission to carry on the project, a building permit, if you will. The server operates from the standpoint that it is better to get forgiveness than to ask permission. Proper leadership will generally not follow that course of action.

4. Will be very thorough and complete, staying with the task until it is completed. The one with this gift will *do the job right the first time*. It is simply amazing what is reported about the timetable of the rebuilding of the wall under Nehemiah: "So the wall was finished on the twenty-fifth day of Elul, in fifty-two days" (Neh. 6:15).

Darrell Robinson says,

> Those who have the gift of leadership readily accept the responsibilities of stepping out to organize, plan, and manage people and programs to achieve goals. The administrator/leader is a take-charge type of person who is able to step in and give direction and orders when needed. The church needs to place

people with the gift of administration/ leadership in positions of leadership.[4]

Doing the job right the first time often falls on deaf ears in the life of the church. Many times people are looking for shortcuts. Sometimes they reason that the work is mostly done by volunteers anyway, so let's not take any more time than is absolutely necessary. But a good leader knows this is a recipe for disaster. The better solution is to work "smarter," not necessarily "harder." If we do the job right the first time, we won't have to go back and do it again.

5. Has a good grasp of the need for faith, knows how to find the will of God, and how to trust God in the work of ministry. Whatever else may be said about leaders in the church, if they do not know how to discover and do the will of God, all else will be of little value. The book of Nehemiah is a classic case study for those with the gift of leading. Nehemiah never ventured out in any aspect of leadership without having spent time in the Word and prayer. He knew how to discover God's will.

A tendency of those with the gift of leading will be to frequent the prayer closet. On the other hand, failures in leadership are often directly related to the lack of prayer and faith in God.

Believing is central to effective leadership. Those with the gift of leading should be well-grounded in their theology. In other words, a leader must believe the right things to be effective in moving the church toward the fulfillment of God's call. The church needs both courageous leaders and committed followers, people who trust God's direction and leadership and obediently follow His will, so they that they can have a positive influence on others.

Dr. Albert Mohler has correctly said,

> The command to believe is central to the Bible. Christianity is founded upon certain nonnegotiable truths, and these truths, once known, are translated into beliefs. The beliefs that anchor our

---

[4] Robinson, *Incredibly Gifted,* 144.

faith are those to which we are most passionately and personally committed, and these are our convictions. We do not believe in belief any more than we have faith in faith. We believe the gospel, and we have faith in Christ. Our beliefs have substance and our faith has an object.[5]

Those with this spiritual gift will normally have the courage of their convictions. They will carry through based on their strongly held beliefs. They are often gifted secondarily in prophecy or teaching, or they are positively influenced by strong teachers in the church. They are willing to take a stand to encourage God's people to move forward in accomplishing His will.

6. An ability to know what tasks can be delegated and to whom they can delegate them (Neh. 4:13). We should note that Nehemiah delegated many assignments but retained the responsibility for the overall result. The one with this gift also desires loyalty and confidence from those he directs (Neh. 5:1-13). He will hesitate to delegate unless the person is reliable.

While not ignoring the actual work on the wall, Nehemiah was not fully engaged in the work itself (again distinguishing this gift from service). What he did was remove obstacles, take off the financial pressure, and maintain the correct legal status.

Another thought here is that leaders will not only properly delegate, but they are generally good at challenging and encouraging their workers. As a general rule, Nehemiah had a cheerful spirit (Neh. 2:1). But as you read through the book, you find over and over that he is constantly encouraging and motivating others to get God's work done.

7. Able to be decisive (Neh. 4, 7). Often those with this gift will take the leadership role if no one else will. This was evident throughout the process that Nehemiah led as he was constantly placed in the position

---

[5] Albert Mohler, *The Conviction to Lead* (Minneapolis: Bethany House Publishers, 2012), 22.

of making decisions. Nehemiah was a man who had exceptional intuition.

Sometimes the decisions that need to be made will not have clear, objective answers. But the leader with a heart tuned in to the things of God will be able to make a decision based on biblical principles and convictions. The willingness to be decisive will often lead directly to the next characteristic.

8. Will endure reaction from friend and foe in order to accomplish his goals (Neh. 4:8-18). In this regard, the leader keeps the pressure on to get the job done. Leaders are very goal oriented and may become frustrated if progress is not made. But they must understand the source of the opposition (whether that source is friend or foe) and endure the opposition to accomplish the goals of the organization.

Nehemiah's foes saw a loss of influence and power coming if the Jews were successful. Nehemiah's friends had to be led to operate with persistence lest they become discouraged in the face of the enemies' attacks. The Bible reports that the result of Nehemiah's leadership was effective, for the people "had a mind to work." Prayer and persistence in the face of both internal and external assaults were hallmarks of his leadership.

9. Dislikes disorder, can't stand a mess (Neh. 1:3-4). The impetus for Nehemiah to take on this difficult task was the ruin of the city that he heard about. Those with the gift of leadership are not going to stand idly by and let things fall apart. They are action oriented and like to see things done in an orderly and decent manner. To see the church in need of repair or the ministries of the church in need of revival will cause them to take action.

10. Has great joy in seeing all the parts come together in a finished product (Neh. 7:1-2; 8:1-18). One of the great delights of leadership is seeing a project come to completion with successful results. Nehemiah had a praise service to celebrate the victory. Churches would do well to celebrate positive events. It seems sometimes that the negative things get all the attention. Leaders are constantly looking for both people and things that they can point to that are the result of God's blessings and the people's obedience to God's call.

11. Needs a current challenge but will normally remain on the "sidelines" until asked to be in charge. We recall that Nehemiah's presence was requested in Jerusalem. While some leaders are self-motivated and will move without being asked, that is not typical of the one with the spiritual gift of leading. Often they will wait until they are asked before taking action to move forward. A church will be wise to be aware of the members who have this gift and keep them employed in leading ministry.

Misunderstandings and Misuses of the Gift of Leading

1. Delegating too much work may make the administrator appear lazy or insensitive. Proper delegation is a must when leading others. Being part of the project is important. Others should recognize that the leader is doing what God has gifted them to do, but on the other hand, we should not create the county-road crew view of five *managers* standing around watching one *worker* with a shovel! Good leaders will, on occasion, get their hands dirty with real work.

2. May appear calloused due to their determination. They must be careful not to view people as human resources but as human beings. This can be helped with expressions of appreciation and due consideration to the effort of those doing the labor. While leadership that directs a group to the completion of a goal sometimes takes dogged determination, there is a time and place for thoughtfulness toward the needs of the workers.

3. They will be very honest about their likes and dislikes and may be unresponsive to suggestions and appeals. This is a misuse of the gift. In the end, the leader often has to make the final decision.

But taking into consideration the suggestions of others is always productive. It is not wise, however, to follow the suggestion of every person who happens along with an idea. But God uses people; therefore, leaders should be open to hear from God, regardless of the sources He chooses to use. Even when we don't follow a given suggestion, thankfulness for the input and serious consideration of the idea will go a long way in maintaining the full support of the workers.

There is also the problem of becoming an autocrat who controls every detail. I recall once when on vacation, I was called and asked what color of paint I wanted used in the classrooms of the new education building that was under construction. That was not a decision I needed to make, and I declined the opportunity. Wisdom is sometimes knowing when your own input is not crucial to the finished product.

4. Impatient with mediocrity and those who tire easily. Those with the gift of leading will sometimes appear bossy because they are constantly telling others what to do (Neh. 13:1-31). It is part of the price of leadership. Mediocrity is unacceptable, especially in the things of God! While a lack of patience can be understood in these circumstances, the leader should be careful to seek the Lord's guidance and not express his or her frustrations. This reveals that it may be time to get before the Lord in prayer.

What is apt to happen, however, is that they will also overlook serious character flaws in those who can get the job done. This may signal approval of ungodly behavior to others and create a spiritual decline. To accomplish God's work, we need to use God's people. Think of the times the church nominating committee put someone in a position of power in the church because the job was related to their secular vocation or experience, notwithstanding the fact that they seldom, if ever, even attended church. I have seen devastating results in such situations.

5. May appear to show favoritism to those who are more loyal. A failure of leading is always going to come when the leader misuses their gift by playing favorites with their special friends. The gifts and abilities of all the church members need to be recognized and used in doing the Lord's work. The fact that someone is more loyal to you as a leader is helpful, but it doesn't mean they are necessarily the best person for the job. Good leadership in the church always involves as many people as possible in the work of the Lord. Clear recognition of the spiritual gifts of those involved in a church project is essential.

6. May fail to give proper explanation and praise to workers. Both proper instruction and praise for work well done are essential. Good leadership, like that which Nehemiah displayed, provides clear direction for others to follow. Expectations may be high, but they should be understood from the start.

The fact that leaders want to get the job accomplished quickly and efficiently may be the primary reason behind their directions being less than clear on occasion and their being light on praise. Leaders should be quick to give proper praise, and church members should do their work as unto the Lord and not expect undue praise for their efforts.

7. May take on projects that are not God's direction and will. This would be a definite misuse of the gift. Leaders, if they are not careful, can run ahead of God. This is why it is important for them to spend adequate time in prayer and Bible study and to be under the sound preaching and teaching of God's Word.

King David decided to build a house for the Lord, and when he mentioned it to Nathan the prophet, he told the king to do whatever was in his heart. The idea was well intentioned, but it was not God's will for David, nor was it the proper time. Nathan spoke without having received clear direction from God. God had to reveal to Nathan in his prayer time that this was not to be done and that David's son would be the one to build the Lord a house (2 Sam. 7:1-17).

Bible Characters Who Illustrate the Gift of Leading

As we have pointed out, Nehemiah is the best example of this gift. If this is your gift, you should carefully study the entire book of Nehemiah. Nehemiah was an eminent example of leadership, and his tremendous faith in God is a precious guide to those who might aspire to lead the church in accomplishing its God given mission.

The book of Nehemiah serves as a practical demonstration of the sovereignty of God worked out in the lives of obedient and willing servants of the Lord. The theme of Nehemiah could be stated this way, "Acting on our faith leads to a greater understanding of God's grace as it operates in and through our lives." Nehemiah was a man of great faith, and much can be learned from his example. You cannot separate the message of Nehemiah from the man Nehemiah, they must be taken together.

A second major theme—and critically important in regard to becoming a man or woman of faith and, consequently, a leader in the life of the church, is that careful attention to the reading and study of God's Word is essential if one is going to accomplish God's will. Opinions varied as Nehemiah approached the difficult assignment he had received from the Lord to rebuild the walls of Jerusalem. He faced much opposition, but he was a man who constantly turned to the Word of God and prayer to determine what course of action to take.

Most believers today could learn a lot from Nehemiah's example. Nehemiah's name means "Yahweh comforts." Anytime you are in difficult circumstances, it is good to know that you serve a God who will comfort you in your affliction (2 Cor. 1:3-7). Leaders, in particular, need this advice as is evidenced from the clarification of the gift in Romans 12:14.

J. Sidlow Baxter wisely comments on the leadership of Nehemiah,

> As we watch this strong, earnest, godly hero, Nehemiah; resolutely leading the rebuilding in the first part of the book, then resolutely resisting compromise and laxity and intrigue in the second part of the book, we find the spiritual message of it all coming home to

us with great force. Let us heed its voice to us. There is no winning without working and warring. There is no opportunity without opposition. There is no "open door" set before us without there being many "adversaries" to obstruct our entering it (1 Cor. 16:9). Whenever the saints say, "Let us arise and build," the enemy says, "Let us arise and oppose." There is no triumph without trouble. There is no victory without vigilance. There is a cross in the way to every crown that is worth wearing.[6]

There are a number of other biblical characters who demonstrate a leaning toward having had the gift of leadership. There was Samuel, who came to serve as prophet and priest in a time when Israel was bereft of leadership. In many ways, he had to clean up the mess left behind by his predecessor, Eli. Samuel is a case study in the business of seeking God through prayer and study of the Word.

Joseph is another example of leadership, particularly those types of leadership assignments where we must go through hard times to be prepared by God for what lies ahead. Joseph becomes a case study in perseverance and patience, faith and obedience.

Joshua was a great leader whose life provides a case study in how to follow a great leader. Most pastors are reluctant to come in to lead a church if they are going to have to follow a well-respected, long-tenured predecessor. Imagine having to follow Moses! But again, we find in Joshua a man accustomed to prayer and study of the Word. He was also one who had learned well from others, in his case, from Moses himself. God may have you in a secondary position of leadership because He is preparing you for greater things in the days ahead.

When we look to the New Testament, we can study any number of the great men who had leadership ability whom God used. When we read the book of James and corresponding passages in Acts, we realize what great strength of character James had. This is a very important aspect of leadership and goes hand in hand with this gift. James writes of the practical implications of the Christian life. He

---

[6] J. Sidlow Baxter, *Explore the Book* (Grand Rapids: Zondervan, 1960), 230-1.

reminds those who would desire positions of leadership that they should make sure they are called: "My brethren, let not many of you become teachers, knowing that we shall receive a stricter judgment" (James 3:1).

Dr. Albert Mohler's excellent book on leadership, *The Conviction to Lead*, has an entire chapter dedicated to the issue of character. I highly recommend that anyone with the spiritual gift of leading obtain and read Dr. Mohler's book. He points out in the book that character is expected of secular leaders. Not perfection, mind you, but "moral stability and conviction." The problem, however, on the secular side is "the fact that we have no common concept of what character really is."[7]

This is not true in Christian concepts of leadership. Mohler explains,

> The Christian leader has to know a far deeper and urgent call to character—a call to character that is not only master of public persona, nor merely a negotiation with the moral confusion of our own age. As followers of Christ, we know that there is no legitimacy to the claim that our private and public lives can be lived on different moral terms. And we also know that the moral terms to which we are accountable are not set by us; they are revealed in God's Word.[8]

When we study the lives of the men God used to build the New Testament church, we see men of conviction and character. They knew what they believed, they knew why they believed, and then they lived their lives in accordance with their beliefs. The one who has the gift of leading could study the lives of Paul, Peter, Timothy, or John and learn much about leadership in the life of the early church.

Church history also gives us numerous men to examine whereby we could gain wisdom in the art of leadership. The following list is not exhaustive by any means, but one could gain much leadership

---

[7] Mohler, *The Conviction to Lead*, 77.
[8] Ibid., 78.

expertise from reading the biographies of men like Martin Luther, George Whitefield, George Mueller, Hudson Taylor, William Carey, A. W. Pink, James P. Boyce, or Charles H. Spurgeon.

Bible Verses That Explain the Gift of Leading

The word *proistemi* is used elsewhere in scripture to refer to the rule or authority of elders (or pastors) in First Thessalonians 5:12, First Timothy 5:17, and the rule of fathers in First Timothy 3:4-5 and 12.

The idea behind this word has to do with leadership and organization for the care and nurture of others. The word is applied to pastors who are called to shepherd the flock of God—that is, they are to spiritually care for them. In First Peter 5:1-9, elders are told to shepherd the people of God, serving as overseers. As such, they are to "stand before" the congregation to provide leadership. It is not in the scope of this book to flesh out the details of pastoral or parental leadership in the church and family. But it is important to point out that both of those forms of leadership have the same word associated with them as the spiritual gift of leading.

The point of this is that those who have this gift and are involved in the administration, organization, and leadership of the church are to do so for the purpose of caring for the needs of the congregation, just as a pastor does for the church family and as a father does for his own family. Individual preferences must be set aside for the good and growth of the local church at large.

In fact, the family may provide a good laboratory to determine if someone is qualified for a greater position of leadership in the church, such as pastor or deacon. In the qualifications for elders, Paul tells us that one who aspires to the office must be "*one who rules* [*proistemi*] *his own house well, having his children in submission with all reverence.*" The importance of the qualification is clarified: "For if a man does not know how to rule his own house, how will he take care of the church of God?" (1 Tim. 3:4-5).

Regarding deacon qualifications, Paul says, "Let deacons be the husbands of one wife, ruling [*proistemi*] their children and their own houses well" (1 Tim. 3:12). Those with the gift of leading can best demonstrate their gift in the home where they provide godly and gracious care for their own families.

How Jesus Demonstrated the Gift of Leading

There is an instruction in scripture to cast our care upon Jesus because He cares for us. Peter says, "Casting all your care upon Him, for He cares for you" (1 Pet. 5:7). Indeed, Jesus is the Great Shepherd (John 10:11-18), which demonstrates His tremendous leadership gift. There was never a servant-leader like the Lord Jesus. The work of a shepherd in biblical times was characterized by two clear things: leading and serving.

We could run through numerous verses from the Gospels to demonstrate the servant model of leadership that Jesus exemplified. If we did so, we would have difficulty covering every single aspect of Jesus's leadership style. Anyone who is in a position of leadership, whether they have the spiritual gift of leading or not, should model their leadership and ministry after Jesus. If the Holy Spirit calls someone into pastoral leadership, it would only make sense that He would in turn give them this gift!

For those with this gift, we should note of Jesus that his assessment of His ministry was, "For even the Son of Man did not come to be served, but to serve, and to give His life a ransom for many" (Mark 10:45). Perhaps the most striking illustration of servant leadership from Jesus is found in John 13 where Jesus washes the feet of the disciples. After completing this menial task of service, He reminded them that He had set an example for them (John 13:14-15).

Conclusion

Often the best leadership is demonstrated by serving, by meeting the practical needs of others. The spiritual gifts are designed so that the body of Christ could function efficiently and effectively as each member takes their place and serves the others through the exercise of their various gifts. To stand in front of others and lead them to meet the needs of the church is a high calling indeed.

It deserves our best effort and requires our full dependence on God to make it so. In that regard, we recall Paul's admonition:

> Therefore, my beloved, as you have always obeyed, not as in my presence only, but now much more in my absence, work out your own salvation with fear and trembling; for it is God who works in you both to will and to do for His good pleasure. (Phil. 2:12-13)

11

The Gift of Mercy

Comforting the saints through the love of God

He who shows mercy, with cheerfulness.
—Romans 12:8

Rejoice with those who rejoice, weep with those who weep.
—Romans 12:15

The gift of mercy enables one to sympathize with and to suffer alongside those who fall into affliction or distress. They are able to both care and share in the needs of others. They are very sensitive and try to see things from God's point of view. The word is the normal New Testament word in Greek for mercy. It is ελεάω (*eleao*), meaning "to show mercy, have compassion on, have pity on, to help one who is afflicted" (ESL). The idea is that of expressing compassion and comfort.

Vine says the gift is, "the outward manifestation of pity; it assumes need on the part of him who receives it, and resources adequate to meet the need on the part of him who shows it...[it] signifies, in general, to feel sympathy with the misery of another, and especially sympathy manifested in act" (VINE). Thayer notes that it is "mercy; kindness or good will towards the miserable and afflicted, joined with a desire to relieve them" (JHT).

The sense of the very word carries with it the idea that the distress that has befallen another is due to no fault of their own. So then, this is "the emotion roused by contact with an affliction which comes undeservedly on someone else. There is in it an element of [*phobos*, "fear"] that this can happen" (TDNT).

Darrell Robinson defines the gift extremely well as "the God-given ability to discern needs in lives of others, to feel compassion for them, and to provide caring support for those in distress."[1]

According to Romans 12:8 and 15, mercy givers should do the following:

- Operate with a cheerful attitude
- Rejoice with those who rejoice
- Weep with those who weep

Romans 12:8 says that mercy is to be performed with "cheerfulness." That word comes from the Greek ἱλαρότης (*hilarotes*), where we get our English word *hilarity*. It means "cheerfulness, readiness of mind" (ESL). Barnhouse makes an astute observation: "Now, we are certainly not going to be good recommendations for the Lord Jesus Christ if we have not learned the great truth that joy is one of the prime requisites of the Christian life."[2]

John MacArthur says,

> The gifted Christian who shows mercy is divinely endowed with special sensitivity to suffering and sorrow, with the ability to notice misery and distress that may go unnoticed by others, and with the desire and means to help alleviate such afflictions.[3]

It is important to mention that the one gifted with mercy is not one who only deals with those going through trials and troubles. We note that the gift is exercised with "cheerfulness" and that the one so

---

[1] Robinson, *Incredibly Gifted*, 146.
[2] Barnhouse, *God's Discipline*, 59.
[3] MacArthur, *Romans 9-16*, 177.

gifted is to "rejoice with those who rejoice." They are also divinely endowed to be a blessing to those who are experiencing good times or events in their lives.

What a joy mercy givers are to the local church! Paul's instructions here go beyond showing mercy without grudging. We all know people who serve in the church yet do so with a negative, put-upon attitude.

> Let nothing be done through selfish ambition or conceit, but in lowliness of mind let each esteem others better than himself. Let each of you look out not only for his own interests, but also for the interests of others.
>
> -Philippians 2:3-4

They vainly attempt to show a low self-esteem but, in reality, are trying to draw attention to themselves. False humility is nothing but pride. It fails to meet the criteria established by the Holy Spirit.

Mercy givers are a great blessing because they help the church keep its ministries other-centered rather than self-centered. Any ministry in the church that is primarily designed for direct contact with people will be greatly enhanced by the addition of those with this gift.

The explanatory verse (12:15) gives two additional concepts. "Rejoice with those who rejoice." This should be easy enough to do, but the flesh tends to react with resentment rather than rejoicing at the success or blessing of others. This may be especially so if the person whose happiness is in question has become so at our expense. When you have competed in an athletic contest, or run for office, or assumed you were going to be chosen for the position or the job, yet someone else got the good news, the flesh resists being happy about it.

If another's great joy makes your own circumstances look rather bleak, it can be hard to rejoice with them. Consequently, we see the need for the divinely motivated individual with the gift of mercy. Are you a help or hindrance? Some people in the church, who set out to help others, actually make the situation worse. When they serve out of a sense of duty or with a resentful attitude, their help is rarely well-received. Sometimes the attitude is, "They got themselves into this so they deserve what they are getting." This was the very attitude of

Job's friends and they nearly drove him to despair. The gift of mercy entails more than just sympathy - it is truly empathy, feeling put into action for the good of others.

A lesson in sportsmanship might help us understand this gift better. I do not recall the college softball teams that were playing, but a young lady hit a home run that would have given her team the victory. The rules required that she touch each base and finally home for the run to count. As she jogged across first base, she tripped and injured her ankle to the point that she could not bear weight on it. If her coaches or teammates tried to help her, by rule she would be called out as coaches cannot assist a runner. The defensive team saw the dilemma. Two of the defensive players picked up the injured runner and carried her to second, then to third, and then to home, allowing her to touch the bases in order. This is what it means to "rejoice with those who rejoice," even when it comes at your expense.

The final admonition, "weep with those who weep," is a little easier to understand. In truth, it is "distinctively Christian to be sensitive to the disappointments, hardships, and sorrows of others...Compassion has in the very word the idea of suffering with someone."[4] It is likely that we are nevermore like God than when we demonstrate compassion to the downtrodden. Mercy givers are those uniquely gifted by God to show the rest of us the importance of showing mercy.

The Basic Characteristics of the Gift of Mercy

1. An ability to empathize with others when they hurt. This ability runs the full spectrum of emotions. They will feel joy or pain equally with others. John wrote his first epistle to give joy and hope to his readers and to cast out fear and torment (1 John 1:3-4; 4:18; 5:13-14). In fact, he expresses one of the primary reasons for his writing: "And these things we write to you that your joy may be full." Then later he writes, "There is no fear in love; but perfect love casts out fear,

---

[4] Ibid., 197.

because fear involves torment. But he who fears has not been made perfect in love."

2. Attracted to people in need (often unusual people). Since they have a deep understanding of people going through distress, they often draw hurting people who will confide in them. Note that in Christ's great hour of distress, He confided in John (John 13:23-26). John is a great example of a mercy because he was not only merciful but firm and straightforward with the truth.

People will regularly assume that because someone is a pastor or minister (vocationally), they are automatically willing to help. Anytime an outsider (someone not a member) comes to a church seeking benevolence they want to talk to the pastor. The assumption is that he will be more sympathetic than a deacon or lay member on the benevolence committee. Since these types of people rarely have an understanding of spiritual gifts, they are often misguided in this thinking.

It is the person with the gift of mercy who is more likely to be sympathetic and feel the pain of a person in need. Of course, benevolence ministry is a place where they might be taken advantage of. While not attempting at this point to give a lesson on benevolent ministries in the church, it is wise for a church to have an exhorter or prophet on the benevolence team.

3. A desire to bring healing and help to those in distress. A great example of this would be the apostle John who took responsibility for Jesus's mother when the Lord was dying on the cross. Robert L. Thomas has well said,

> "Showing mercy" is a special "know how" in consoling the mourner, relieving the sufferer, accomplishing acts of various kinds of assistance, or something of that sort for the benefit of distressed people...In the contemporary scene the world is full of distressed people, which means many open doors for service by Christians with the gift of showing mercy.[5]

---

[5] Thomas, *Understanding Spiritual Gifts*, 201.

4. Deeply loyal to close friends. Mercy givers will react harshly if a close friend is attacked. In Luke 9:54, James and John asked the Lord if He wanted them to call down fire on the Lord's enemies! While they were deeply loyal, they would characteristically also have a need for close friendships, particularly those who have mutual commitment. This is demonstrated in John's close relationship to Christ, even referring to himself as the "disciple whom Jesus loved" (John 13:23; 19:26; 20:2; 21:7, 20).

5. Deeply emotional with great concern over people hurting on the inside. They can sense genuine love and, therefore, are more vulnerable to deep and frequent hurts from those who fail to love sincerely. John's use of the word *love* throughout his Gospel and epistles indicates his concern in this area. In fact, he used the word *love* more than any of the other Gospel writers.

When people are facing troubling times—whether the cause is physical illness or injury, financial setback, or some other emotional trauma—often the greatest need is simply for reassurance that someone genuinely cares. Since all the gifts are designed for evangelism, this deep concern for hurting people is very valuable in laying a foundation for sharing the gospel. The opportunity to share Christ will often present itself when there has been a genuine expression of concern for the hurting person's situation. It is perhaps trite but nonetheless true—people don't care how much you know until they know how much you care.

It is the person with the gift of mercy who will be the first to react negatively to the condemnation offered by street preachers. There is nothing wrong with street preaching *per se*. However, often such preaching is extremely judgmental. It may present the truth, but the problem is, it doesn't necessarily present the whole truth. It lays out the penalty for sin but often fails to give the power available for salvation. Christ came to save sinners, not to condemn them.

There is nothing wrong with being straightforward and firm in presenting the penalty for sin. Death is a steep price to pay (Rom. 6:23). But the solution must be given with compassion. This was the approach that the apostle John took in First John. For example, in chapter 1, he was not shy to present the fact that we have all sinned but also that sincere confession brings forgiveness and cleansing. In chapter 2, he reminds us that Christ is our "Advocate," that He himself became the "propitiation" (the payment) for our sin. This is the proper approach and the one that a mercy will insist upon.

6. A desire to remove the source of pain or hurts. Protection is almost a natural instinct for the one with this gift. Often they will go to severe lengths to accomplish their goal (see misuse number 7 below). John's first epistle was a plea for Christians to stop hurting and hating one another (1 John 3:11, 15).

We can distinguish here between exhorters and those with mercy. The exhorter tries to help the person benefit from his hurts, but the one with mercy tries to remove the source of the hurts. The mercy gift places greater emphasis on mental or spiritual distress as opposed to physical distress.

The mercy will also have a problem with people who are harsh and irritable. They are hurt when someone is hateful, regardless of toward whom the hate is directed. The mercy recognizes that hateful feelings are what marked believers before they were saved, and such feelings are not appropriate, especially among the saints of the Lord (cf. Tit. 3:1-8).

7. Tendency to avoid firmness and decisions for fear of offending someone. In a sense, I think it is fair to say that a mercy wants everyone to be content. They do not like to rock the boat. This may cause them to avoid being firm or decisive. They must see, however, that greater hurts may occur if they fail in this regard. They will follow and be compliant until they realize that a greater danger looms if they remain neutral. John's boldness when faced with denying the Lord, which would cause greater hurt in the long run, especially in his spiritual life, demonstrates this (Acts 4:13-20).

8. Tendency to measure acceptance by physical closeness. John demonstrates this in his closeness to the Lord (Mark 10:35-37, John 13:23-26). Sometimes a mercy giver will measure acceptance from others by their willingness to touch and be physically close or to spend quality time with them. This is a danger that must be carefully guarded against. Getting too close to someone physically can lead the person you are trying to help to make false conclusions about your intentions. You also run the risk of becoming too emotionally involved to provide effective biblical counsel and comfort.

9. Will be attracted to prophets (because opposites attract) as firm truth is balanced by gentle love. We might note that John spent more time with Peter than any other disciple (Luke 22:8; Acts 3:1-11, 8:14).

Misunderstandings and Misuses of the Gift of Mercy

1. May fail to be firm and therefore appear to be wishy-washy in trying not to offend. They will often fail to take disciplinary action when it is necessary. There is a danger of being taken advantage of. For this reason, it is important for mercies to have moral freedom. That is, they need to have their walk with God and their spiritual disciplines in order. It is imperative for them to have dealt with any bitterness in their life in order to be effective in the exercise of their gift.

2. A tendency to take up the offenses of others who are hurt. Before comfort is given, it is wise to seek the help of a prophet to see why the hurt was caused and an exhorter to give steps of action to properly respond to the hurt. It is a misuse of the gift to take up an offense on another's behalf until the facts behind the hurt are established.

3. Depending too heavily on emotions rather than reason and logic. The problem here is a danger in rejecting sound biblical doctrine that appears harsh to them. They may tolerate evil if they do not understand why people suffer. They may encourage and sympathize with those who are suffering as a direct result of disobeying God. Seeking the advice of a prophet, teacher, or exhorter can be a great help to correct this.

4. Reacting wrongly to God's purposes in allowing people to suffer. It is a misuse of the gift to give people a pass and enable them in their wrong response to what God may be doing in their life. Sympathizing with someone who is suffering as a direct result of their disobedience to God's standards is unbiblical. Understanding their circumstances and what may have led them into their predicament is one thing. Condoning their wrong actions is another.

It is critical for a mercy to understand God's purposes through suffering. Whether suffering has a direct correlation to sin or not, either that of the sufferer or someone else, sometimes God has purposed the suffering for the spiritual growth or maturity of the person, or simply as a consequence to their actions. (To better understand suffering, study James 1, 1 Peter 3 and 4, and Romans 5).

5. May tend to be possessive in friendships of the time and attention of others. This can occur simply from the motivation to get close enough to the situation to provide the necessary comfort. But once a biblically compassionate response has been given, the mercy should consider backing off lest their intentions be misunderstood. Monopolizing someone else's time, even if the intent is good, can lead to dissatisfaction, especially from members of the mercy's family who may feel slighted.

They also misuse the gift when they become overly troubled personally over other people's needs. They will sometimes stress out because they cannot find a suitable solution or find a way to provide comfort that seems to alleviate the problem. This can be especially true when they try to help someone who rather revels in their misery.

The misery lover will be the one to take advantage of the mercy giver, but the mercy will become frustrated because there is seemingly no way to move the miserable out of their misery.

6. Overreacting to insincerity in others and shutting them off rather than helping them. The church has its share of insincere people. Sometimes they are that way because they are lost; they have never really come to saving faith in Christ. A mercy needs to learn to recognize that situation because what that person really needs is a faithful witness to what true salvation entails.

There are others in the church who are genuinely saved, but they are trying to live the Christian life in the energy of the flesh. This can appear as insincerity. There is nothing more frustrating than trying to live the Christian life on your own. It can't be done! We can only live as Christians through the indwelling power of the Holy Spirit.

All believers need to learn to walk in the Spirit (Gal. 5:16ff). Mercies need to be spiritually mature enough to determine whether the person they are dealing with is truly walking in the Spirit. This means they need to both know and exercise the fruit of the Spirit.

7. Persons of the opposite sex will be drawn to one with mercy. The one with mercy may become too intimate with others, and this should be checked in any relationship with the opposite sex. Members of the opposite sex may be drawn to a mercy because of their sensitivity, understanding, and willingness to listen.

Because of the emotional nature of this gift, it is imperative that safeguards be established, especially where a counseling relationship might be needed. In general, a mercy should limit their work to members of the same sex unless accompanied by their spouse or, in some cases, by another believer, perhaps a church leader, teacher, or pastor.

Bible Characters Who Illustrate the Gift of Mercy

John the apostle clearly had the gift of mercy as we have pointed out in looking at the characteristics of the gift. Anyone with the gift would do themselves a great favor by becoming thoroughly familiar with his writings. John is known as the apostle of love, yet he was a very firm and direct individual. His love was sincere. He deeply cared about people, but he never compromised the truth.

Another excellent example of the gift is Dorcas of Joppa. We read of her life in Acts 9 where we are told, "At Joppa there was a certain disciple named Tabitha, which is translated Dorcas. This woman was *full of good works and charitable deeds* which she did" (Acts 9:36, emphasis mine). The church was obviously blessed by this woman's deeds of charity. So beloved was she that when she became sick and died, the church called immediately for Peter to come.

When Peter arrived, the evidences of her ministry of mercy were shown. Peter, by the power of the Holy Spirit, raised Dorcas back to life. That was a miracle designed to bring credentials to the ministry of Peter and the preaching of the Word. This attracted much attention, and many were reached with the gospel. But it was the effect of Dorcas's ministry of mercy that laid the foundation for the preaching and teaching of the apostles (cf. Acts 9:36-43).

In the church today, people will be more open to the gospel when they see that believers actually do love and serve one another for Jesus' sake.

Epaphroditus is another example of mercy. He was sent by the church at Philippi to relieve the sufferings being experienced by Paul in prison. So dedicated was Epaphroditus to the task that he became sick nigh unto death (cf. Phil. 2:25f). The ministry of this man reveals an important aspect of this gift and, in a sense, the others as well. "It entails hard work and unselfish service... Exercise of the gift puts oneself into the background and considers only the positive value it can impart to others."[6]

Bible Verses That Explain the Gift of Mercy

The Bible has a great deal to say about the mercy and grace of God. Mercy is the foundation of our salvation. Surely if God can extend mercy to us, we should be willing to extend it to others. In Psalm 119,

---

[6] Ibid., 201.

that great psalm on the trustworthiness of God's Word, the psalmist cries out to the Lord for mercy. "Deal with Your servant according to Your mercy, and teach me Your statutes" (v. 124).

He knows he can cry out for mercy because of what the Word of God teaches on the subject. He was saved by the mercy and grace of the Lord; therefore, he has no problem appealing to mercy. He remembers the day that mercy came running to his aid. He knows the reality of salvation and how truly deep is the Father's love for him.

So the psalmist, likely David, knows that this great God will never fail and that He will "teach *him His* statutes." Again, he is ever after knowledge, wisdom, and understanding. He wants to grow in the Word and needs the mercy of God to do so. In essence, this is an appeal to be strengthened by the Holy Spirit in the inner man.

While he is waiting on the mercies of the Lord, which are new every morning, he is desirous of being fortified in the Word of God.

There is a connection that John Phillips rightly points out in his commentary. The need of God's mercy is inextricably connected to a need to grasp God's laws. "Mercy and morality go together." He notes a classic example, that of Absalom and David. David forgave the somewhat justifiable sin of Absalom, but Absalom had taken the law into his own hands. David ignored this. He forgave and banished Absalom and then, almost inexplicably, welcomed him back. But in all of this, Absalom was unrepentant. There was never any reconciliation.[7]

Here is a truth that we would do well to grasp. It defines the connection of mercy and morality. You cannot receive forgiveness until you repent. Think about that and let it sink in. So far from repentance was Absalom that he became resentful. The mercy he received, he squandered, and it bred rebellion. Note again the psalmist's appeal: "Deal with Your servant according to Your mercy, *and* teach me Your statutes." Mercy and morality hold hands. Reconciliation and repentance are kissing cousins.

---

[7] John Phillips, *Exploring the Psalms: Psalms 89-150* (Neptune, NJ: Loizeaux Brothers, 1988), 377.

The one with the gift of mercy will do well to remember this vital connection.

Other references to the mercy of God are found in the following verses: Ephesians 2:4; Titus 3:5; Luke 1:50, 72; Romans 15:9, 9:15-18; Philippians 2:27; Jude 21-23.

There are numerous commands given to us to exercise mercy: Matthew 5:7, 9:13, 23:23; Luke 10:37; James 2:13. Some general references to mercy are Romans 11:30-31, 1 Corinthians 7:25, 2 Corinthians 4:1, 1 Timothy 1:13-16, 1 Peter 2:10.

We are commanded to request mercy through prayer (Heb. 4:16; Gal. 6:16; 1 Tim. 1:2).

How Jesus Demonstrated the Gift of Mercy

Of course, God Himself is mercy, and the Lord Jesus (who demonstrates all seven gifts) is our greatest example of mercy. The examples of Jesus demonstrating mercy are too many to list, but there are several that should be considered as we look to our Lord for clarity on the subject.

Jesus was moved with compassion at the death of his friend Lazarus. His tears were not so much for the loss of His friend as they were for the misunderstanding of truth in those others who were weeping. Where was their faith in God's promise of mercy revealed in the gift of eternal life?

In John 11:33, the Bible says of Jesus, "He groaned in the spirit and was troubled." *Groaned* is the word εμβριμάομαι (*embrimaomai*), which means "speak harshly to; criticize harshly; be deeply moved." It carries with it the idea of indignation and is used again in verse 38. But at what was Jesus indignant?

The word *troubled* is ταράσσω (*tarasso*), which means "trouble, disturb, upset, stir up (as water)." Thus, it means to agitate. Jesus was indignant and agitated over the ravages of sin. Death is an enemy, and the fear of death is a powerful tool that Satan uses against the Lord's people. As our merciful High Priest, Jesus was concerned over their misunderstanding of His capability to bring mercy and destroy the power of death (cf. Heb. 2:14-18). Like Jesus, we need to have compassion for the lost.

This same compassion was expressed by Jesus when He lamented over the condition of Jerusalem. "O Jerusalem, Jerusalem, the one who kills the prophets and stones those who are sent to her! How often I wanted to gather your children together, as a hen gathers her chicks under her wings, but you were not willing!" (Matt. 23:37). We know from many examples that Jesus not only had compassion for sheep without a Shepherd, but He went to seek and save the lost. We need to have that same mercy for their souls.

When Jesus ran across the hurting and humbled, He was moved with compassion and mercy. In fact, as His works were made known, many cried out to Him for mercy. This is demonstrated in the following text:

> When Jesus departed from there, two blind men followed Him, crying out and saying, "Son of David, have mercy on us!" And when He had come into the house, the blind men came to Him. And Jesus said to them, "Do you believe that I am able to do this?" They said to Him, "Yes, Lord." Then He touched their eyes, saying, "According to your faith let it be to you." And their eyes were opened. And Jesus sternly warned them, saying, "See that no one knows it." But when they had departed, they spread the news about Him in all that country. As they went out, behold, they brought to Him a man, mute and demon possessed. And when the demon was cast out, the mute spoke. And the multitudes marveled, saying, "It was never seen like this in Israel!" (Matt. 9:27-33; cf. 15:21-28, 17:14-21, 20:29-34).

At the outset of His earthly ministry, Jesus declared that He had come to be a minister of mercy.

> The Spirit of the Lord is upon Me, Because He has anointed Me to preach the gospel to the poor; He has sent Me to heal the brokenhearted, To proclaim liberty to the captives And recovery of sight to the blind, To set at liberty those who are oppressed; To proclaim the acceptable year of the Lord." (Luke 4:18-19)

Jesus made mercy the subject of several parables. In Matthew 18, Jesus tells the story of the "unforgiving servant," who had no mercy even though great mercy had been extended to him (Matt. 18:23-35). The story is a great lesson in the need for and art of forgiveness. Merciful attitudes lead to forgiving actions.

In another parable, the one about the Good Samaritan, Jesus makes a clear and convincing appeal to love our neighbors and explains just who our neighbor is: the man or woman whose need we have the ability and resources to meet. Who in the story was a true neighbor? The people who heard the story could easily see that the neighbor was the one "who showed mercy." Jesus's command was that we should "go and do likewise" (Luke 10:25-37).

Anyone who has the motivational gift of mercy should study the Gospels with particular attention to the words and actions of Jesus as He encountered people in need of mercy and encouragement.

Conclusion

There are so many ministries in the life of a local New Testament church that mercy givers can easily find an effective place to serve. The need for visiting hospitals, nursing homes, and those members of the church who are homebound is always great. Then there are the homeless shelters, soup kitchens, clothing closets, and crisis pregnancy centers that all need people with the gift of mercy to share the love of God with their clients. There are preschool ministries, senior adult ministries, and benevolence and bereavement ministries. All these are well suited to the gift of mercy.

But perhaps even greater is the need for the gift of mercy, simply in the Sunday School classes and in the pews of the sanctuary. Many of God's people are hurting in ways that are not seen by most. The mercy who is sensitive to the leading of the Holy Spirit can be a great blessing to the average believer, who simply needs a word or touch of encouragement. I think it is true that often the mercy giver ministers somewhat as an angel unaware. As they dispense the mercy of God through their words and actions, they really never fully know the extent of the blessing they bring.

There is an instruction in Paul's second letter to the Corinthians that applies to all but would be particularly true of a mercy. Paul says,

> Blessed be the God and Father of our Lord Jesus Christ, the Father of mercies and God of all comfort, who comforts us in all our tribulation, that we may be able to comfort those who are in any trouble, with the comfort with which we ourselves are comforted by God. (2 Cor. 1:3-4)

The mercy, as the recipient of the comfort of God, is able to give that same comfort to the beleaguered saints they find in trouble's way.

Blessed is the congregation who receives the ministry of those gifted with mercy!

12

Using Your Motivational Gift

Understanding your purpose as a servant of the Lord

As each one has received a gift, minister it to one another,
as good stewards of the manifold grace of God.
—1 Peter 4:10

One of the most detrimental things that can happen in the life of a believer is to know your motivating spiritual gift and yet not use it effectively in the service of the Lord. Another area that gets neglected is the effect your motivating gift has on other areas of your life. Everything we do should be approached on the basis of our giftedness as the Holy Spirit is the motivator who has gifted us. He is the One who is to guide and direct our lives.

In this chapter, we will begin with some cautions that should be considered as you find your place of service using your gift. Then we will consider the significance of the gifts in the areas of your personal life, your family, and in your church.

Having learned the seven motivational gifts, you should be well aware of what your gifts are. If not, it is imperative that you continue to study so that you will know how the Spirit has gifted you to serve the church. You have at least one motivating gift, and likely, the Holy Spirit has gifted you in at least one other secondary area.

Note the command Peter relates to us in regard to using our gifts:

> As each one has received a gift, minister it to one another, as good stewards of the manifold grace of God. If anyone speaks, let him speak as the oracles of God. If anyone ministers, let him do it as with the ability which God supplies, that in all things God may be glorified through Jesus Christ, to whom belong the glory and the dominion forever and ever. Amen. (1 Pet. 4:10-11)

Peter emphasizes the basic truth that every believer has at least one motivational, spiritual gift. Another point is that God is the One who gave you your gift, just as He gave you your salvation. With the gift, there comes a responsibility to take what God has given you and to become one of the "good stewards of the manifold grace of God." Not only has God gifted you, but according to Peter, He will empower and enable you to use your gift.

In other words, you don't operate in the spiritual gifts through the energy of the flesh but with "the ability which God supplies, that in all things God may be glorified through Jesus Christ" (1 Pet. 4:11). It parallels perfectly the Christian life that is "Christ in you, the hope of glory" (Gal. 2:20). The Christian life isn't what you do for God but rather what God does in and through you to bring the most glory to Himself.

We often think of the motivational gifts as *grace gifts*. The only way we can be good stewards of the grace of God is to minister faithfully in our grace-given giftedness. The reality of all this is that God has made you part of His plan of redemption, reconciliation, and restoration. He uses you as an agent to minister his "manifold grace" to others through using your gift. That is why it is so important for people to know, understand, and use their gifts.

Some Cautions in Using Your Gift

There are some important cautions when you begin to use your gift. In all things, the true disciple of the Lord needs to be balanced and maintain a biblical approach in serving others. Consider the following cautions when you begin to employ your spiritual gift:

1. Do not evaluate others on the basis of your gift. Your temperament is based on your gift (not the other way around), and your disposition will reflect your gift. Rebellion and selfishness can allow demons to pervert your gift. Remember that the Lord gifts each believer, and we need one another. In fact, we need each of the seven gifts operating, particularly in the church, for the church to be successful.

If you set up a false standard for the actions of others that is conformed to your specific gift, you will put others at a disadvantage. Use your gift, try to understand the giftedness of others, and allow the Holy Spirit to be the one who brings conviction and change when needed in others. Simply put, don't try to be someone else's "Holy Spirit."

T. W. Hunt says,

> Christ's self-emptying is the supreme example of humility. To have the mind of Christ, we must deliberately humble ourselves by becoming other-directed, first to God and then to others. We are in a position to build the kingdom when we humble ourselves. Because of Christ's humility, He was able to obey radically. If I am humble, I can obey in the same way Christ did. He enables my humility in His office as the Righteous Servant. His example is my goal.[1]

2. Do not become proud in your gift. Arrogance will lessen your effectiveness for the Lord. Our service for the Lord should always be a humble service. We serve the Lord not because we have to but because we want to! There is no greater privilege on this earth than to have the title *servant of the Most High God!*

In each of the seven motivational gifts, our greatest example is Jesus Himself. In an overall sense, as relates to all the gifts, His

---

[1] T. W. Hunt, *The Mind of Christ* (Nashville: Broadman & Holman Publishers, 1995), 100.

most powerful example was that of humble obedience to the will of the Father. Paul reminds us of the majestic extent of His humility: "And being found in appearance as a man, He humbled Himself and became obedient to the point of death, even the death of the cross" (Phil. 2:8).

Jesus often reminded the disciples that He had come not to do His own will but that of the Father (cf. John 4:34, 5:30, 17:4; Rom. 15:3). Over and over, Jesus demonstrated humility through obedience to all that the Father had designed and prepared for Him.

When Peter calls on us to use our gifts as "good stewards of the manifold grace of God," he goes on to remind us that service brings suffering, service should always should operate under authority, and that service will always be best suited when one is "submissive... and... clothed with humility." Plainly, "God resists the proud, But gives grace to the humble" (cf. 1 Pet. 4-5).

If the motivational gifts are about anything, they are about humble service and obedience to the call of God.[2] To serve effectively will necessitate the elimination of pride and the desire to develop the mind of Christ (cf. Phil. 2:5-11).

3. Do not try to force others to see your gift or their own. If God can give gifts, He can reveal them. This is a personal and private matter for the most part. That doesn't mean you can't encourage others—what it means is that you can't force anyone to grow spiritually. As we have said previously, the spiritual gifts are one of the most misunderstood teachings of the Christian life. We need to be reminded that if the Holy Spirit can confer gifts upon each believer, He can also reveal them.

---

[2] A great complementary study to the spiritual gifts would be T. W. Hunt's book *The Mind of Christ* (Nashville: Broadman & Holman Publishers, 1995). Chapter 8 is titled "Humble and Obedient" and is an excellent study of humility. Hunt says, "It is strange that some of us give lip-service to the lordship of Christ, but in practice we ignore His teachings...Jesus' teaching on humility is among the best known of His teachings, and yet the power and nobility of humility remains the best-kept secret in the Christian world" (p. 96).

What we can do is encourage the study of the gifts in the Word and seek to determine what our gifts are and use them to the glory of God and the good of the church (cf. Rom. 12:3-5). When Peter mentions the spiritual gifts in First Peter 4, the instructions he provides prior to mentioning the gifts applies in the context.

> But the end of all things is at hand; therefore be serious and watchful in your prayers. And above all things have fervent love for one another, for "love will cover a multitude of sins." Be hospitable to one another without grumbling. (1 Pet. 4:7-9, cf. vv. 10-11).

If we follow those instructions, then we will be much more effective in ministering our gifts to one another "as good stewards of the manifold grace of God." A serious approach to serving the Lord, coupled with prayer, fervent love, and hospitality without complaining, will make us ready for effective ministry in the use of our spiritual gifts. Peter makes it clear that the bottom line of our service through the gifts is "that in all things God may be glorified through Jesus Christ."

4. Do not underestimate the value of the gifts of others. All the gifts are necessary in the life of the church. Biblical truth will sometimes offend, and often it should. Nonetheless, we have no license to be offensive in our approach or disposition. If you offend someone in the exercise of your gift, you should be concerned.

Again we can look to Peter's instructions about the gifts for guidance in this area. He reminds us not to think it strange that we might suffer. Is he suggesting that we might suffer for trying to use our spiritual gifts to encourage and edify the church? Yes, that is exactly what he is talking about. We should not think it strange that the world would ignore us, express hatred toward us, or even persecute us.

But in the context of First Peter 4, the judgment is that which "begins at the house of God" (v. 17). Sometimes the harshest reaction you will get in using your gift is from fellow church members.

The solution is the proper operation of all the gifts. We can never underestimate the value of the other gifts and should be encouraged when we see them operating in the life of the church.

5. Do not use your gift as an excuse not to manifest the other gifts. Each and every gift is essential to the proper function of the church and valuable to every member. Since you have the giver of the gifts, you are capable of all seven. While this is difficult for many people to understand, one of the main reasons the gifts are given is to help all of us learn to be obedient in those areas that are not our gifted areas.

For example, if you do not have the gift of giving, that does not excuse you from meeting financial needs where you see them and where God clearly speaks to you. In fact, the giver has the goal of encouraging others to give as God has prospered them. If you are not gifted with mercy that does not excuse you from showing mercy where it is clearly needed.

Under normal circumstances, God will use the appropriate person with the proper giftedness to meet the need. But all of us have commands in scripture that relate to each of the seven gifts. He may call you to accomplish a task from time to time that is not up your alley, so to speak, but you are the one person whom God has in place to meet the need. The point is to understand where you are primarily gifted and to understand how the Holy Spirit is normally going to use you in the service of the Lord through the local church.

Significance of the Gifts in Your Personal Life

1. Build all your activities around your primary gift. Your every activity, whether work, home, recreation, or whatever you do, should reflect an understanding of the operation of your gift. The gift you have was given by the Holy Spirit, who dwells within you. That gift, by the operation of the Spirit, should control your life. You are not a regular member of society anymore.

This is a very important principle. As scripture says, we have been bought with a price and are not on our own to do as we please (cf. 1 Cor. 3:16-17; 6:19-20). We are servants of the Most High God and, as such, need to submit to His direction and guidance in all our decisions relative to life. Whatever plans we make, we should take into consideration how we might be most effective in using our gift as we carry out those plans (cf. James 4:13-17).

2. Let your gift establish your ministry. It is essential for every Christian to have a ministry. Ministry is not the "job" of the pastor, church staff, elders, deacons, or Sunday school workers. It is a requirement of the Christian faith. If you establish a ministry in your personal life, you will help free your pastor to do his primary task, that of equipping the saints (Eph. 4:11-13). As we have stated previously, "every member a minister" should be the motto of every church.

Too often, the church fills ministry needs with whomever the nominating committee can find to fill a slot. People are often frustrated because they are serving outside their giftedness; they are working out of a sense of duty and not of love. There are times when your church will need you to step up to the plate and perhaps take a position not best suited to your ministry. Trust the leading of the Holy Spirit and depend on His wisdom and guidance as you serve.

But the best approach, both for the church and the individual member, is for any given ministry of the church to be established because God has raised someone up who is spiritually gifted to operate or engage in that ministry. We might consider shutting down a ministry where there appears to be no one gifted to do it rather than forcing someone into a position to which God has not called them.

On numerous occasions, I have been asked as a pastor why the church wasn't doing this or that ministry. Often the answer was that God had not raised up anyone to coordinate or staff such a ministry. When asked if God was calling that person to "do" the ministry, this often ended the conversation!

Most pastors would agree, many in the church have the idea that we pay the church staff to "do" ministry, and the rest will sit back and be ministered to. This was not the method of Jesus, and it is not the model of the New Testament church. Thankfully, over the years, I have seen many believers come to understand that ministry is a calling for every Christian. They have discovered their spiritual gift and found joy in serving the church for Jesus's sake!

3. Admit your deficiency in certain areas and let others fill the void in your life. Sometimes we let false humility keep us from receiving the ministry of a fellow believer. For example, someone with the gift of service offers to assist or complete a service task for you which you are perfectly capable of doing. You might even do the task better than them. But you may be robbing them of a Holy Spirit motivated opportunity to use their gift. This is an area where we sometimes let our pride get in the way.

I have personally been somewhat hardheaded in this regard in years past. Thankfully, through the leading and teaching of the Holy Spirit, primarily in this area of spiritual gifts, I have learned to let people do their ministry. Even if it means we have to come behind them and "fix it." People need the Lord, the old song said, and people in the church need to know they are needed in the life and ministry of the church. If you are a church leader, involve as many people as you can in the ministry.

If you say to a mercy, "I don't need your sympathy," you are going to hurt their feelings. You may think you are tough enough or spiritual enough to handle your situation. But not only will you hurt the feelings of one sent to minister to you, you may very well grieve the Holy Spirit Himself.

This can be particularly hard for those brought up with a strong work ethic and a mind-set that you never accept "charity." I was one of those who had to learn this lesson the hard way. The details are not significant, but at one point, I was praying that God would meet a particular financial need I had. Out of the blue, an offer came for help. But it came from an unexpected, and, to some degree, unwelcome, source. I initially rejected the offer.

The individual, a person with the gift of giving, said to me, "You are a pastor, and God told me to give this money away to someone who needed it. Do you know anyone else who needs it?" Talk about getting hit in the face with a dose of reality. God's message was clear, "Don't ask Me to meet your needs and then get picky about the people I choose to use to meet the need!" I repented of my pride and accepted the gift.

Learning to receive God's grace is sometimes more difficult than we realize. If we are of the "you have to earn it to feel good about it" crowd, we will not make good receivers, or givers for that matter. God places people in our lives with specific giftedness to meet needs, sometimes needs we may not even realize we have. It is in the best interest of our spiritual lives to receive what God provides through whom He chooses to provide it.

4. Recognize the worth of your gift in proportion to others. So often in the ministry of the church, the gifts will complement one another. An exhorter will give godly counsel, and an administrator will come along beside and help get the counselee's affairs in order. The exhorter gave proper direction to improve the future, but without the practical instruction of the administrator, the exhortation might have created frustration.

We cannot emphasize enough that every gift is important and needed. This means that every person is important and needed. Let's not get this out of proportion. A feeling of being needed is not an emotional crutch we need to hang on to. There is a very real sense in which God does not *need* any of us. The point is that He has chosen, by His own sovereign grace and will, to use us as "fellow workers" (cf. 1 Cor. 3:5-15). You will likely experience no greater joy in the church than in seeing the results of your Holy Spirit-motivated ministry being used to change lives for the better.

Significance of the Gifts in Your Family

When I came to understand the spiritual gifts and began to try to determine the gifts God had given my children, it was very beneficial to my family and particularly to the way I went about my responsibilities as a parent. All of us have heard our children say, "You don't understand me." We have most likely heard this from our spouses and extended family members as well.

I have no illusions that understanding and operating in your spiritual gifts, coupled with an attempt to know and understand the gifts of your family members, will solve all the problems of tension in your home. However, I do believe it could go a long way in helping to produce that outcome. Consider the following points as you think about the way the gifts impact your family:

1. Helps you see why other members of your family act the way they do. This does not excuse bad behavior, but it does help explain, and sometimes mitigate, the actions of family members. There is no question that you can better understand one another when you know how they have been gifted by God.

You might ask, "How does this work in the situation where my children are too young to be saved, or they have reached an age where they could be saved but have not yet surrendered their life to Christ?" Since an unbeliever doesn't have the Holy Spirit, they will naturally not have a spiritual gift. I admit this is a tough question.

If you have unsaved children, you are praying for them to be saved on a daily basis (or at least you should be!). You are asking the Holy Spirit to put a hedge of protection around them and to provide for their needs. From the standpoint of the sovereignty of God, we know that God has foreknowledge of who will be saved. I believe the tendencies of the gifts can be seen in those God is working with and bringing to saving faith. While you cannot be certain, you can see patterns.

By way of example, I am aware of a case in which the youngest child of three had made two professions of faith and had been baptized twice. He had been a leader in the youth ministry, a leader of an evangelistic outreach team, having led a number of people to Christ. He was also a talented singer, using his voice to sing in church and youth meetings. The parents recognized in him the primary gift of giving. This provided much-needed understanding of certain actions that were prominent in his life. As it turns out, he turned from the Lord and was apparently never really saved. The parents hold out the hope that one day he will yet be saved. They are convinced that he will have the gift of giving. It is part of his nature.

Obviously, this is not an exact science. But one of the good things is that you can lead your children to investigate the gifts and help them discover and know how the Holy Spirit might be planning to use them. In the process, this might end up being the very means whereby you can use your gift in their life to lead them to saving faith in Christ.

2. Helps you see the completeness of your family. Most families will find all seven gifts as primary or secondary gifts within their family. It is amazing how God has the ability to bring families together and to see how His work through the gifts can provide families the opportunity to engage in ministry to others.

Perhaps if families put as much time in getting their children active in using their spiritual gifts as they did in getting them to travel sports-team events, the church and the child would be eternally better off! I am an avid sports fan, a high school sports official, and was a longtime coach and leader in youth sports as my boys were growing up. But we did not let sports, or other activities, interfere with that which was most important. The good news is that you can do both, but you must lead your family to put the things of God in the right and proper perspective.

3. Gives each member of the family a chance to belong and contribute to the success and well-being of the family. Children learn from watching, and they learn from instruction. That is why attendance at church activities is just as important, in fact, from an eternal perspective, much more important, as attendance at school. But most of us would agree that hands-on training is the best teacher of all.

For this reason, it is important to get your children involved in doing ministry by such things as going on mission trips, taking them to volunteer for yard work at the church or on visitation to the nursing home. Better still is to help them discover how God has gifted them then challenge them to learn, know, and do the will of God relative to their gifts.

4. Helps keep you from pushing others where they do not belong. For this reason, it is critical that parents understand how the Holy Spirit has gifted their children. Many parents try to force children into areas of service, education, or vocation that are not suited to their gifts. This frustrates the child, brings heartache to the family, and diminishes the effectiveness of the cause of Christ.

Many have been the mama-called preachers, men with no call from God but a call from mama. They were pushed into an area of church ministry and service for which there was no call or giftedness from God. The best path, if you desire that God should call your child into full-time ministry, is to get on your knees and take it to the Lord in prayer. I sensed for many years that God might call my oldest son, who clearly had the gift of prophecy, into the pastorate. I prayed hard about it, and so did his mother.

To be honest, knowing the heartaches so often associated with pastoral ministry, we prayed that God might not call him to that work. But we did not want to be the ones calling him. As a senior in high school, one Sunday night, he came down the aisle, surrendering his life to full-time preaching! God had been dealing with him for years; and it was God's call that he responded to, as it should have been.

The other side of the story are those whom God calls, but their parents or family put pressure on them not to follow the call because of personal reasons or just plain selfishness. No believer, and no believing child, will ever experience the fullness of God's joy until they know and are using their spiritual gift. To let our children follow the call of God will sometimes mean letting them go. The good news is that we will have eternity to talk about it as we celebrate the goodness of God forever.

Significance of the Gifts in Your Church

To some extent, we have covered all these points in the previous chapters. This section serves as a summary for why the gifts are so critical to the life of the New Testament church. I am firmly convinced that the struggles and tensions so often manifested in the life of a church could be soothed and ameliorated with a thorough understanding of the work of the Holy Spirit, particularly in regard to the gifts. Recall some of the primary reasons the gifts are significant in the life of the church:

1. Builds up the fellowship. This is what we are supposed to be doing! The goal for all of us should be to make others better—to help them grow in their relationship and walk with the Lord. Paul says, "But the manifestation of the Spirit is given to each one for the profit of all" (1 Cor. 12:7). The very purpose of the gifts is the "profit" or benefit of others.

While Paul was not specifically addressing spiritual gifts in Philippians 2, he did speak of the "fellowship of the Spirit." His instruction to the church was plain (emphasis mine):

> Therefore if there is any consolation in Christ, if any comfort of love, if any *fellowship of the Spirit*, if any affection and mercy, fulfill my joy by being like-minded, having the same love, being of one accord, of one mind. (Phil. 2:1-2; cf. vv. 3-4)

It seems to me that the "fellowship of the Spirit" would lead us to meet the needs of others, to be concerned about how we might minister to the church and the lost around us. The best preparation for that kind of ministry is to know and use your spiritual gift.

2. Causes members to respect the function of others. If you can see that God is the giver and that He has gifted each person, it will give you a greater respect for what that person is doing under the leading of the Spirit. In a similar fashion to how God uses the gifts in a family setting, so He does in the life of the church. If we truly understand that it is "God who works in you both to will and to do for His good pleasure" (Phil. 2:13), then we can have respect for what others bring to the table in the church.

We refer back at this point to chapter 4 where we outlined the basic truths about spiritual gifts. Recall, every believer has at least one spiritual gift, and that is their primary motivation for ministry. If this is true, then we should learn to respect the work of the Holy Spirit in the lives of our fellow believers in the church. The truth is, we need one another!

3. Helps you accept responsibility in line with what God has gifted you to do. Knowing and using your gift helps to keep you out of other people's business! It also means that you have a gift and therefore are, in your own right, a blessing to the church (cf. 1 Cor. 12:12-27). Jerry Vines rightly says,

> This means that every believer is given gifts individually. Each believer is given one or more…God has given you spiritual gifts because you are important to Him. You have God-given capacities. God does not waste His gifts on unimportant people. You are special to Him![3]

4. Helps you seek to develop the gifts of others. One of the greatest joys in my life has been watching as people in the church discover and begin to use their gifts. As you become more comfortable with your gift, you begin to see the value of gifts to the church; and as a result, you will encourage others to find and use their gifts. The more the gifts are developed, the greater the church's capacity to fulfill its mission.

5. Gives praise to God for the manifestation of the gifts. One of the designs of the gifts is that the credit—the glory, if you will—goes back to God who is behind it all. Peter said that the gifts are always

---

[3] Vines, *Spirit Life*, 106.

exercised through "the ability God supplies, that in all things God may be glorified." Paul, in Ephesians, speaks of God being given glory in the church (Eph. 3:21) then, in chapter 4, refers to the "grace... given, according to the measure of Christ's gift." (Eph. 4:7). Then he refers to several of the ministry gifts given to the church.

Appropriate understanding and encouragement of the spiritual gifts causes the body of Christ to grow in spiritual maturity, to increase in faith, and ultimately to come into the "fullness of Christ." The body then grows and edifies itself in love. What could bring more praise to God?

6. Will cause all things done in the church to be judged on the basis of whether they bring praise to God and edification to the body. This simply amplifies the previous point. Most churches could use a good dose of evaluation. The ministries and programs of the church should be evaluated on the basis of whether or not God is being praised and whether or not the church is being edified. Part of this evaluation would include whether or not people are being witnessed to and won to saving faith in Christ.

If it is good for the individual believer to examine himself to determine his standing with the Lord (2 Cor. 13:5), then it should not be too much of a stretch to say the church should, on occasion, examine itself and its ministries for their application in genuinely helping the church to pursue its mission.

7. Will cause a desire for balance in the manifestation of the gifts. If you've heard banging from the laundry room, it could well have been that the load in the washer got out of balance. Churches get that way sometimes. When the church is out of balance, where the emphasis seems to fall in one area or just a few, there can be a lot of clanging going on but little "cleaning."

When a church has a proper and balanced view of spiritual gifts, all the appropriate emphases of ministry can be realized. In fact, there will be a desire for this. The two areas that are most likely to get out of balance are evangelism and discipleship. Both are part of the Great Commission. But some churches will major on one and minor on the other. Balance is needed! Both are things to major on, and each complements the other.

8. Eliminates the need for a nominating committee! We have alluded to this benefit previously. If God wants a "ministry" done, He will gift and then raise up someone to do that ministry. There is no need for a nominating committee to beg people to serve. The reason that happens so often is because in most churches, people are placed in areas of service that are not suited to their gifts. Not to mention the fact that the nominating committee is often involved in putting people in positions of power rather than of service.

Some churches have helped to alleviate this problem by shifting from a committee concept (where the emphasis is on making decisions) to a ministry-team concept (where the emphasis is on service). Often we make our plans and set up our programs and then tell God we want Him to bless what we have decided to do. A better idea is to find out what God is already blessing and then get in on it. We won't have to ask God to bless it because He already has!

Paul's advice to Timothy in his leadership of the church at Ephesus would be well applied in our churches today: "Be diligent to present yourself approved to God, a worker who does not need to be ashamed, rightly dividing the word of truth" (2 Tim. 2:15). We are soldiers of the Lord Jesus Christ, and the command we have been given is to be diligent in the carrying out of our orders. We can best accomplish the mission by understanding and utilizing our motivational spiritual gifts in the local church.

Part III

Context
Keeping the Spiritual
Gifts in Balance

13

The Relationship of Evangelism To Spiritual Gifts

Is there a gift of evangelism?

But you shall receive power when the Holy Spirit has come upon you; and you shall be witnesses to Me in Jerusalem, and in all Judea and Samaria, and to the end of the earth.
—Acts 1:8

We had just announced a new outreach ministry in our church, and I had encouraged the membership to sign up. A part of the ministry included attending a class to be taught on how to be more effective in sharing the gospel with the lost. One of our men came up to me after church that day and said, "Pastor, I'd love to help with the new ministry, but I wanted you to know that I don't have the gift of evangelism." I wasn't the first pastor to hear such a report. Sadly, statistics tell us that the vast majority of church members never share their faith. I recall one survey some years ago that said that only five percent of a church's active attendance participates in any meaningful form of outreach ministry.

The question we need to answer is whether or not the excuse the gentleman gave for not participating in the outreach class was valid. Here was my response, "Sir, I know that you do not have the gift of evangelism. Neither do I have the gift. Evangelism is not a gift, it's a command." As I recall, he maintained his reticence and did not participate in our class. If we look at the Great Commission as expressed in Acts 1:8, we do not see any parenthetical opt-out. The verse doesn't say that those with the gift of evangelism will "receive power"; it says "*you* shall receive power." In the context, there can be no denying that the "you" is a reference to the church or, more specifically, to all believers.

The verse plainly says, "*You* shall be witnesses to Me." I looked up the word phrase *you shall be* in the Greek and discovered that it actually means "you shall be." At this point in the text, it's in the future tense because at the time, the Holy Spirit had not yet come upon them. But you only have to move forward one chapter to bring it into the present tense! In Acts 2, the believers were filled with the Holy Spirit, and the greatest evidence of their being filled was that they went out and told others about Jesus.

So the reality is that you are a witness. You are either going to be a good one or a not-so-good one. When you were saved, you were indwelt by the Holy Spirit, so there is nothing for which you need to wait to become a witness for your faith in Christ. You have all the power, knowledge, and wisdom you need to share Christ with others. I would acknowledge that the way the Holy Spirit has gifted you will have an impact on the way you witness. But you are not afforded the option to say that you don't witness because you do not have the gift of evangelism. Some other Christians may be better at it than you are, but that is no reason for you not to do the best you can with the help of the Holy Spirit to win the lost to saving faith in Christ.

What about the Gift of an Evangelist?

There is only a one-letter difference in the word *evangelist* and the word *evangelism*. But that one letter makes a huge difference. It is true that God has given a group of men as a ministry gift to the church who are called evangelists. "And He Himself gave some to be apostles, some prophets, *some evangelists*, and some pastors and teachers" (Eph.

4:11, emphasis mine). As I mentioned in chapter 2, these men might be called *Great Commission specialists.* Their task is to encourage and instruct churches in developing evangelism strategies to reach their Jerusalem, Judea, Samaria, and the uttermost part of the earth. They are men skilled at winning souls and come to a church for the purpose of leading out in revival, teaching evangelistic methods, and reaching out to the lost.

The biggest job evangelists have is encouraging all the members of the church to be active in outreach and witnessing. They do this through both modeling and teaching. There are many methods of sharing one's faith. The key is that when the gospel is shared, we should "tell the truth."[1]

The Motivational Gifts and Evangelism

It is perhaps true that, in some sense, there is a "gift of evangelism." The truth is, since evangelism is a command, in one way or another, each of the seven motivational gifts is one of seven ways that God motivates His people to share their faith. Darrell Robinson says, "Every gift is for evangelism!" Regarding, for example, the gift of administration, he says, "God wants to use those with the gift of administration/leadership to use their gift to reach the lost for

---

[1] One of the best works available related to the subject of telling the truth in evangelistic efforts is *Tell the Truth* by Will Metzger (Downers Grove, Illinois: InterVarsity Press, 1984). We might lament the shallow, weak, and unbiblical approach in much of contemporary evangelism. A wrong approach, one that often puts "results" over "accuracy," produces false converts! Metzger gives a proper foundation to correct this weakness in the church's modern approach to witnessing. He says, "Let us be willing to reexamine our theology of evangelism by Scripture, for otherwise our evangelism may be infected by prejudice, pragmatism and sin. If, however, we are convinced there is a *theological* reason behind our methodology, then we *may* be justified in evangelizing accordingly...A scriptural doctrine of evangelism should be the controlling element in any practice of evangelism" (p. 15). The rest of Metzger's book fleshes out this premise superbly.

Christ."[2] And the same could be said of each of the gifts, which we will consider in their relation to evangelism.

The individual with the gift of *prophecy* may want to emphasize the fact that all are sinners, that Christ paid the price for our sin in His death (cf. Rom. 5:8), and that repentance is the only viable option. Without repentance, there can be no salvation. The prophet is well equipped to deal with this need in the life of one being drawn by the Holy Spirit. The use of Acts 3:19-20 would be more than sufficient:

> Repent therefore and be converted, that your sins may be blotted out, so that times of refreshing may come from the presence of the Lord, and that He may send Jesus Christ, who was preached to you before. (Acts 3:19-20)

If your gift is *service*, you might want to emphasize the fact that Christ came to not to be served but to serve: "For even the Son of Man did not come to be served, but to serve, and to give His life a ransom for many" (Mark 10:45). You would speak to the fact that what He did made it possible that one could be saved because of His ministry to us and that the greatest privilege of life is that, through faith in Him, you might become one of His servants forever! This is seen in Paul's statement to Titus: "Who gave Himself for us, that He might redeem us from every lawless deed and purify for Himself His own special people, zealous for good works." (Titus 2:14).

If your gift is *teaching*, you might emphasize the many proofs of the resurrection. You should research the facts and make yourself competent in the realities related to the death, burial, and resurrection of the Lord. In a gracious way, you present Jesus as the Resurrected Lord and Savior. No other religion has a resurrected Savior. The teacher would be quite familiar with First Corinthians 15 as the biblical text for emphasis on the importance and reality of the resurrection. As a teacher, you may be confronted with the point that you cannot "prove" the resurrection happened. From an absolute human standpoint, this is true, but the good news is that you don't

---

[2] Robinson, *Incredibly Gifted*, 144.

have to prove the resurrection! What the lost have to do is prove that He did not rise from the dead!

If your gift is *exhortation*, you may wish to focus on the future, specifically heaven. What can the unbeliever do about his situation when he stands before God in judgment? Surely, he will admit he is a sinner and in need of a Savior. How will the sinner's life be changed for the better by coming to the Savior? The exhorter might take the approach of John the Baptist, who came, saying, "Repent, for the kingdom of heaven is at hand!" (Matt. 3:2). This is the particular ability of the one with the gift of exhortation.

If you have the gift of *giving*, your approach to soul-winning might come from John 3:16: "For God so loved the world that He gave His only begotten Son, that whoever believes in Him should not perish but have everlasting life." There is no greater gift than the free gift of eternal life in Jesus Christ, our Lord! The giver knows the greatness of the gift of Christ and can use Ephesians 2:8-9 to make his point: "For by grace you have been saved through faith, and that not of yourselves; it is the gift of God, not of works, lest anyone should boast."

If your gift is *leading* or *administration*, then you can witness by making emphasis on the fact that Christ is Lord, that He is the *Supreme Leader* of all things and all people. Submission to the lordship of Christ is essential for one to be genuinely saved. This person will be well acquainted with the Roman road to salvation and will be able to apply Romans 10:9-10 effectively to the listener's heart:

> That if you confess with your mouth the Lord Jesus and believe in your heart that God has raised Him from the dead, you will be saved. For with the heart one believes unto righteousness, and with the mouth confession is made unto salvation.

For the one with the gift of the *mercy*, the emphasis in witnessing will surely be on the mercy and loving-kindness of the Lord. There are so many verses that speak to the mercy of God in salvation. One passage that could be used effectively by the mercy giver is Titus 3:5-8:

> Not by works of righteousness which we have done, but according to His mercy He saved us, through the washing of regeneration and renewing of the Holy Spirit, whom He poured out on us abundantly through Jesus Christ our Savior, that having been justified by His grace we should become heirs according to the hope of eternal life. This is a faithful saying, and these things I want you to affirm constantly, that those who have believed in God should be careful to maintain good works. These things are good and profitable to men.

The point should be abundantly clear at this conjuncture. Regardless of your spiritual gift, you have a mandate given in the Great Commission to share the gospel, to witness to the lost, to rescue the perishing. Each of us will have a different approach based on our gifts, and often God will use several different individuals with various gifts in the life of those He is bringing to saving faith. One of the greatest joys of the Christian life is to lead a poor, lost sinner to the Lord.

One of the greatest things that can happen in the life of a local church is to have the membership begin to understand and use their spiritual gifts for the very purpose of soul-winning. "The fruit of the righteous is a tree of life, and he who wins souls is wise." (Prov. 11:30). Not only is it wise, but it is one of those things that can bring the very breath of heaven into the church. Jesus said, "I say to you that likewise there will be more joy in heaven over one sinner who repents than over ninety-nine just persons who need no repentance" (Luke 15:7). If that is the case, then what unspeakable joy should be filling the hearts and lives of believers as the church becomes a soul-winning lighthouse for the lost! I have never seen a church have more joy than when people are walking the aisles week after week!

May God be pleased to raise up people in your church who understand their gifts and use them to edify the saints and evangelize the sinners!

Having the Gospel Conversation

Regardless of your motivational gift then, the task is for you to learn to have the "gospel conversation." That is, you must learn how to use your gift to get into a conversation about the gospel with the lost people you know. All of us have the opportunity to share Christ with the lost, but we often look the other way and excuse ourselves out of the situation.

It is not that hard to start a conversation. Most people are willing to engage in conversation with you, particularly if they realize the direction you are going is one from which they may opt out. If they do, you have discharged your duty to the Lord! It is not your job to get results; it is your job to share the gospel. You cannot make people listen, nor do you need to!

Some people are harder to talk to than others. Sometimes those closest to you will be the most difficult to engage in conversation about the gospel. Strangers may present a problem in that there is the unknown factor of how they might respond.

But we must remember that their response is something that they are responsible for, not us. There is a tremendous example in the Bible of one of God's great men who confronted one of the most difficult types of people to reach. We have a very important conversation between Paul and Felix, who was governor of Judea from AD 52-59. The story is found in Acts chapters 23 and 24.

After Paul's arrest in Jerusalem, the Roman commander Claudius Lysias discovered that Paul was a Roman citizen and sent him to the governor Felix in Caesarea (Acts 23:23f). The high priest and others quickly came to make their charges against Paul before Felix (Acts 24:1-9). Felix was quite intrigued by Paul, and he listened to his defense. Paul was held for a long period of time in Caesarea for the final two years of Felix's tenure. Later, when Festus replaced Felix, Paul appealed to Caesar, and the long process of his being sent to Rome began. Paul was able to have a similar conversation with King Agrippa II (Acts 25:13- 26:32), who had inherited Phillip's kingdom (most of the area of Palestine) with headquarters in Caesarea Philippi.

Felix was an extremely difficult and wicked individual. He had numerous people murdered, many crucified, just because he felt they stood in the way of his upward progression in the empire. His third wife, Drusilla, was Jewish, and she was a woman whom Felix had lured from her first husband. Amazingly, Paul was willing to confront this sin in their lives when he spoke before them.

The point of all this is to say that if Paul could witness in such dire circumstances to a man with such great power, literally the power of life and death, then the reality is that we too can share the gospel. We can share the gospel in the most difficult of circumstances and before the most obstinate sinners we know. Paul's example, found in Acts 24, is of particular significance in this regard.

When we have the gospel conversation, if we are going to be successful in sharing the truth of the message of salvation, we must be willing to bring up the issue of the conviction of sin. No one will ever be converted to the Savior unless they first feel and respond to the conviction of their sin. But this type of conviction is never convenient, is it?

Do you ever get up on Sunday morning and think to yourself, "I can't wait to get to church and hear the pastor's message. I sure hope he preaches on all the sins I've committed this week; I can't wait to get under some of that old-time conviction!" Or do you rather sit in the pew or the Sunday school classroom and think, "Go away for now, I don't want to hear it." Even though you know the message is right and you know you are guilty, you simply don't want to address your guilt.

This is the very experience that Felix had in his gospel conversations with Paul. Notice how Paul's direct conversation with Felix plays out:

> But when Felix heard these things, having more accurate knowledge of the Way, he adjourned the proceedings and said, "When Lysias the commander comes down, I will make a decision on your case." So he commanded the centurion to keep Paul and to let him have liberty, and told him not to forbid any of his friends to provide for or visit him. And after some days, when Felix came

with his wife Drusilla, who was Jewish, he sent for Paul and heard him concerning the faith in Christ. Now as he reasoned about righteousness, self-control, and the judgment to come, Felix was afraid and answered, "Go away for now; when I have a convenient time I will call for you." Meanwhile he also hoped that money would be given him by Paul, that he might release him. Therefore he sent for him more often and conversed with him. But after two years Porcius Festus succeeded Felix; and Felix, wanting to do the Jews a favor, left Paul bound. (Acts 24:22-27)

We can note in this passage Paul's straightforward presentation of the gospel message to Felix. His words brought Felix under *conviction*. This conviction of sin is essential in the gospel message because without it, no one can be saved! We should recall the words of our Lord Jesus regarding the work of the Holy Spirit:

And when He has come, He will convict the world of sin, and of righteousness, and of judgment: of sin, because they do not believe in Me; of righteousness, because I go to My Father and you see Me no more; of judgment, because the ruler of this world is judged. (John 16:8-11)

These are the very things Paul spoke to Felix about; as we see in Acts 24:25! But note Felix's comment in response: "Go away for now; when I have a convenient time I will call for you."

Conviction was the clarion call of the gospel message as preached by the apostles in the early days of the church (Acts 2:22, 36, 38; Acts 26:16-18). In Matthew 3:1-12, we have John the Baptist delivering this same type of message. We know that the people John the Baptist preached to were convicted because they came confessing their sins and were bringing forth fruit worthy of repentance. It made a change of heart and lifestyle, it was real. When you truly repent and believe the gospel, it changes your life from the inside out.

There are two reasons that I have chosen to go into some detail on evangelism in a book about spiritual gifts. It is impossible for you to use your spiritual gift if you are not saved! There may be some reading this book who are like Felix. They need to repent when they face conviction so that they can obtain a clear conscience and be saved.

The majority who are reading this book are saved. You are reading because you want to be more effective in the service of our Lord. You want to lead others to be more effective in using their gifts for the glory of God and the good of the church. I can assure you, God wants to use you as an agent of conviction to lead others to Christ following Paul's example. Remember, evangelism isn't a gift—it's a *command*!

Please note the process that Paul went through, using his spiritual gifts of exhortation, prophecy, and teaching to share the faith with Felix.

Number one, we note that Paul had been building a case for a conversation "concerning the faith in Christ" (v. 24). We have to go back and read and study the prior comments in Acts 24 made by Paul to Felix, verses 10- 21, to see how Paul accomplished this first essential point in sharing the faith. In order to gain a hearing before others, there are two things we must do, and these are demonstrated here in the life of Paul.

First, we are to have a **visible witness** by maintaining a clear conscience: "This being so, I myself always strive to have a conscience without offense toward god and men" (v. 16). Paul was not ashamed of his faith. He readily confessed that he worshipped God as a Christian and that he believed the Bible (v. 14).

There is a difference in believing the Bible and claiming to be a Christian and in living that way! Note, Paul said, "I...always strive." His desire was a clear conscience before God and others. He was saying, "I don't want to offend God or other men." How do you do that? Might I suggest living by the Ten Commandments, summarized in the Great Commandment of our Lord? If your life is filled with sin and compromise, you will not get a hearing from others.

The second thing we must have is a **verbal witness** by focusing on Christ's resurrection.

> I have hope in God, which they themselves also accept, that there *will be a resurrection of the dead,* both of the just and the unjust...

unless it is for this one statement which I cried out, standing among them, "*Concerning the resurrection of the dead* I am being judged by you this day"(vv. 15, 21; emphasis mine).

Some say, "Well, I never actually say anything about Christ, but they can tell I'm a Christian by the way I live." That's wonderful, but no one ever got saved by merely observing another's behavior, even if it is correct Christian behavior. Your lifestyle is important; it's the platform from which you gain the opportunity to share your faith, but that sharing must be done verbally.

Recently I had someone tell me they didn't like the idea of outreach visitation. I asked what they preferred, and they said they believed in "lifestyle evangelism." I said, "That's great, but the problem with lifestyle evangelism is no one ever gets saved!"

As we use our spiritual gifts in evangelism, it is always best to do it God's way. You cannot get saved in your own time and on your own terms; you must come to God His way. When we share our faith, we must do it just as Paul did when he confronted Felix, we actually have to open our mouths and tell people about Jesus.

The way you get someone to listen to the gospel is that you do what Paul did, you focus on the Resurrection, you focus on life after death issues. This is truly the Great Commission in action. The very thing that makes the gospel of the Lord Jesus Christ different from every other religious thought or concept is the fact that Jesus rose from the dead! Build a case and share the gospel!

Number two, we note that Paul not only was building a case, he was more than willing to *bring conviction*, reasoning with the lost from the Word of God (v. 25; cf. Isa. 1:16-20, John 16:8). Once Paul had built his case, he was able to bring Felix under conviction. He reasoned with him from the Word of God. You and I are God's ambassadors for this very reason:

> Wash yourselves, make yourselves clean; Put away the evil of your doings from before My eyes. Cease to do evil, Learn to do good; Seek justice, Rebuke the oppressor; Defend the fatherless, Plead for

the widow. "Come now, and let us reason together," Says the Lord, "Though your sins are like scarlet, They shall be as white as snow; Though they are red like crimson, They shall be as wool. If you are willing and obedient, You shall eat the good of the land; But if you refuse and rebel, You shall be devoured by the sword"; For the mouth of the Lord has spoken." (Isa. 1:16-20)

Paul spoke to Felix about righteousness, self-control, and judgment. These are the very things the Holy Spirit brings conviction in according to John 16:8-11, with self-control being needed to deal with sin.

Paul begins his conversation with Felix by declaring, "Here's the standard, you must be righteous." Just how righteous must one be? According to Jesus in the Sermon on the Mount, "Therefore you shall be perfect, just as your Father in heaven is perfect" (Matt. 5:48).

Jesus told the rich young ruler that he would have to keep all the commandments to go to heaven (Matt. 19:16f). Of course, we know that the gospel message deals with the fact of the "great exchange," our sin for His righteousness. But the beginning point is a recognition of the fact that there is a standard.

What is righteousness? It is *being* right so you can *do* right. Simply put, it is knowing the difference in right and wrong, which, by the way, is not up for a vote of the Congress or any other group. God's standard is explained in the Word, so Paul reasoned with Felix from the Bible.

We need to recall whom it was that Paul was dealing with: Felix and his third wife, Drusilla, whom he had lured from her husband and had committed adultery with. Paul was marching down the same road that John the Baptist dared to travel. Do you know why John got his head cut off? Because he dared to tell a public official, in his case, King Herod, that his marriage to Herodius (his brother Phillip's wife) was wrong! In other words, God's standards apply to everyone.

Paul followed up the standard of righteousness with the need for self-control, and this is because of *sin*. Felix had all the excuses down pat. We read that he was knowledgeable of both Jewish law and the

Christian faith. Earlier in chapter 24 of Acts, verses 14and 22, we read (emphasis mine),

> But this I confess to you, that according to the Way which they call a sect, so I worship the God of my fathers, believing all things which are written in the Law and in the Prophets…But when Felix heard these things, *having more accurate knowledge of the Way*, he adjourned the proceedings and said, "When Lysias the commander comes down, I will make a decision on your case."

So the truth is that Felix knew what was right and wrong; he just had no self-control. He lived by the hedonistic philosophies: "If it feels good, do it" or "Everyone else is doing it." He knew nothing of self-control or denial of self.

But God's standard is *absolute*; and to conform, we must have self-control, which is a fruit of the Spirit. In other words, to be righteous, you must be saved. You must have a relationship with Christ and be filled with the Spirit. The reality is that, on your own, you have no power to overcome sin. You either control your urges, or your urges will control you! And you can't do that without the help of the indwelling Holy Spirit.

Once Paul had established the standard of righteousness and spoken of Felix's need of self-control to overcome his sin, he then reminded Felix of the righteous sentence of God, "the judgment to come." The consequences of a life of sin are misery in this life and an eternity of separation from God and being cast into hell fire in the next life. That, sadly, is a place where "stop, drop, and roll" won't work!

When Paul spoke of these things, the Bible says "Felix was afraid"; but sadly, he loved his sin more than his eternal security. He had no real fear of God but simply a certain dread that if Paul was right, he might one day be in big trouble. He needed to heed the admonition found in Hebrews 9:27: "And as it is appointed for men to die once, but after this the judgment."

We might say that Felix was under the *bondage of convenience*; for which repentance is the only answer (v. 25; cf. 2 Cor. 6:2). Note the response of Felix to Paul: "Felix was afraid and answered, 'Go away for now; when I have a convenient time I will call for you.'" Here are some representative thoughts of what Felix's attitude must have been:

- "I don't want to give up my friends."
- "I don't want to give up my sins."
- "I don't want to give up my lifestyle."
- "I'll sow my wild oats, and at a more convenient time of life, I'll get saved. Besides, I might get under conviction to go to church or to have to tithe, and what would my friends say?"
- "Look, Paul, I'd be a hypocrite, and God knows that's no good. I'm enjoying my life of sin, and I'll think about what you've said, and I'll call you again at a more convenient time."

Do you know what Felix was doing? He was sinning away his day of grace! "He who is often rebuked, and hardens his neck, will suddenly be destroyed, and that without remedy" (Prov. 29:1). A critical question for anyone reading this is, Are you like Felix? Are you thinking you'll have a more convenient day? We must make it clear, conviction is *never* convenient! Hear the Word of the Lord in this regard:

> We then, as workers together with Him also plead with you not to receive the grace of God in vain. For He says: "In an acceptable time I have heard you, And in the day of salvation I have helped you." Behold, *now is the accepted time.* Behold, *now is the day of salvation.* (2 Cor. 6:1-2, emphasis mine)

Paul was explaining to Felix that you cannot come to God on your *terms* or in your own *time,* you must come on *His* terms and in *His* time. It may cause you to have to give up some things and make some changes in your life, but you gain much more than you lose. Think about it. Wouldn't it be good to give up hell for heaven, guilt for grace, sin for salvation?

But notice Felix's response: "We'll talk about this again later." But Jesus said, "Fool, this night your soul will be required of you" (Luke 12:20).

The only answer is *repentance*! But Felix did what he said he would do, and for two years, he called on Paul and conversed with him (vv. 26-27). And each time, Paul reasoned with him on righteousness, self-control, judgment to come, and faith in Christ. The *blessing of conversion* comes when one is saved and released from bondage. It is interesting to see how this played out between Felix and Paul.

> Meanwhile he [Felix] also hoped that money would be given him by Paul, that he might release him. Therefore he sent for him more often and conversed with him. But after two years Porcius Festus succeeded Felix; and Felix, wanting to do the Jews a favor, left Paul bound. (Acts 24:26-27; cf. Acts 26:28).

Felix had put Paul in physical bonds, but the truth was that Paul wasn't the one who needed to be released from bondage. Felix was the one in bondage and in need of release—how ironic!

For someone who has been putting off becoming a Christian or who is resistant to the gospel message like Felix, or perhaps almost persuaded like Agrippa, we need to be forthright in sharing the gospel message. Again, when Paul confronted Felix with the gospel, each time he spoke to him "about righteousness, self-control, and the judgment to come." I believe Paul's conversation with Felix may very well be summarized by his words to the Romans about the subject in chapter 3, verses 9-26. From that passage, we can find four basic points that Paul most certainly shared with Felix.

First, Paul said, "Felix, you are not going to heaven on the basis of your own personal *righteousness*" (and neither are any of us). I can hear Paul quoting his letter to the Romans,

> What then? Are we better than they? Not at all. For we have previously charged both Jews and Greeks that they are all under sin. As it is written: There is none righteous, no, not one; There is none who understands; There is none who seeks after God. They have all turned aside; they have together become unprofitable. There is none who does good, no, not one." (Rom. 3:9-12)

Then Paul would go on to say, "Felix, on your own, you have no *self-control*, but you are clearly, like every other person, under sin." Paul would then add to that:

> Their throat is an open tomb; With their tongues they have practiced deceit; The poison of asps is under their lips; Whose mouth is full of cursing and bitterness. Their feet are swift to shed blood; Destruction and misery are in their ways; And the way of peace they have not known. There is no fear of God before their eyes. (Rom. 3:13-18)

You might simply change the personal pronouns to the second person to see how Paul might have said these things to Felix. He was a most despicable man, but without his personal recognition of his sin and his repentance, there would have been no hope for him to be saved!

Paul would say to Felix, "Listen dear friend, the *judgment of God* is real, and it is coming soon. You have no assurance that you will have another day to make your life your life right with God so repent and believe the gospel today. Felix, no one can escape the judgment of God!"

Then Paul would continue his quote from his letter to the Romans:

> Now we know that whatever the law says, it says to those who are under the law, that every mouth may be stopped, and all the world may become guilty before God. Therefore by the deeds of the law no flesh will be justified in His sight, for by the law is the knowledge of sin. (Rom. 3:19-20)

Paul would then plead with Felix, "Your only hope is a *relationship with Jesus*. Surely, after all I've said Felix, you know that you cannot be righteous before God on your own, but God has made a way for you."

> But now the righteousness of God apart from the law is revealed, being witnessed by the Law and the Prophets, *even the righteousness of God, through faith in Jesus Christ*, to all and on all who believe. For

there is no difference; for all have sinned and fall short of the glory of God, being *justified freely by His grace through the redemption that is in Christ Jesus,* whom God set forth as a propitiation by His blood, through faith, to demonstrate His righteousness, because in His forbearance God had passed over the sins that were previously committed, to demonstrate at the present time His righteousness, that He might be just and the justifier of the one who has faith in Jesus. (Rom. 3:21-26, emphasis mine)

This is the gospel message we must proclaim to others. We, regardless of our spiritual gifts, need to be asking others, "Do you have a relationship with Jesus? Have you repented of your sin and turned to Christ in faith, yielding control of your life to Him?" As church members, using our spiritual gifts, we need to be building a case so that we can share Christ with our friends and family members.

I would pray that after reading this chapter, you would commit yourself anew to sharing the gospel. Would you ask God to give you the courage of Paul to speak even to the most hardened of sinners? He is faithful and will answer your prayer!

14

A Correct Understanding of Service in the Church

*The need for a correct concept of service and
a confirmed check on salvation*

*And God is able to make all grace abound toward you,
that you, always having all sufficiency in all things,
may have an abundance for every good work.
—Second Corinthians 9:8*

*Examine yourselves, as to whether you are in the faith.
Test yourselves. Do you not know yourselves, that Jesus
Christ is in you? - unless indeed you are disqualified?
—Second Corinthians 13:5*

Spiritual gifts are a wonderful thing when understood and properly taught and utilized in the life of the church. But a correct understanding of our purpose in serving God is essential. In addition to that, it is important that we clarify the reason that some get so frustrated in trying to serve the Lord. The reason may well be that they are not genuinely saved! We have a hard time in the church when it comes to suggesting that a member of the church, particularly an active and long-standing member, might indeed be lost.

A quick corrective to this mind-set can be made from the scripture's insistence on making certain that we examine ourselves as to our relationship with the Lord. Paul says, "Examine yourselves as to whether you are in the faith. Test yourselves. Do you not know yourselves, that Jesus Christ is in you?—unless indeed you are disqualified" (2 Cor. 13:5). This is a serious warning. Paul was concerned about his own standing with the Lord and expressed that in First Corinthians 9:27, where he also expressed concern for the believers in Corinth.

A similar Old Testament warning comes from Jeremiah: "Let us search out and examine our ways, And turn back to the Lord" (Lam. 3:40). There can be no doubt that many who attend church never serve the Lord or others in any meaningful way. If salvation means that one's life has been radically changed (which it most certainly does), and if a church member's life evidences no outward change, how can we continue to give them assurance that they are indeed saved?

It is important when establishing a biblically based ministry utilizing spiritual gifts in the church that we correctly understand what it means to serve the Lord and that we are certain of our own saving relationship to Christ.

A Correct Concept of Service

At this point, we want to interject an important concept regarding our understanding of ministry or service to the Lord in general. Our goal in this book has been to determine our motivation for ministry. What motivates you to serve God? Why we do what we do is extremely important, perhaps even more important than what we do. We all know that bad motives can ruin good deeds. This is biblical:

> Though I speak with the tongues of men and of angels, but have not love, I have become sounding brass or a clanging cymbal. And though I have *the gift of* prophecy, and understand all mysteries and all knowledge, and though I have all faith, so that I could remove mountains, but have not love, I am nothing. And though I

bestow all my goods to feed *the poor*, and though I give my body to be burned, but have not love, it profits me nothing. (1 Cor. 13:1-3)

This next concept may seem strange to many, but I want to warn you about the debtor's ethic. The appeal to serve God often comes packaged this way: "After all God has done for you, what will you do for Him?" Or, "God gave His life for you. Out of gratitude, surely you will give your life for Him?" I am as guilty as anyone of using this mind-set of "guilt motivation" and of being motivated by it. But there is a subtle danger. Your service to God is not an installment payment on your debt! You can never repay God because you owed a debt you could not pay. Every Christian will be eternally in God's debt. Fortunately, there was One who paid our debt for us!

As John Piper reminds us, the Bible does not seem to list gratitude as a motive for obedience or service to God. What does the Bible use to motivate us to serve instead? The promise of divine enablement and reward![1] Our labor for God is also His gift to us! It is primarily a privilege to serve God, not so much a duty. While there are aspects of our service that could be considered duty we should serve out of love. "Or who has first given to Him and it shall be repaid to him? For of Him and *through Him* and to Him are all things, to whom be glory forever. Amen" (Rom. 11:35-36). We might note that this text immediately precedes our text on spiritual gifts in Romans 12! (Cf. Rom. 15:18)

We exercise our gifts in the energy of the flesh to our own detriment. There is a tendency in the church for everyone to do what is right in his own eyes. But the gifts can only have lasting effect if we exercise them the way Peter instructs us to use them.

As each one has received a gift, minister it to one another, as good stewards of the manifold grace of God. If anyone speaks, let him speak as the oracles of God. If anyone ministers, let him do it as

---

[1] For an excellent take on this subject, please see John Piper's *Brothers, We Are Not Professionals* (Nashville: Broadman & Holman, 2002), chapter 5: "Brothers, Beware of the Debtor's Ethic."

with the ability which God supplies, that in all things God may be glorified through Jesus Christ, to whom belong the glory and the dominion forever and ever. Amen. (1 Pet. 4:10-11)

God is the supplier, and if we are to serve Him well, then we must avail ourselves of His grace, making us even greater debtors to His mercy and grace. Paul says:

> And God is able to make all grace abound toward you, that you, always having all sufficiency in all things, may have an abundance for every good work. As it is written: "He has dispersed abroad, He has given to the poor; His righteousness endures forever." Now may He who supplies seed to the sower, and bread for food, supply and multiply the seed you have sown and increase the fruits of your righteousness, while you are enriched in everything for all liberality, which causes thanksgiving through us to God. For the administration of this service not only supplies the needs of the saints, but also is abounding through many thanksgivings to God, while, through the proof of this ministry, they glorify God for the obedience of your confession to the gospel of Christ, and for your liberal sharing with them and all men, and by their prayer for you, who long for you because of the exceeding grace of God in you. Thanks be to God for His indescribable gift! (2 Cor. 9:8-15)

We should note David's prayer to the Lord regarding the offerings that had been given for the building of the Temple:

> Yours, O Lord, is the greatness, The power and the glory, The victory and the majesty; For all that is in heaven and in earth is Yours; Yours is the kingdom, O Lord, And You are exalted as head over all. Both riches and honor come from You, And You reign over all. In Your hand is power and might; In Your hand it is to make great And to give strength to all. "Now therefore, our God, We thank You And praise Your glorious name. But who am I, and who are my people, That we should be able to offer so willingly as this? For all things come from You, And of Your own we have given You. For we are aliens and pilgrims before You, As were all our

fathers; Our days on earth are as a shadow, And without hope. "O Lord our God, all this abundance that we have prepared to build You a house for Your holy name is from Your hand, and is all Your own. (1 Chron. 29:11-16)

Gratitude functions properly as a motive only as it gives rise to increased faith and keeps us fully dependent on God for all things. Whatever your situation, and whatever your calling and giftedness, you must keep trusting God for more grace. You will be evermore indebted to Him, but you will be evermore eternally blessed for it. This, my friends, is life-changing because it takes you out of the driver's seat and enthrones God in His rightful place in your life.

A Confirmed Check on Salvation

Let's be perfectly honest with one another. We are well aware that some of the people who are church attenders rarely, if ever, serve in ministry to others. They don't have the problem of a debtor's ethic; instead they have substituted religion for true faith. Quite often, this type of individual actually comes to see God as though God were in his or her debt.

Why do I say that? My experience has shown me that, over the years, it really doesn't matter what is preached or taught; there are some who are not going to do anything about it. They hear the message and may or may not agree with it. Perhaps they are of the opinion "Well, that's the preacher's view, but it has no real meaning to me." For those who can hear the blessed trumpet of the gospel over and over again and never lift a finger to serve the Lord through the ministry of the church, must we not inquire as to whether they are saved?

As a pastor and evangelist, it concerns me greatly that there are some who apparently have no desire to serve God. Is it possible that the New Testament emphasis on serving God is wrong? Or is serving God through the spiritual gifts the natural result of a relationship with Jesus?

I am of the scripturally inspired belief that my task as a pastor is to win the lost and save the saved! The Puritans understood this much better than we do. Many are offended if the pastor suggests that those who regularly attend church might be lost.

When it comes time for the funerals of those who never professed in this life any commitment to Christ or His church, we are even expected to say, "Well, he might have made his life right with God on his own." But the Bible says nothing about that. That is the maudlin sentimentality of a worldly attitude, pervasive in a church that has lost its horrifying fear of hell.

How did Paul instruct Timothy in this regard? "Take heed to yourself and to the doctrine. Continue in them, for in doing this you will *save both yourself and those who hear you*" (1 Tim. 4:16, emphasis mine). Not only would Timothy's preaching save those who heard him, it would save Timothy! It is entirely possible that the word *save* in this context is meant in the sense of "rescue." But Paul was not instructing Timothy in regard to his evangelistic preaching to the lost.

When we turn to the passage, we will find in verse 12 that Timothy was instructed to be an example to "the believers"! It seems then that the correct biblical approach to preaching in the church is to challenge the very salvation of the elect. As Paul further instructs Timothy, we discover that the salvation of the elect is not automatic (cf. 2 Tim. 2:10-13). As John Piper says, salvation comes through means, and the means of salvation includes perseverance! All that Paul did was intended for the salvation of those he preached to.

> Now if we are afflicted, it is for your consolation and salvation, which is effective for enduring the same sufferings which we also suffer. Or if we are comforted, it is for your consolation and salvation. (2 Cor. 1:6)

This a point about which we need to be clear. We are not suggesting a doctrine of "sinless perfection." What we are saying is that one who is a true believer—one who has been justified, sanctified, and will one day be glorified—cannot live in a habitual state of sin. Sin bothers a true believer. And in the context of spiritual gifts, it should bother any true believer if he or she is not using their gifts to serve others and glorify God.

People do not end up in hell because of the particular commission of a sin or the omission of some duty to God. The Bible teaches that all have sinned and fall short of God's glory (Rom. 3:23). But the sins—gross or not, many or few—are a result of being separated from God, of being lost. In other words, we don't become sinners because we sin. We sin because we are sinners. It is our nature.

But if you are a true believer, God has forgiven you of your sin. You received the forgiveness of God when you repented. So we are not suggesting that one might be lost if they have committed this or the other sin. We are saying that if you are genuinely saved, such sin will bother you, and the evidence that you are saved is that you will repent and you keep on repenting! If you say you have not sinned, the Bible says you are a liar! (cf. 1 John 1). Paul speaks of true repentance: "For godly sorrow produces repentance leading to salvation, not to be regretted; but the sorrow of the world produces death" (2 Cor. 7:10).

We should be concerned for our fellow believer's progress in sanctification, as well as our own. But when all is said and done, and the body lies cold in the grave, it should be our chief desire that the soul of the departed will be, at that very moment, warmly embraced by the Savior, our Lord Jesus Christ, in heaven. Let us be concerned that the believers persevere in final salvation!

These comments should in no way be construed to propose that we believe a saved man can lose his salvation. However, the truth is that all any of us have outwardly is the appearance of salvation. That the appearance was no apparition will be manifest in your continued faithfulness until death. Jesus said, "But he who endures to the end shall be saved." (Matt. 24:13). He also said, "Be faithful until death, and I will give you the crown of life" (Rev. 2:10).

There is a very good starting point for understanding this personally. It is the moment in time when you come to feel the weight of your sin and see yourself for the awful sinner you really are. It is a weight that is heavy on your heart. It breaks your heart that you have so wickedly behaved in light of the eternal love of the Lord (cf. Psalm 51). In this condition, you cannot but beg His mercy and forgiveness.

You then place full faith and trust in Him alone as your Savior; and you come, as best you know how, to yield your life to Him. You run up the white flag of surrender and begin a lifelong quest to remain under that banner. What great joy and freedom such action will give you. You will be free from the burden of religious duty and self-righteous haggling. You will know you are undeserving of His loving-kindness, yet you will also know that you are the unmerited recipient of His unfailing grace. Hallelujah, what a Savior!

In summary, we serve God because He commanded us to serve Him. We serve Him in the full knowledge that the Christian life is not what we are doing *for* Him but what He is doing *in* and *through* us by His Spirit. We serve Him because He enables us to serve, and it is a grand privilege to be a slave of the Most High God! We serve Him because we are looking forward to the fulfillment of His glorious promises, which include our divine rewards. We serve Him so that we will be prepared to worship and serve Him throughout eternity.

We also recognize that the prerequisite to our service is our salvation experience. Since we cannot serve Him in our own strength or ability, we must be indwelt by the Spirit, filled (controlled) by the Spirit, and empowered by the Spirit. That happens at the moment we are saved by grace. As Paul explains it, first we are saved by grace: "For by grace you have been saved through faith, and that not of yourselves; it is the gift of God, not of works, lest anyone should boast" (Eph. 2:8-9). But then he goes to indicate that saving grace has a real and effective result in our lives: "For we are His workmanship, created in Christ Jesus for good works, which God prepared beforehand that we should walk in them" (v. 10).

The reality of the Christian life is that those who are saved are called, gifted, and empowered to serve. We are God's "workmanship," His prized possession, and He created us for accomplishing good works for the kingdom cause. The only evidence of one's salvation is that they are serving God, and the way God has designed for that to take place is through the motivational spiritual gifts.

There is a saying I have encouraged in the churches I have been privileged to serve as pastor. It is taken from the oft-repeated phrase used by Baptists in regard to the security of our salvation: "Once saved, always saved." But a better way of saying it is, *"Once saved, always serving!"* May God bless your service to His people through your local church.

15

The Truth about Tongues

*The most abused concept in the modern
church related to spiritual gifts*

*For God is not the author of confusion but of
peace, as in all the churches of the saints.
—First Corinthians 14:33*

This chapter could serve as an addendum to the book. We have
covered the motivational gifts and clearly explained the ministry and
manifestation gifts in previous chapters. However, no book on spiritual
gifts would be complete without addressing the issue of "speaking in
tongues." I do so in full understanding that there are many who have a
different conception of the practice. It is not my intent to hurt feelings
but rather to expose the truth by a serious consideration of the scripture.

There is no question that many Christians have been confused
about this subject. The problem is exacerbated by the fact that the
"unknown tongues" practice is encouraged and implemented in
churches through the elevation of experience over scripture, as we
shall see. Dr. John MacArthur, in his excellent work on the subject
entitled *Strange Fire*, rightly says:

> By elevating the authority of experience over the authority of
> Scripture, the Charismatic Movement has destroyed the church's

immune system—uncritically granting free access to every imaginable form of heretical teaching and practice.[1]

This is a serious charge, and therefore the subject is one that must be given crucial attention, especially in the evil days in which we live. We cannot afford to be wrong on such an important subject.

Defining the Problem

There can be little question that the most confusing aspect of spiritual gifts relates to the much misunderstood biblical gift called *tongues*. We have previously explained what the gift actually refers to in chapter 2 under the ministry and manifestation gifts.

The phenomenon is called speaking in tongues. It is purported to be a sign of the baptism of the Holy Spirit, which, according to its adherents, occurs subsequent to salvation. Many of these adherents argue that it is the one and only proof of having the Holy Spirit in your life. Few believe it is required to prove you are saved. But most, if not all of them, believe that all Christians should speak in tongues and that those who do not are, at worst, lost and, at best, living in rebellion to God and are second-class citizens spiritually.

As we know, the actual biblical gift was the ability to speak (or perhaps "hear") in a foreign language. Acts 2 is very clear that the first instance of speaking in tongues had to do with foreign languages. The purpose was the propagation of the gospel and the affirmation of the gospel message that was being preached by the apostles. The need for such a gift unquestionably ceased when the New Testament was written and the church was well established.

The unknown tongue itself, as is practiced today, is unintelligible

[1] John MacArthur, *Strange Fire* (Nashville: Nelson Books, 2013), xvi. Dr. MacArthur deals with the entire charismatic movement in his book, including the prosperity gospel, the signs and wonders movement, and the problem of unknown tongues. It is not my intent in this chapter to deal with the entire movement but to focus on the issue of tongues. I highly commend the reading of Dr. MacArthur's work for a fuller understanding of the problems evident in this false movement.

speech, referred to variously as an "utterance," a "tongue of fire," "holy spirit language," or "a heavenly language." Usually, those who claim to have it base the claim on an experience that has occurred in their life at some point. Some few claim to have a tongue that is a known language, but this is rare, and the effect is essentially the same when there is no one to translate.[2]

Our goal is to determine what the scriptures teach about this subject. The goal is not to disparage any individual person who speaks in tongues but rather to clarify what the scriptures actually have to say regarding this area of spiritual gifts. Many of those who follow this practice today do so because they have fallen prey to the teachings of false prophets. It is hoped, if such persons are still reading, that they will seriously consider the biblical teaching contained here on the subject and amend their ways.

The subject becomes more confusing to many because when this practice is undertaken in the church, there is usually no interpretation. We should note that the problem of interpretation is significant in this regard as babble, or unknown tongues, have no objective interpretation possible. What passes as interpretation, which biblically means "translation," is at best something the interpreter makes up and at worst the curses of demonic forces at work in that person.

Of course, scripture clearly demands that any tongue spoken in the church be interpreted. Some try to avoid this by saying that they only speak a heavenly language in their private devotions. They do not speak in public because it would violate the rules found in First

---

[2] It is interesting to note that the beginning of the modern charismatic movement, a new addition to professed Christianity in the early 1900s, began with unknown gibberish being spoken. The claim of those in the movement was that these were actual foreign languages. Proof that the tongues—which, at the time, were both spoken and written—were known languages was severely lacking. One of the early proponents of the practice, Charles Parham, claimed that people would be able to go as missionaries without language school training if they had the gift. Those who did go to the mission field under this misguided belief should not have been surprised when they discovered that they were not understood by the foreigners they were attempting to speak to! Again, Dr. MacArthur does a superb job in exposing the false foundation of this movement in *Strange Fire* (ibid, 19-36).

Corinthians 14. However, the vast majority of tongue talkers are encouraged to do so publically and often. Sometimes nearly an entire congregation will be babbling in tongues at the same time.

For those who limit the practice to private conversations with God, they can't understand it, so it doesn't edify them. It just makes them feel good or spiritual about themselves. Recently I heard a new wrinkle on the issue of what is often called a personal, private prayer language. It seems that the reason for this so-called gift is to bypass Jesus and speak directly to God in the language of heaven.

This would be laughable except for the fact that it so nearly borders on blasphemy. No one can get to God via bypassing Jesus! The members of the Trinity do not bypass each other as they are in perfect accord (John 14:6). The truth is, such languages are not heavenly at all, but they certainly could be demonic (cf. Jas. 3:5-6).

While the issue of spiritual warfare is not something that many professing believers want to tackle, the truth is that demons may very well be behind the phenomena of unknown tongue speaking. Demons would have several reasons for encouraging the phenomena of unknown tongues. Here are several:

First, the practice of a so-called gift of unknown tongues causes pride in those who supposedly "have it," as opposed to those who do not have it. Many years ago, I was taking a long cross-country flight, and a flight attendant had noticed that I was reading my Bible. She struck up a conversation with me and determined she could convince me that not only were unknown tongues necessary but that I would be speaking in one before we touched the ground.

I ended up having to repudiate her unbiblical concepts as she was insistent that she was on a higher spiritual plane than me— pun intended. Sadly, the wrong emphasis on this "gift" creates the "haves" and the "have-nots," and I gladly admit I'm a have-not in this regard.

There are many in the charismatic movement who use the term the *full gospel* to refer to their particular brand of practicing the faith. The implication is that those who do not speak in an unknown tongue have less than the full gospel. But there is no portion of the gospel message in scripture that I do not believe. I believe in all of the gospel and nothing more than the gospel. The truth is that those who insist on this gift are what I call *gospel plus* because they have added a false element to the true message of the Bible.

Second, this so-called gift causes people to depend on an unknown—and, therefore, non-edifying—tongue rather than just straightforward praise to God. It essentially eliminates the need for study of the Word of God. If you have this gift, you do not need to read the Word and pray it back to God, and ultimately, there is no need to study or to praise the Lord in a language you can understand.

Third, this gift divides local churches because it creates confusion (cf. 1 Cor. 14:34). I have known of many churches that have split or gone through tremendous grief because unknown tongue talkers got loose. They were not confronted, and their pride and false doctrine were allowed to drive a wedge through the church.

The Purpose of the Gifts

In previous chapters, we have covered the purposes of the true gifts of the Spirit. We summarize it here and recall that they are for the service of God through ministry to others (Rom. 12:1- 5). The gifts are used to meet the needs of the church so that each member takes his or her proper place within the body. We serve God through serving the church, and you cannot serve God without taking your place within the life of the church. It is not possible to please God and be separated from the church at the same time. As we know, the bottom line of the gifts is to edify or profit others (1 Cor. 12:7).

As Dr. Jerry Vines says, "Spiritual gifts are not toys to play with, they are tools to build with." The gifts were never intended to make us super spiritual, to make us feel good about ourselves, or even to draw us closer to God, although the latter may be a result. The concept is clearly, and always, meeting the needs of others.

When we try to logically, theologically, or systematically find a purpose for speaking in unknown tongues, we will find that there is no scriptural support. Regardless of the subject, it is critical to theological understanding to have a solid doctrinal foundation for any practice that is claimed to be revealed, encouraged, and empowered by the Holy Spirit. In this regard, the issue of tongues creates insurmountable problems: What would cause people to insist on speaking in unknown tongues and to insist you must also do it to prove you have the Holy Spirit?

Let's consider the only objective standard, which for the believer is the Word of God. This standard is often, if not always, ignored! What the Word teaches is our only real question. Let me say again, it is not my purpose to make an attack on anyone who believes differently from what is taught here on this subject. I am not trying to belittle or discredit any individual person who is charismatic or Pentecostal in their beliefs. Many of them are good, sincere, and well-meaning people. However, there are some in the movement who are false prophets. These we would treat in a somewhat different manner because scripture requires us to.

My purpose is to discover what the Bible teaches and to encourage all believers to adhere to that alone. We must be guided by the Word, not our experience or anyone else's view of their experience. In the process, we may mention the name of a charismatic leader. The issue at hand is to help us all understand why what we are often told by our charismatic friends, family, and acquaintances is actually wrong.

Typically, the strongest argument the proponents of unknown tongues come up with is this: "I (or someone I know who is very spiritual) had an experience, and you cannot deny the experience." The truth is, not only can you deny the experience, you should deny it if it does not line up with the Word.

The problem with our charismatic friends is that they are using a subjective standard based solely on the experiences of men. But there is no way to prove or disprove the correctness of any experience unless we submit it to the Word of God.

Not only do those in the charismatic movement insist that others must speak in an unknown tongue to give evidence that they "have the Holy Spirit," they also often claim that every believer should have and exercise all the spiritual gifts. We have previously shown that this is not an accurate understanding of the Bible's teaching on spiritual gifts.

If we consider the motivational gifts from Romans 12, we find that they were given by the Spirit and they are gifts that are "gifts differing" (v. 6). Not everyone has the same gift, nor should they desire to have all of them. The push for tongues is an emphasis on a gift that Paul said would "cease" (1 Cor. 13:8). For those seeking to be used by God through the use of spiritual gifts, Paul says that the speaking gifts that edify others should be the ones most sought after (cf. 1 Cor. 12-14). The motivational gifts, the ones given to us at salvation by the Holy Spirit and listed in Romans 12, do not include tongues.

In listing both the manifestation gifts and the ministry gifts in First Corinthians (ch. 12, vv. 8-11 and 27-31 respectively), it is clear from the use of rhetorical questions that there is no expectation of any believer having, or receiving, all the gifts. Of course, the manifestation gifts are results that the Spirit produces in individual believers through the exercise of motivation and ministry gifts. But note this clear statement from Paul: "But one and the same Spirit works all these things, distributing to each one individually as He wills" (1 Cor. 12:11).

Jimmy Swaggart is an ardent supporter of the charismatic teaching that every Christian should speak in unknown tongues and possess all the gifts. His comments are representative of all who espouse this false teaching. Referring to speaking in tongues, Swaggart says,

> The great truth, that this is *not* an optional experience but something intended for *every* Christian, *came to me while I was preaching* [*sic*, emphasis mine]…that the baptism in the Holy Spirit is not a voluntary or elective move on the part of the Christian—it is an *obligation*.[3]

His justification is wrongly based on Acts 1:4, which is a clear reference to a onetime event. Swaggart's teaching plainly contradicts the overall teaching of scripture.

---

[3] Jimmy Swaggart, *How to Receive the Baptism in the Holy Spirit* (Baton Rouge: Jimmy Swaggart Ministries, 1982), 8-9.

The Practice of Tongues in the New Testament

To get to the bottom of what is meant by tongues in the New Testament, the best solution is to understand the words in their language and historical context. We can begin by defining the words in the Bible that reference this gift.

In defining the words for "tongues" in Greek, we find that the definitions are very similar to the words we use to describe the same things. There are two primary words used in Acts and First Corinthians that define the gift known as tongues.

First, there is the word γλωσσα (*glossa*), which primarily means "a language." It is defined as, "1) the tongue, a member of the body, an organ of speech; 2) a tongue - the language or dialect used by a particular people distinct from that of other nations" (JHT).

Normally then, the word occurs in the plural because it refers to various languages. When it occurs in the singular, it could refer to an unknown ecstatic babble. While the babble may be of different styles, since it has no meaning at all, it is all one tongue. We might call it gibberish. In First Corinthians 12:10, there is a reference to "kinds of tongues," which is a way of referring to language families.

The bottom line is that the word can only mean two things: "a known spoken language" or "the organ that is found in one's mouth useful for taste and in forming the words we speak."

The other word for "tongues" is the word διάλεκτος (*dialektos*), which means "a dialect." In fact, this is the Greek word from which we get the English word *dialect*. It used in Acts 2:6 and 8. There is really no getting around the meaning of this word. It is defined as "conversation, speech, discourse, language...the tongue or language peculiar to any people" (ESL).

In the context of Acts 2, the idea behind the gift was to attract the attention of people by speaking words they would clearly understand. It seems obvious that Peter preached in Greek, a common language that most would understand.

It is important for us to consider the *historical situation* from the book of Acts. The issues that are significant are *evidence, subsequence,* and *seeking*. The common teaching of the charismatic movement is that the reception of the Holy Spirit is something *subsequent* to salvation—you are saved, but the Holy Spirit comes later, in response to your faith or some other thing. The other thing includes *seeking* (tarrying, waiting, praying, etc.).[4]

We must ask, what biblical *evidence* is there to support the charismatic teaching on the subject of tongues? The charismatic position can resort only to the historical narratives in the book of Acts to provide any evidence for speaking in tongues, specifically Acts chapters 2, 8, 10, and 19 (which we will refer to later).Some may attempt to use First Corinthians 14 and a few obscure Old Testament passages ripped from their context, but these passages provide even less evidence for the modern practice of unknown tongues.

We will begin by focusing our attention on the passages in Acts. In the four places where tongues are "evident," there is no question that in Acts 2, the tongues spoken were languages and dialects. Therefore, there is no reason to believe that somewhere along the way, it mystically changed to an unknown babble. This would have been very offensive to the Jews since such ecstatic babble was used in the pagan religions to worship demons, as Paul clearly reminded the Corinthians (cf. 1 Cor. 12:1-3).

If we just looked at the book of Acts, we would find many other

---

[4] Again we might refer to the previously mentioned definitive charismatic work from Jimmy Swaggart. He says, "There is a real and definite difference between being born *of* the Spirit and being baptized *in* the Spirit. A person is not baptized in the Holy Spirit at the moment he is saved. The baptism in the Holy Spirit is an experience completely separate from salvation; it can only come *after* salvation, and it must be consciously *sought* by the believer (Luke 11:13)" (ibid. 11). This teaching clearly negates centuries of orthodox Christian theology, not to mention the Bible. Swaggart goes on to blame "spiritual lethargy within the Christian church" on the belief that "that conversion is an experience complete within itself." But the Word of God plainly teaches that salvation is a complete experience, and when you are saved, you receive all of the Holy Spirit and the gifts He intends to motivate you with to get you involved in kingdom ministry (cf. Luke 24:49; John 7:38-39, 14:16-18; Acts 1:4-5; Rom. 8:9, 15-17; 1 Cor. 6:19-20; 2 Cor. 1:22; Gal. 4:6; Eph. 1:3-14; 1 John 2:20, 27).

passages in that book where people were clearly saved and there was *no evidence* of tongues. Those passages are found in Acts 2:41-2; 4:4; 5:14; 8:5-6, 37-38; 9:17, 31, 42; 11:21; 12:24; 13:12, 48-52; 16:5, 14-15, 30-34; 17:4, 10-11, 34; 18:8, 27-28; 19:20; and 28:24. Twenty-two references in all to people being saved with no evidence of their having proved it by speaking in tongues. If we were keeping score, that would be 22-4, in favor of getting saved without the evidence of tongues!

Let us not forget that the tongues spoken of in each of the four places in Acts where it is mentioned is a reference to speaking, or quite possibly hearing, a known language. It is extremely rare to hear a charismatic teacher even mention known languages, but when they do, they readily admit that the vast majority of tongues in the modern era is of the unknown variety and, therefore, beyond objective interpretation.

As to the issue of *subsequence*, a delay between being saved and receiving the Holy Spirit, you will find it in Acts 2 and 8. An entire doctrine of tarrying for the receiving of "Holy Spirit baptism" is based on two passages. The concept is not taught in the epistles, which is where we form our doctrinal understandings. While tongues is mentioned in Acts 10 and 19, there is no subsequence in those passages.

Swaggart says, "There is a difference between being born *of* the spirit and being baptized *in* the Spirit...it [Holy Spirit baptism] can only come *after* salvation, and it must be consciously *sought* by the believer."[5] It is important to remember that Acts is *narrative*, not *normative*. In Acts 2, the subsequence found is due to the promised coming of the Holy Spirit in fulfillment of Joel 2:28-29. Once that occurred, there was only one other need for a slight delay, which is found in Acts 8:14-17, when the Samaritans were saved. Their receiving of the Holy Spirit was delayed for confirmation of the apostles Peter and John. The phrase *as yet* is οὔπω (*oupo*), which means "something hasn't happened that should have." The hatred between Jews and Samaritans had to be cut off when it came to the

---

[5] Ibid. 11.

start of the Christian church. What we have in these chapters is known as *historical transition.*

In no case in Acts, or anywhere else in scripture, is there the slightest evidence of waiting or tarrying or begging or seeking for evidential gifts of the Spirit's presence in the life of a believer. Mr. Swaggart refers to Luke 11:13 for support. It says, "If you then, being evil, know how to give good gifts to your children, how much more will your heavenly Father give the Holy Spirit to those who ask Him!"

This is a comparative statement. Earlier, Jesus reasoned that even human fathers would, to the best of their ability, give good gifts to their children. That being so, then "how much more" would God do good for His children! If we ask for the Holy Spirit, we will receive Him. That's what happens when we are saved because scripture is clear that when you are saved, you will receive all of the Holy Spirit you are ever going to get (cf. Eph. 1:3; Rom. 8:9,15-17; John 14:16-18).

But Mr. Swaggart claims that the real movers and shakers of the Christian world today are those who have come forward to accept this gift of an unknown tongue, the only supposed evidence that one has truly received the Holy Spirit. But rather than go to scripture, Swaggart goes to a method he claims was given to him directly by God! Again, he says all who receive the Holy Spirit will speak in tongues, no exception. The purpose of the book of Acts is to declare the historical record of the first-century church, not to teach prescriptively what was to continue happening.

We find a third place in Acts where tongues is mentioned, chapter 10:44-48. Once again, tongues was the speaking, or hearing, of a known language, one which the speaker did not know but one which was plainly a spoken language with rules of grammar and an established vocabulary.

We'll speak more of this later, but the truth is, tongues as a gift in the New Testament was designed as a sign to unbelieving Israel. Paul explains,

> Brethren, do not be children in understanding; however, in malice be babes, but in understanding be mature. In the law it is written:

"With men of other tongues and other lips I will speak to this people; And yet, for all that, they will not hear Me," says the Lord. Therefore *tongues are for a sign, not to those who believe but to unbelievers*; but prophesying is not for unbelievers but for those who believe. (1 Cor. 14:20-22, emphasis mine)

This turns the whole charismatic-babble doctrine on its head because the teaching is universally that tongues are not given to evidence to other believers that you "have it," but rather to provide proof of the gospel message's veracity.

In Acts 10, we have the Gentile "Pentecost" because the same thing happens here as did in Acts 2. They spoke in other languages to confirm the reality of their salvation to others, in particular to the unbelieving Jews. It was to prove to the Jews that the Gentiles had the same Holy Spirit they had received on Pentecost. When you include Acts 10:47 in the context, you see that Peter is equating receiving the Holy Spirit with salvation!

Later, when Peter is defending the taking of the gospel to the Gentiles at the Jerusalem Council (Acts 11:15-17), he clearly states that their receiving of the Holy Spirit was the evidence of their having been saved. This was the reason, in this one case, for subsequence so that it could be clearly known that the gospel was for all people. The elders in Jerusalem received this testimony and declared, "Then God has also granted to the Gentiles repentance unto life."

The final time we find tongues mentioned in Acts comes in chapter 19, verses 2-6. When Paul arrived in Ephesus, he found some disciples of John the Baptist. Simply put, they were not saved until Paul arrived and shared with them the gospel of Christ. When they received the Lord and were baptized, they also received the Holy Spirit. Then they spoke in other languages, similar to the day of Pentecost. This was again a judgment sign to Israel that God's Word and the plan of salvation had gone to the Gentiles.

Interestingly, Swaggart says that the things that hinder one from receiving this gift are "unbelief " and "failing to yield to God."[6] He

---

[6] Ibid. 24-28.

claims that speaking in tongues is the only evidence of the Holy Spirit's control. I would beg to differ and say that submission to the authority of the Holy Spirit, as evidenced by obedience to the Word of God, is the only true proof that the Holy Spirit has converted and indwelt your life.

In another very interesting statement, Swaggart admits that he doesn't know why God chose tongues as the sign of Holy Spirit filling or baptism. But he says he knows "scripturally" that He did. The problem is, he quotes not one scripture to back up his claim.[7]

Without trying to be mean, Jimmy Swaggart was big on tongue talking and little on obedience. He could slay people in the Spirit but could not control his own sexual desires. He disgraced the ministry and was in no way an example of holiness. My point is that his life certainly does not prove any real benefit from this business of speaking in tongues.[8]

The real evidence of the work of the Holy Spirit in the life of the believer is holiness, not emotional excess or babbling in an unknown tongue. Paul reminded the Corinthians that they were to "cleanse [themselves] from all filthiness of the flesh and spirit, perfecting holiness in the fear of God" (2 Cor. 7:1). Walking with God is not a matter of how loud you shout but how straight you walk! Your hallelujahs without holiness will be hollow.

A Closer Look at First Corinthians 14

Outside the book of Acts, the only place a charismatic teacher can go for support for their false teaching on tongues is First Corinthians 14. But if we study the chapter carefully, we will find that it is far from something that encourages the modern practice of unknown tongues.

---

[7] Ibid. 43-45

[8] Swaggart's moral problems are well documented in other sources, such as Wikipedia (https://en.wikipedia.org/wiki/Jimmy_ Swaggart). John MacArthur also exposes Swaggart, along with numerous other charismatic leaders in *Strange Fire* (62).

On the contrary, Paul is unmistakably condemning the practice and encouraging a proper understanding of both the spiritual gifts and Christian worship.

A breakdown of the chapter will reveal the truth about tongues as they were practiced in Corinth and will give us principles to understand why the practice has ceased for today. First of all, we need to remember that the all the tongue talking that Paul approved of would have been speaking in known languages for the purpose of reaching the lost with the gospel and authenticating the veracity of the apostolic preaching.

The need for that type of gift in Corinth would have been minimal at best. It would seem apparent that some in the church at Corinth were claiming a true spiritual gift but were, in fact, simply using an ecstatic babble, something brought over from their pagan days before they were saved (cf. 1 Cor. 12:2-3). This may be the reason that some in the church who had crossed over into some type of ecstatic utterances were not using interpreters. You cannot interpret or translate nonsense.

Paul is very thorough in his exposé of the problem with tongue talking in Corinth.

Paul's Comparison of Prophecy and Tongues (1 Cor. 14:1-5)

In the charismatic movement, the declaration that tongues is the primary and most important of the gifts is undeniably true. For example, Kenneth Hagin, known by many as the father of the Word of Faith movement, said, "Of these [referring to the gifts in 1 Cor. 12], the gift of tongues is the most prominent."[9] An article in *Charisma* magazine says,

> A spirit language is the greatest gift the Holy Spirit can give a believer. Jesus is the greatest gift God could give for the redemption of the world, and the Holy Spirit is the greatest gift Jesus could give to His church. Of all the resources in heaven and the eternal universe, nothing is more valuable, beneficial or important for the

---

[9] Kenneth Hagin, *Prevailing Prayer to Peace* (Tulsa: Kenneth Hagin Ministries, 1979), 40.

> Holy Spirit to give the individual child of God than her own spirit language (1 Cor. 12:31; 14:4).[10]

But this is not the testimony of Paul. He plainly says that the most important and useful gift is prophecy. "Pursue love, and desire spiritual gifts, but especially that you may prophesy" (v. 1). He is no doubt referring to the motivational gift of prophecy, which can lead to the manifestation gift of prophecy, the conviction of sin leading to repentance.

Why is this most important? The task of the church is to speak forth the Word of God so that people can understand it, see their need of a Savior, and then repent and believe the gospel! Paul says if you are going to desire a gift, you should desire to preach the gospel, not blabber utterances that no one can understand anyway.

The words *tongue* and *tongues* are going to prove vital to our understanding of this passage. One possible view is that *tongue* refers to ecstatic utterance and *tongues* refers to languages. This would fit fairly well, and yet there is at least one exception in verse 19 where Paul is clearly referring to using a language, singular. Another view is that it simply means "your mouth with which you speak" or "one language" or, in the case of the plural, "more than one language."

The latter seems to be the case in verse 2 because men can't understand it but God can. This is not a commendation of speaking something God understands but men don't. Bear in mind, while God may very well have His own language, he understands every human language. In every case in scripture where God speaks to men, He does so in a language those men understood. There is absolutely no need for you to speak to God in some language that only He knows since He knows the language you speak!

If we have learned anything in our study of spiritual gifts, I hope we have learned that the purpose of the gifts is that they are to edify and profit others. "Mysteries" (v. 2) is simply truth revealed. If the

---

[10] Bill Hamon, "10 Reasons for Speaking in Tongues," *Charisma*, November 14, 2014, http://www.charismamag.com/spirit/supernatural/17419-10-reasons-for-speaking-in-tongues.

tongue is going to do that, it would have to be a known language. A person speaking in a foreign language may very well be sharing the truth of God, but it's not doing any of the hearers any good because they can't understand it.

So in verse 3, Paul declares the great difference that plain, straightforward preaching makes! It edifies, exhorts, and comforts!

By contrast, tongues (v. 4) are, at best, only good for self-edification. This is neither a compliment nor an encouragement. Remember that the context is spiritual gifts, which are for the good of others. Paul is asking what good can come from something no one understands. An argument may come forth that, at least, this individual is edifying himself. But that is self-seeking, clearly condemned by James (James 3:13ff; cf. Phil 2:1-4). It also breaks the spirit of the love chapter (1 Cor. 13:5), where Paul says, "Love does not seek its own."

In verse 5, Paul makes it clear that the only possible way tongues could be valid for the church would be for the tongue talker to know his interpreter and to speak in a known language that is then translated to the church. But if you know the same language the church knows, why in the world would that be necessary? Again, the key is that "the church may receive edification."

Paul's Illustrations (1 Cor. 14:6-12)

Paul begins by referring to himself. "If I come to you speaking with tongues," obviously referring to languages they did not speak, what good would that do them? A message is neither helpful nor good if it is not edifying to the church. Why do charismatics put this high premium on unintelligible speech? Most interpretations have proven to have little, if any, connection with what was spoken. You cannot translate when there is not an objective standard.

Paul says, "If I'm going to edify you or help you grow in your Christian walk, then what is communicated must be something you can understand." He demonstrates the principle through several illustrations.

His first illustration is musical instruments, "things without life"

(v. 7). In order to make music, the instruments must make sensible, distinctive sounds. Chords and notes are put together for a reason. Variation and order are essential. I often kid about playing a piano by ear and saying I would but it gives me a headache. This is what Paul is referring to, the useless idea that noise, without *distinction*, can communicate anything. The word *distinction* is διαστολη (*diastole*) and signifies "a setting asunder (*dia*, asunder, *stello*, to set, place, arrange), hence, a distinction; in Rom. 3:22 and 10:12" (VINE).

Then Paul refers to the military "trumpet" (v. 8), and this sound is even more important because it means life or death. It would seem from the context here that we have a word that tells us that Paul may be dealing with ecstatic utterances, not known languages. He uses the word *uncertain*, αδηλος (*adelos*), which "denotes (a) unseen; with the article, translated which appear not (*a*, negative, *delos*, evident), Luke 11:44; (b) uncertain, indistinct, 1 Cor. 14:8" (VINE). Either way, if the congregation doesn't speak the language, it does them no good to hear the tongue.

Meaningless sounds are not instructive to anyone, so Paul says. You must speak to people in words "easy to understand" (v. 9). Otherwise, it could be said, "For you will be speaking in the air" or "You are just a lot of hot air." Grunts and groans don't communicate messages that can be understood. If you want to be understood, you must speak clearly, and how much more so should that be when communicating the precious truth of the Word of God? The phrase is one word in Greek, ευσημος (*eusemos*), "intelligible, clear, distinct" (DBL); "well marked, clear and definite, distinct" (ESL).

Paul then turns to the most commonsense argument of all against "unknown tongues," and that is the use of languages (vv. 10-11). Here, the word is φωνή (*phone*); it can mean simply "voices or sounds"—"a sound, a tone; of inanimate things, as musical instruments; a voice... of a language" (ESL). While there are many of them, they all have meaning; none are "without significance." This word is αφωνος (*aphonos*), "lit, voiceless, or soundless (*a*, negative, and *phone*, a sound), has reference to voice, dumb, silent; without meaning" (VINE).

Without meaning, a voice or noise is useless. But regardless of that fact, both the hearer and the speaker must know the meaning. In essence, Paul says in verse 11, "Suppose I have a legitimate tongue [a foreign language], if my hearer doesn't know it we will be as foreigners [barbarians] to each other." *Barbarian* is an onomatopoetic word from βαρβαρος (*barbaros*). All the sounds are alike, and therefore, they are meaningless.

Paul attempts again to be positive about the Corinthians themselves and commends them for being "zealous for spiritual gifts" (v. 12). But he knows they have gotten off track and wants them to understand that the most important thing is for them to "excel" in edifying others. That is the very purpose of the spiritual gifts in the first place.

Since true tongues (the ability to speak in a known foreign language) are not helpful unless the hearers know the language, or unless there is effective interpretation available, how much more useless is the gibberish that is practiced today? If you are eager to do it God's way, then seek "for the edification of the church" and do not cause confusion.

Clearly, the gifts Paul refers to are public, not private! *Seek* means "a continual, habitual action." Communication is the key that is being stressed. The gospel is the message that needs excellent communication. We might say, "Share the gospel. Use words when necessary!" Since we have enough trouble communicating in English, we certainly should not confuse our conversation further by the use of nonsense and unintelligible speech!

The Practical Effects of Tongues in the Church (1 Cor. 14:13-19)

Paul's next comments are rather sarcastic, and the failure to recognize his manner of speech has caused many to go astray when considering this passage. Whether you are speaking a known language or not is entirely irrelevant here. The point he is making is that no one present in the congregation can understand you.

Paul makes three points about speaking in tongues here that

would be true whether he was referring to speaking in a language that none of the hearers understood or in an unknown gibberish that no one could understand. First of all, such noise would be unfruitful (vv. 13-15). The Spirit of God never bypasses the mind in an attempt to reach only the emotions (cf. Rom. 12:2).

Paul says that if you think you have some known tongue you can speak in, that's fine; but you would be better off seeking to *interpret*, which literally means "to translate." He explains, "For if I pray in a tongue, my spirit prays, but my understanding is unfruitful" (v. 14). This is a reference to man's spirit, and likely, Paul is referring to the empty emotional chatter involved in their former pagan religions. If he spoke in a known foreign language that he did not know, he might well be speaking something that could be understood, but he couldn't understand it! So if you are going to seek God to use you in this manner, don't pray that you could mysteriously speak a language others don't understand— but seek to translate, to interpret, so that you can be an instrument of edification to others.

Paul's conclusion in verse 15 is that there is absolutely no place for mindless activity in worship. Whether praying or singing, it must involve both the mind and the spirit; and for that to occur, one must be understood (cf. Eph. 4:23, Col. 3:10).

Second, Paul makes the point that whether you are preaching or praying, if you don't speak in words that can be understood (vv. 16-17), the "uniformed," the lost sinner or the immature believer, will receive nothing from what you say. He can't say amen. He can't agree or disagree because you have left him in the dark. He cannot be edified. Even if your gift was a true tongue, a known language, and what you said really did do a good job of "giving thanks," it is still a waste of time because it didn't help anybody.

Third, Paul makes the point that languages that are not understood by the hearers will do nothing more than cause confusion (vv. 18-19). Paul does acknowledge the true gift of speaking in known languages and says he has it. Let's remember that he was an apostle, and that office has ceased and, along with it, this gift. In other words, he was not critical because he did not have the gift, an accusation charismatics often throw at those who oppose them.

What is very plain is that Paul would never use an unknown utterance in church because it would confuse people and lead to chaos in worship. Paul's choice between "five words" that could be understood and "ten thousand" in a language that could not be understood is clear.

The Purpose of Tongues in the New Testament (1 Cor. 14:20-22)

Paul makes an *appeal for maturity* among the believers. He references their moral problems and pleads for them to be mature in understanding and to put away evil behavior. There is a great danger in getting overly emotional about anything. We can also understand that Paul knew that when you let your emotions run ahead of your thinking, you can easily be led into moral failure.

I recall a Church of God pastor I knew many years ago. He related to me one day that he had taken seriously a fellow pastor's warning not to let ecstatic utterances and emotional frenzies take hold in the worship service. In essence, he was told that one minute he'd be praying in the spirit with some woman at the altar, and the next they would be playing in the flesh. I think we can easily draw the conclusion that nonbiblical belief in the church can easily lead to nonbiblical behavior both in and out of the church.

The church at Corinth could have been described by Ephesians 4:14, "that we should no longer be children, tossed to and fro and carried about with every wind of doctrine, by the trickery of men, in the cunning craftiness of deceitful plotting," It was difficult to teach the Corinthians as they thought of themselves as more advanced in theology than others were. But they had allowed their experiences to rule over truth. The scriptural admonitions to study the Word and test the spirits should be sufficient to warn of the danger of failure in regard to those necessary disciplines in the church (cf. Acts 17:11; 1 John 4:1).

At this point, Paul gives us an explanation of the purpose of the true gift of tongues. It was a sign to unbelieving Israel.

> Brethren, do not be children in understanding; however, in malice be babes, but in understanding be mature. In the law it is written: *"With men of other tongues and other lips I will speak to this people; And yet, for all that, they will not hear Me,"* says the Lord. Therefore tongues are for a sign, not to those who believe but to unbelievers; but prophesying is not for unbelievers but for those who believe.

Here, Paul quotes from Isaiah 28:11-12 (cf. Jer. 5:15). The Old Testament stated that Israel, and later Judah, would be judged for their sin; and foreigners, speaking languages the Israelites did not understand, would come and take over. Assyria captured Israel, and then Babylon captured Judah. Paul is referencing these events and putting forth a warning that if the people did not hear the apostles as they spoke at Pentecost, the same judgment would fall on them again. This occurred in AD 70 and marked fulfillment of that judgment. As a consequence, there was no longer a need for that sign to unbelieving Jews.

The Procedure for Tongues in the New Testament (1 Cor. 14:23-40)

Paul sets up a hypothetical situation. He says, "If the whole church comes together in one place and all speak with tongues," whether those were known languages or just gibberish, "the uninformed or unbelievers" present will think you are "out of your mind." The KJV uses the word *mad*, which is an excellent translation. The word means "a frenzied rage," and it is where we get our word *mania*. Tongues must be understood if they are to be used at all, and that is exactly what we find happened with the unbelieving Jews at Pentecost (Acts 2).

But Paul asks a very pertinent question at this point. What happens if, instead of this *en masse* speaking in tongues, the Word of God is preached? This would result in the conviction of sin as "unbelievers or an uninformed person" are "convinced," literally cross-examined or "called to account" (ESL) by God's Word. The person sees himself as he really is; the secret sin of his heart is brought to light.

Such conviction naturally leads to the recognition of one's need for a Savior. Paul says the result of such "prophecy" could well be that someone would begin to truly worship God, "falling down on his face." He will see and later report to others of God's great work of saving grace among His people. This, by the way, is true spirituality. What Paul is talking about here is that which leads to holiness of life, not ecstatic emotionalism that leads to chaos.

Paul seems to accept the fact that there were some in the church at Corinth who were going to insist on using their gift, or natural ability, to speak in foreign languages. Let's be clear, there is nothing in this passage of scripture that should lead us to believe that Paul would ever accept the modern concept of "unknown tongues," gibberish in the so-called language of heaven (*sic*).[11]

But if known languages were to be used in the church, then Paul wanted them to follow some rather strict regulations for their public demonstration (vv. 26-28). The first thing that he wanted them to

---

[11] There are some in the charismatic movement who loudly claim that there is some sort of heavenly language. I would certainly be open to the idea that such is true. The problem is that if it is so, God has not told us that in the Bible. The teaching sometimes takes First Corinthians 13:1—"with tongues of men and of angels"— as a proof text. But this has to do with love and is simply a comparative statement. *Tongues*, in this case, means "languages." Suppose you were eloquent in the speaking of several languages but you had no love—what good would that do? There is no evidence from the Bible that angels have their own heavenly language that men can learn. Every spoken word from angels came in the language best understood by the humans they were speaking to! Will we speak one language in heaven? I think it is likely that we will, but it will most likely be Hebrew! It will certainly be the one God desires it to be. In this verse, Paul is speaking of skill and eloquence, not some mystical, unknown language.

Another misused verse in this regard is Romans 8:26: "Likewise the Spirit also helps in our weaknesses. For we do not know what we should pray for as we ought, but the Spirit Himself makes intercession for us with groanings which cannot be uttered." This is a communication within the Godhead that we cannot utter and so is not an instruction to speak in some mystical language. It is simply saying that God the Spirit intercedes for you.

know is that when they got together, the most important issue was that everything spoken or done would lend itself to the edification of all present.

It seems that in Corinth, when they gathered for worship, everyone had something to say! It was, in a sense, mass hysteria. This was not orderly or appropriate. Often we find people who want to attend a Bible study where there is no qualified teacher, but everyone just gets together and shares their opinion about what a particular passage means to them. While people are entitled to have opinions, that doesn't qualify their opinions as biblical teaching or Bible study. Small-group studies where questions are allowed is all well and good, but someone present needs to have to studied the Word in context and should be prepared to instruct the others in "what saith the Lord."

There is always a doctrinal basis for Christian behavior. Purity of doctrine is essential in the church, and we really don't have time for the foolishness that is so often a kissing cousin to ecstatic utterance. For Paul, confusion was out, and building up was in. There is only one thing that can ultimately build up the church, and that is God's Word.

In verses 27 and 28, Paul gives them the strict regulations for any use of true biblical tongues. These are the standards to be used in public worship forums:

1. Only three people could speak, preferably only two (v. 27).
2. Those who speak must speak one at a time. It would be hard enough to listen to a language you did not understand, but imagine the confusion if multiple people were speaking in various different languages (v. 27).
3. There must be an interpretation in a language that all can understand (v. 27). Let's understand that Paul is referring to the presence of a translator, someone who knows both languages and can effectively translate from one language to another.

4. If there was no interpreter/translator present, then anyone with a tongue was required to keep silent (v. 28). The Spirit does not work through those who are out of control or allegedly slain in the spirit. All His gifts are given to and operated through the conscious and aware minds of believers.
5. Women were not to speak in tongues publically (vv. 33-35) and were required elsewhere in scripture to refrain from teaching men (cf. 1 Tim. 2:11-12).
6. All that was done in worship was required to be done decently and in order (v. 40).

It would not take much effort on the part of any discerning Christian to recognize that each of the aforementioned regulations are violated on a regular basis by those in the charismatic movement who insist on speaking in unknown tongues. Further, we should realize that Paul is referring to the use of known foreign languages, and his instruction has no place for babble.

There has been much harm to unsuspecting believers by the charismatic movement in this regard. Some have been wrongly taught, and others have been coerced into becoming "more spiritual" by a somewhat forced learning of how to speak in tongues. One might think that if you have to be taught how to speak in a tongue, then it might not be a gift of the Holy Spirit after all. I can give a number of references to places where the "how-to's" of tongue talking could be found. But let there be no doubt, if you want to know how, you can be taught.[12]

Many years ago, I had just finished preaching a two-part sermon series on the *Truth about Tongues* using much of the content found in this chapter. After the second message and after the service had ended, a young lady, married and in her twenties, came forward with her husband. She was weeping, but I soon realized they were tears of

---

[12] There are numerous works where charismatic false teachers give the instructions on learning to speak in tongues. Two examples are Kenneth Hagin's *The Holy Spirit and His Gifts* (Tulsa: Rhema Bible Church, 1993) and Gordon Lindsay's *Gifts of the Spirit, Volume 4* (Dallas: Christ for the Nations, 1976).

joy! She had been set free that night from a terrible and debilitating spiritual unease that she had carried for years.

It seems that she had been raised in a Pentecostal church. Over the years, she had heard people speak in tongues and, of course, had been told that in order to manifest that she had the Holy Spirit, she too must speak in a tongue. She prayed that God would give her the tongue, but He did not.

She was embarrassed. She was made to feel, and genuinely felt, that she was spiritually inferior to others in the church. She wondered if she was even saved. She desperately wanted to speak in a tongue but was overcome by the feeling of inadequacy. So she did what many in that movement do: she began to fake a tongue. She told me that she didn't think she was very good at it. She still felt spiritually weak and inadequate, but she was able to convince others in her church that she was now one of the "haves."

But the chicanery eventually began to weigh very heavily on her spirit. Oh, she continued to tarry, to wait, to beg God for the "real thing," but it never came. Finally, after getting married, she left that church and, coming to our community, began attending the church I pastored. When she learned the truth about tongues, she was beyond relief. She didn't need to speak in an unknown tongue! Those who did were not exercising a spiritual gift but more likely were under the influence or control of demons, and she could now find her true motivational gift and serve God!

She was free from worry, guilt, embarrassment, and the feelings of spiritual inferiority that had developed in her life. It is shameful, the pressure that some in the charismatic movement put on people to prove their spirituality by means of ecstatic utterances and emotional outbursts. When you learn the truth, it will absolutely set you free! (John 8:31-32).

Paul continued to emphasize the priority of prophecy in the New Testament. When he set up regulations for the use of known languages in the church, he also set forth a procedure for prophecy, or preaching, in the church (vv. 29-33). The procedures Paul gave for preaching in the church were designed to create order and an atmosphere that would best provide for the edification of the church. Here is a summary:

1. Only two, or at most three, were to speak (v. 29).
2. Other prophets (preachers) had to pass judgment; in other words, discern what was being preached. They were to measure the message against their knowledge of the Word of God (vv. 29-30).
3. They were to speak in turn; that is, "one by one." Even if the language used is understood by everyone, if several are speaking at one time, no one can get much out of it (v. 31).
4. The clear purpose of preaching was for learning and encouragement (v. 31).

Paul follows these procedures with a principle that is very important for us to understand. He says that "the spirits of the prophets are subject to the prophets" (v. 32). In other words, they are never out of control or out of mind. God does not bypass our minds. The idea that a preacher can prance across a stage and look up into the ceiling and declare that he just received a revelation from God was foolishness to Paul. A preacher, if he wants to deliver a message from God, needs to be a prayer warrior and a humble student of the Word, one who has studied and prepared, one who has received a word from God by his close study of and attention to the Word of God.

Paul reminds them that peace, not confusion, is God's way (v. 33). I once asked a lady, who was concerned about the problems (literally, confusion) her speaking in a private prayer language was causing in her marriage, to manifest the tongue so I could take authority over it and test it. She said, "Well, I can't do it anytime I want." I asked her why not since verse 32 says the spirit is subject to the prophet. She said, "Usually I can," and then she did. The results of that encounter were phenomenal, to say the least, but she repented of her pride, and the problem ended.

Paul then deals with the role of women (vv. 33-35), in particular as it relates to the issue of tongues. He emphasizes that this is a universal requirement; it is not cultural or geographical (cf. 1 Tim. 2:9-15). I believe Paul is referring to two things: First, a woman is not to speak in tongues in the church. Second, she is not to preach or prophesy in the assembly.

Paul explains this position as one resulting from the consequence of the fall (1 Tim. 2:11-12). This is God's design and one that He has purposed for the church. But Corinth was doing what many charismatics do today, permitting women to speak in tongues and to preach. Paul declares this to be improper. He says it would be best for them learn from their husbands. The Corinthians, as many today, were set on doing it their way.

We then find another very important and general principle stated in verses 36-38. No believer can overrule God's Word. You can't alter it, you shouldn't ignore it, and you will be defeated if you disobey it. Those who are truly spiritual will be able to acknowledge that Paul's words are the Lord's commands. If anyone does not recognize this, he is not to be recognized by the church. Paul's teaching is absolutely authoritative.

So here is the summary (vv. 39-40). Prophecy is the superior gift. At the time, true tongues, those done in a manner fulfilling all biblical demands, were not to be rejected. Both of these things reference the group or church as a whole. Finally, the bottom line of all the instruction is that all things are to be done decently and orderly. May it be so in the church for His glory!

The Personal, Private Prayer Language

We have one last issue to address in regard to the truth about tongues. There are some who will not speak in an unknown tongue publically because they understand the regulations set in place for tongues in the church in First Corinthians 14. However, they are still convinced that a gibberish or ecstatic babble can be a true gift of the Holy Spirit. Since, as they wrongly believe, the gift exists for their own personal edification, they practice it in private—hence the term *personal, private prayer language.*

There are numerous problems with the idea. First, one of the clear and unmistakable facts about spiritual gifts is that they are designed to profit or benefit others (1 Cor. 12:1-7; 1 Pet. 4:10- 11). All who practice the personal, private prayer language are doing so without even an intended benefit to others. Self-seeking is routinely condemned in scripture. For this reason alone, we could rule out this practice.

Second, the use of spiritual gifts is clearly for the edification of the believers. This was the emphasis throughout Paul's exhortation on the subject in First Corinthians 14. It is a given that this practice does not edify others, but neither can it edify the person practicing it. The question would have to be asked, How does the practice of a personal, private prayer language build up the person using it? Does it lead them to be more spiritually mature? Does it cause them to live a holier lifestyle? By its very nature, it cannot do these things.

Third—and here is the greatest danger—its only capability is to produce pride in the one who does it. They will perceive themselves as one of the "haves" and thus superior to others who are "have-nots." It may make them feel good about their supposed closeness to the Lord, but the practice has no basis or foundation in the scripture.

Finally, we might note that Jesus never spoke in tongues. This is interesting because as the Creator and the One who confused language at the Tower of Babel, He would have known all languages and been able to converse with anyone, regardless of what human language they spoke. But there is no indication anywhere that Jesus spoke to God in some language that others could not understand. In fact, the opposite of that was true because the disciples heard Him pray and recorded what was said! Jesus invited them to pray along with Him.

Men ought always to pray and not faint in the process (Luke 18:1). There is good news! God can hear you if you speak in your native tongue! May the heavens be filled with our voices of praise!

And they sang a new song, saying: "You are worthy to take the scroll, And to open its seals; For You were slain, And have redeemed us to God by Your blood Out of every tribe and tongue and people and nation."
—Revelation 5:9

Appendix I

Discerning Your Spiritual Gifts - Survey

How to Take the Survey: These questions will assist you in discerning your gift but it is imperative that you be completely honest. There are no "right answers" *per se*. It is best to answer the questions according to your true motives and feelings rather than what you think the answers ought to be. Answer each question with a numerical value based on the following scale:

Almost Always (Yes) - 5; Often - 4; Sometimes - 3; Rarely - 2; Almost Never - 1; Never (No) - 0

1. Hypocrisy in others really bothers you; to the point that you feel you should do or say something about it: ____
2. It is normal for you to neglect your own responsibilities and needs in order to be of help to others: ____
3. You normally are more focused on the details, even to the point that you sometimes miss the big picture: ____
4. You are a decisive person, quick in making decisions: ____
5. You always tithe no matter what your other financial obligations might (in other words, tithe first, bills second): ____
6. When receiving or giving instructions you prefer them spelled out clearly and plainly: ____

Almost Always (Yes) - 5; Often -4; Sometimes -3; Rarely - 2; Almost Never - 1; Never (No) - 0

7. You find that you often and rather easily develop close bonds to and with others: ___

8. You tend to make quick value judgments: ___

9. You are inclined to over-emphasize practical needs at the expense of spiritual needs (you see meeting the practical needs of the day as urgent and needing your attention before attending to spiritual matters such as your prayer and Bible reading time): ___

10. You are tempted to give all the knowledge you have on a subject when conversing with someone: ___

11. You enjoy encouraging others in their spiritual growth: ___

12. You are motivated to share your personal assets to enhance the ministry of an individual or church (beyond the tithe): ___

13. When given leadership responsibilities you realize the need to be careful of the pride of power: ___

14. It is hard for you to be firm at times with others, even when necessary: ___

15. Your tongue is sometimes thought to be sharp or harsh: ___

16. Others characterize you as somewhat aggressive (or maybe even pushy): ___

17. You are very concerned that Scriptural truths should take priority; then human experience be measured by that truth: ___

18. You are discouraged with the lack of progression in those with whom you're sharing spiritual directions or truth: ___

19. You can discern and make wise financial investments: ___

20. You have motivation to organize that for which you are responsible: ___

21. You find it easy to rejoice when others rejoice: ___

22. You are impulsive: ___

23. You tend to have genuine affection for others: ___

24. You enjoy accumulating knowledge and digging out facts: ___

25. You enjoy personal counseling with others: ___

Almost Always (Yes) - 5; Often -4; Sometimes -3; Rarely - 2; Almost Never - 1; Never (No) - 0

26. You tend to purchase quality items that will last: ____
27. You are very thorough: ____
28. You recognize the hurting and enjoy providing comfort to them: ____
29. You sense a degree of pride in your speaking ability: ____
30. You do things for others even if it means your own personal sacrifice and discomfort: ____
31. Following a sermon or lecture, you review your notes and look up all the Scripture references: ____
32. You talk a lot (you have a strong "verbal need"): ____
33. You are motivated by value over price: ____
34. Following the rules is important: ____
35. You are fairly serious (as opposed to the "life of the party" type): ____
36. You discern and draw conclusions quickly: ____
37. Meeting needs that will free someone to do something else is enjoyable to you: ____
38. You are more concerned with obtaining truth than with communicating truth: ____
39. When asked for your advice, you find that you can hardly wait until they've done to answer, perhaps even interrupting: ____
40. You are able to see needs (financial) that others sometimes overlook: ____
41. You consider yourself to be a leader: ____
42. You are pleased (and perhaps somewhat proud) of your ability to empathize with others: ____
43. You are motivated to reveal unrighteous motives or actions by presenting God's truth: ____
44. You are able to recognize personal needs and have a desire to meet them: ____
45. You really enjoy research and detailed study: ____
46. You enjoy and prefer the one-on-one ministry approach: ____

Almost Always (Yes) - 5; Often -4; Sometimes -3; Rarely - 2; Almost Never - 1; Never (No) - 0

47. You enjoy hosting people in your home, friends, family, and sometimes even strangers: ____
48. You use people in reaching your goals rather than meeting their needs: ____
49. You tend to feel strong sympathy with the misery of others: ___
50. You categorize individuals when you find out what church they attend: ____
51. Others see you as diligent, sometimes even doing more than is really necessary: ____
52. You tend to authenticate and validate new insights and information by resource books, commentaries, and other such authorities: ____
53. You are motivated to stimulate the faith and develop the character of others: ___
54. God has made it possible for you to have resources to give, sometimes you even find it relatively easy to make money: ____
55. You have an unusual ability to see the overall picture and to clarify long-range goals: ____
56. You find it easy to empathize with others: ____
57. You enjoy, or you would enjoy, speaking to groups: ____
58. You really enjoy meeting the practical needs of others: ____
59. You prefer the study Bibles over paraphrased editions in your own personal study: ____
60. You are persistent and consistent in praying for others (on your own and one-on-one with them): ____
61. You are motivated to give anonymously (with a view to encouraging the recipient to look to God for their provision): ____
62. You have a keen desire to see tasks completed as quickly as possible, although done in a thorough way: ____
63. When a person is in distress you find it easy to identify with that person: ____

Almost Always (Yes) - 5; Often -4; Sometimes -3; Rarely - 2; Almost Never - 1; Never (No) - 0

64. You tend to be direct, or frank; in other words, you readily tell people what you think: ____
65. You enjoy manual projects: ____
66. Word definitions, historical backgrounds, and biblical meanings are extremely important to you: ____
67. You are an enthusiastic person: ____
68. You can readily identify with Matthew and Zaccheus in their ability to keep clear financial records: ____
69. You find it easy to delegate work: ____
70. You are a very loyal friend: ____
71. It is easy for you to personally despise that which is evil: ____
72. Doing things for others without regard to whether you receive any credit for doing it is natural to you: ____
73. You especially enjoy word studies dealing with the original Greek: ____
74. You enjoy telling others what to do: ____
75. When someone comes to you with a material need you are able to make a quick decision as to the validity of the need: ____
76. You enjoy leading or presiding over others and/or groups: ____
77. You tend to feel uncomfortable around people who are specific and reasoned in their analysis of things before making decisions: ____
78. You sense when something is not what it appears, you effectively discern right and wrong and do so immediately: ____
79. You believe that the best way to love someone is to meet their physical or practical needs: ____
80. You enjoy searching out and validating truth which has been presented: ____
81. You are able to be patient with one who shows slow progress, as long as they are paying attention and trying: ____
82. You feel you have a good business sense: ____
83. If a building permit is required you get it first, then you build: ____

Almost Always (Yes) - 5; Often -4; Sometimes -3; Rarely - 2; Almost Never - 1; Never (No) - 0

84. Protecting the innocent is almost a natural reaction for you: ____

85. It is important for people to show outwardly that they have made a decision/commitment (for example to come forward to receive Christ; or come to the altar publicly to pray): ____

86. You are pleased with your ability to help others: ____

87. You really enjoy studying the Bible and researching the background and word meanings: ____

88. You are good at discerning where people are in their spiritual walk with Christ: ____

89. You would teach (or like to see taught) courses on responsible Christian stewardship in the church: ____

90. You are motivated to coordinate the activities of others for the achievement of common goals: ____

91. You are tempted to tell people that which will make them happy rather than exactly the truth that they need to hear, but which might hurt them: ____

92. You are open and direct about almost everything: ____

93. It is difficult for you to say "no" to requests from others: ____

94. When you have a chance to give a talk, you find it hard to come up with illustrations, preferring rather to give a straightforward presentation of the truth: ____

95. You tend to be overly conscious of both your successes and your failures: ____

96. You are somewhat turned off by emotional appeals for money, preferring to give based on logical need: ____

97. You tend to be competitive: ____

98. You are guided by emotions more so than logic: ____

99. You tend to see people as groups rather than individuals: ____

100. You like to be appreciated but you are not interested in public acknowledgment: ____

101. You especially enjoy presenting truth systematically (rather than topically): ____

Almost Always (Yes) - 5; Often -4; Sometimes -3; Rarely - 2; Almost Never - 1; Never (No) - 0

102. When giving someone an answer to a question they've asked you, you tend to give them everything you know on the subject: ___

103. You measure spiritual success by material assets: ___

104. One of your favorite biblical characters is Nehemiah: ___

105. You are adept at mentally and emotionally relating to a person's need and giving them aid: ___

106. People sometimes accuse you of being judgmental: ___

107. You appreciate clear instructions on how to do a job: ___

108. You sense a need to validate other's statements (to make sure they are accurate or true): ___

109. You are very encouraged by people who are diligently pursuing righteousness in their personal walk with the Lord: ___

110. You enjoy helping other Christians organize their finances: ___

111. You overlook character faults in people that you need to help you reach a goal: ___

112. You judge other people primarily by their sensitivity or lack thereof: ___

113. You see right and wrong as a clear cut, black-and-white issue in most cases: ___

114. You dislike red tape and unnecessary restrictions when doing a job: ___

115. It greatly bothers you when someone uses a Scripture out of context: ___

116. When talking to a group or an individual, you are very sensitive to their response or lack of response to you: ___

117. You take a genuine interest in the needs of strangers: ___

118. Helping a group to clarify its goals and then to determine how to reach those goals would be a great joy to you: ___

119. You feel a heaviness of spirit when people don't agree with you: ___

120. You speak quickly, rather than listening and hearing a person out: ___

Almost Always (Yes) - 5; Often -4; Sometimes -3; Rarely - 2; Almost Never - 1; Never (No) - 0

121. You would rather do the job yourself than delegate it to others: ____

122. If Hebrew or Greek were offered as a course of study, you would likely take one or the other if otherwise possible in your schedule: ____

123. Mentoring younger believers is a very critical aspect of the church's education ministry: ____

124. You are a frugal person, managing your money in a biblical and effective manner: ____

125. You enjoy scheduling: ____

126. When playing a sport or a game you do not have a strong competitive spirit, desiring more that other participants be happy and enjoy themselves: ____

127. If you see someone who has unrighteous motives which he is covering up, you often have a strong desire to expose his motives: ____

128. You have a good ability to recall the specific likes and dislikes of people: ____

129. You have a large vocabulary: ____

130. You really like the biblical character Barnabas: ____

131. You believe that love of money can be very destructive: ____

132. You are someone not easily sidetracked if the objective has been clearly established: ____

133. You are offended when a person with physical or mental difficulties is made fun of: ____

134. You grieve deeply over sinful patterns in others: ____

135. You enjoy doing a job extremely well: __

136. You are especially concerned with thorough scholarship in Christian literature: ____

137. You will overlook practical matters around the house and concentrate instead on talking with people: ____

138. Tithing is the starting point for giving, not the end: ____

Almost Always (Yes) - 5; Often -4; Sometimes -3; Rarely - 2; Almost Never - 1; Never (No) - 0

139. You feel that Christians and their organizations are usually too disorganized: ____

140. You have a hard time saying "no" when you think it will hurt the person: ____

141. You deeply desire to see real repentance, accompanied by works that evidence a true change: ____

142. You prefer short-range goals and jobs, as opposed to long-range ones: ____

143. You are accused of lacking warmth and feeling: ____

144. You can readily identify with people's problems and relate to them: ____

145. You have a desire to make money for the primary purpose of giving it to the Lord's work (in other words, would this be the way you would most enjoy serving the Lord): ____

146. You have both a desire to lead your group and yet a need to wait to do so until you are invited: ____

147. Others would say that you are very loyal and that you would stand up for them if needed: ____

148. You are especially sensitive to the motives and character of people: ____

149. Given the opportunity to do a job in an organization, do you get very frustrated with "proper channels" and red tape, desiring to just do the job, perhaps even helping out of your own funds to avoid red tape: ____

150. You see personal experiences as a danger if used to serve as a foundation for truth: ____

151. You avoid systems of information which lack practical application: ____

152. You tend not to spend much on yourself: ____

153. You enjoy teaching other Christians time management and organizational skills (in a group or individually): ____

154. You are often attracted to people in need: ____

Almost Always (Yes) - 5; Often -4; Sometimes -3; Rarely - 2; Almost Never - 1; Never (No) - 0

155. A strong emphasis on truth and authority (more so than love) marks your thinking about values and morals: ____

156. You tend to stick with a job till you get it done, even if it takes till all hours of the night: ____

157. Once you see a passage of Scripture interpreted one way, it is difficult for you to see it any other way: ____

158. You clearly recognize how guilt can block people from moving forward in the spiritual walk: ____

159. You save money by getting the best buy, not the least expensive product: ____

160. You are a caring person who wants to see things done right: ____

161. You have a strong drive to do that which will make people happy (sometimes even at the expense of truth or justice): ____

162. You are able to identify with the sins of a person you are talking to: ____

163. You prefer to do practical ministry within the body of Christ, leaving the teaching and other more spiritual leadership to others: _

164. You really appreciate the thoroughness of an author like Luke: ____

165. Hope for the future is an important theme in your dealing with others: ____

166. Your generosity to outsiders is sometimes resented by your family: ____

167. You find that organizing things seems to come natural and that it is very important: ____

168. You lack firmness unless it is something that will bring healing and harmony to the body of Christ: ____

169. You try to change people to your point of view in certain areas of life: ____

170. You feel that others sometimes spend a lot of time on spiritual or religious things in order to get out of hard work: __

Almost Always (Yes) - 5; Often -4; Sometimes -3; Rarely - 2; Almost Never - 1; Never (No) - 0

171. You tend to get on tangents and "rabbit trails" easily: ____
172. You have a great love for spiritual maturity and desire to see people grow in their faith: ____
173. In giving to the Lord's work, your primary concern is that the group to which you give be one which is strategic (a multiplying, reaching or discipling ministry): ____
174. You find yourself sometimes having a greater concern that your church or group reach its goals than in meeting the varying needs of individual members of the church: ____
175. One of your favorite biblical characters is the Apostle John because of his emphasis on love and the way he cared for others: __
176. God's reputation is extremely important to you: ____
177. People who aren't willing to get in and do hard work especially bother you: ____
178. You have a lot of books and study projects you've started and not finished: ____
179. There is a "cause and effect" sequence that is obvious with Scriptural principles and life experience: ____
180. You have a burden to get other Christians to give more generously to the Lord's work: ____
181. You don't like a mess; distinguishing major objectives and not getting bogged down in details is essential to you: ____
182. You avoid making decisions if you think someone might react negatively: ____
183. You are honest to a fault: ____
184. You tend to be calm and quiet: ____
185. You find yourself inwardly challenging the knowledge and/or background of those who teach you: __
186. When helping someone and they don't respond well, you tend to lose interest in helping them: ____
187. You despise slothfulness: ____

Almost Always (Yes) - 5; Often -4; Sometimes -3; Rarely - 2; Almost Never - 1; Never (No) - 0

188. You are a goal setter: ____
189. You resist being rushed through an activity, preferring to feel and enjoy it: ____
190. You express your thoughts and ideas verbally: ____
191. You get impatient with those who seem to have a lack of stamina: ____
192. You find a greater joy in researching the truth than presenting it: ____
193. You enjoy setting courses of action for others to follow and grow in their faith: ____
194. You keep excellent records of your personal finances: ____
195. You believe in doing the job right the first time: ____
196. You have an unusually strong desire to see unity among Christians: ____
197. You consider yourself persuasive in speech: ____
198. You are more like Martha than Mary: ____
199. This statement would really bother you: "Truth is discerned more by the Spirit than by the intellect." ____
200. Though you know that you are not, you sometimes appear to be unsympathetic to others: ____
201. You rejoice when you discover that a financial need met was an answer to prayer: ____
202. You are more concerned with the end result than with the "how to:" ____
203. You have a real sensitivity to atmospheres of joy or distress in a group: ____
204. You are distressed over abuse of authority: ____
205. It frustrates you that when you've agreed to do a job you discover there is a time-limit: ____
206. You prefer expositional preaching/teaching to that which is topical: _

Almost Always (Yes) - 5; Often -4; Sometimes -3; Rarely - 2; Almost Never - 1; Never (No) - 0

207. You are willing to spend a great deal of time with someone who needs help: ____
208. When giving a gift (other than money) to a Christian ministry, you are very concerned that it be of high quality: ____ -
209. You tend to stick with proven ways that work rather than wanting to try new things and ideas: ____
210. You resent those who are not sensitive to the feelings and personal needs of others: ____

Appendix 2

Discovering Your Spiritual Gifts
The Key to the Spiritual Gifts Survey

There are seven gifts. The questions are arranged so that the seven gifts will apply consecutively.

1. Gift of Prophecy (Prophet, Preacher)
2. Gift of Service (Server or Helper)
3. Gift of Teaching (Pastor/Teacher)
4. Gift of Exhortation (Exhorter)
5. Gift of Giving
6. Gift of Leadership (Administration, Organization)
7. Gift of Mercy

In other words, questions 1, 8, 15, 22, etc., apply to the "Gift of Prophecy." Questions 2, 9, 16, 23, etc., apply to the "Gift of Service," and so forth through the seven gifts. The question numbers are listed under the gift to which they apply.

After you have taken the survey you can score it on the form provided on the next page. Each answer should have a numerical value (write your score from the questions beside the corresponding question number in the Survey Profile). There are thirty questions related to each gift. Total your score on each gift and write that number at the bottom of the column corresponding to the question numbers for that gift. The maximum score on a gift is 150. If any one category is overwhelmingly prominent, you may be fairly certain this is your gift, unless you know of some reason the results of the test might be distorted, such as prior training for a job, or anything which might cause you to answer predominantly in that category. Most people will have a primary and secondary gift.

If there is no one or two categories which dominate with a somewhat higher score then you may want to study through the material and take the test again at a later time. It is not wise to compare scores with others. The idea behind the survey is not to get a high score but to see which gift or gifts seem to stand out in your case. Each person brings a different set of circumstances and mind set to the survey.

Have fun with the survey. It is a self-evaluation, your answers will not be "graded" by anyone else. Consider it a tool to be used to determine how you can best serve the Lord. If you are confused by the results continue to study the gifts and seek the advise of a seasoned Christian who understands the gifts and how to evaluate them in others.

"As each one has received a gift, minister it to one another, as good stewards of the manifold grace of God. If anyone speaks, let him speak as the oracles of God. If anyone ministers, let him do it as with the ability which God supplies, that in all things God may be glorified through Jesus Christ, to whom belong the glory and the dominion forever and ever. Amen." (1 Peter 4:10–11)

Appendix 3

Spiritual Gifts Survey Profile

1	2	3	4	5	6	7
Prophecy	Service	Teaching	Exhorting	Giving	Leading	Mercy
1	2	3	4	5	6	7
8	9	10	11	12	13	14
15	16	17	18	19	20	21
22	23	24	25	26	27	28
29	30	31	32	33	34	35
36	37	38	39	40	41	42
43	44	45	46	47	48	49
50	51	52	53	54	55	56
57	58	59	60	61	62	63
64	65	66	67	68	69	70
71	72	73	74	75	76	77
78	79	80	81	82	83	84
85	86	87	88	89	90	91
92	93	94	95	96	97	98
99	100	101	102	103	104	105
106	107	108	109	110	111	112
113	114	115	116	117	118	119
120	121	122	123	124	125	126
127	128	129	130	131	132	133
134	135	136	137	138	139	140
141	142	143	144	145	146	147
148	149	150	151	152	153	154
155	156	157	158	159	160	161
162	163	164	165	166	167	168
169	170	171	172	173	174	175
176	177	178	179	180	181	182
183	184	185	186	187	188	189
190	191	192	193	194	195	196
197	198	199	200	201	202	203
204	205	206	207	208	209	210
Prophecy	Service	Teaching	Exhorting	Giving	Leading	Mercy

Total your score by question on each gift. Write the numerical value (0 to 5) that you gave each question beside the question numbers on the chart. At the bottom of the column corresponding to the question numbers for each gift total your responses. This will give you your spiritual gift "quotient" for each of the gifts.

About the Author

Thomas E. Rush has served as a pastor and military chaplain for over 35 years. He received a B.S. in Industrial Management from the Georgia Institute of Technology, a Master's of Divinity from Southeastern Baptist Theological Seminary and a Doctor of Ministry degree from Immanuel Baptist Theological Seminary. He has preached in numerous revivals and Bible Conferences across the nation and led many seminars on the subject of Spiritual Gifts. He has done a lifetime of research and study on the subjects of evangelism, discipleship and spiritual growth. He currently serves as an Evangelist with TREAD Ministries and resides in the metro Atlanta area. His wife Victoria is a treasured partner in ministry and together they have three sons and nine grandchildren.

Dr. Rush can be reached for conferences, revivals and seminars through his website and blog page: www.pastortomrush.com

Or at:
TREAD Ministries
Tom Rush Evangelism and Discipleship Ministries
PO Box 1910
Monroe, Georgia 30655

Printed in the United States
By Bookmasters